INTRODUCTION BEHAVIORAL ECONOMY

JOHN LOK

ISBN 979-888591487-1

Contents

Preface v

Prologue ix

Macro And Micro Economic Strategy Measurement Consumer Behaviors

1. Economic Environment Influences Fuel Price Change 3
2. How Applying Micro Economic Method Predict Future Householders Accept To Use Secondary Energy Useful Behaviors 13
3. Environment Pollution Influences Householder Behaviors Change 26

Economic Methods Measure Energy Consumer Shopping Behaviors

4. The National Income Measurement Behavioral Economy Method 51
5. Applied More Economic Method Solves Energy User Behavioral Challenge 55

Pollution Factor Influences Traveller Behaviors

6. Emotion Labor Factor 61
7. Pollution Factor Influences Travel Behavioural Consumption 76
8. Pollution Influences Traveler Behavior 81
9. Pollution Environment Influences Travellers Self-driving Journey Choice 89
10. Informal Economic Solves Pollution Influences Tourism Industry Development Challenge 93
11. How Living Economic Environment Influences Our Daily Living 105
12. Environment Impacts Consumption Desires Change 128
13. Gdp Measurement To Quality Of Human Life 147
14. Behavioral And Environmental Economic Prediction To Traveler And Energy User Behavior 165

Preface

Introduction

The objective of macroeconomic behavioral methods is to control the short run behavior of an country's economy development. Is it useful to be applied to assist developing countries' economic development. If we think of stability as a situation in which the main macro variables are at a desired or target level. This book divides three parts, In first part chapter one concerns how economic environment can influence global fuel price change, I shall indicate on how economic environment can influence the relationship between airline freight service fuel consumption useful price change .Can economic measurement can predict when airline fuel price changes to airline freight service industry I shall indicate what factors cause the fuel price will raise as well as what the other external threats can cause risk to airline industry. Moreover, I shall also compare the different fuel price rising factors and other external threats whether which is the most effort to influence airline industry failure. Then, I shall give recommend how global airline industry can apply behavioral economic method to predict when the fuel price will rise possibly.

In first part chapter two, I shall indicate how developed country, such as US how to apply micro economic method to predict and measure second energy will be accepted to be used by global householders to replace primary energy . What are second energy to bring human beneficial advantage and why it has more advantages more than primary energy. Is it technological product invention image or story ? Do global householders need to use primary energy to be essential energy consumption product to replace secondary energy in our future daily life ? What are the economic factors and how and why economic factors which can influence householder electricity energy consumers to impact their behaviors how to choose electricity energy every day. These factors can include housing quality factor, every country's regional house prices factor, wealth effects on householder final consumption factor, environmental impacts of householder activities factor, the effect of occupancy and building characteristics on energy use for space and water heating factor, householder income and electricity energy acceptable consumption factor, householder individual attitude to electricity energy efficiency and conservation factor, cooking fuel and lighting electricity energy education to the householder factor, householder individual electricity energy comfortable physical feeling factor, knowledge about electricity energy usage, energy performance and energy efficiency factor, weather impact on the householder electric energy consumption factor, the annual average temperature weather change factor, the electricity energy consumption characteristics to the country's residential sector factor and the socio-demographic and psychological influence to residential electricity energy consumption factor.

In first part chapter three, I shall indicate one good strategy can solve the challenge how to implement inflationary policy can achieve rising GDP income and keeping consumers desires won't reduce effect when unemployment ratio is still high in the country.

I write this primary energy consumption topic to explain why secondary energy will be one kind of the best man-made renew used form of energy to supply to human to use, instead of primary natural resource energy. But, I also indicate two kinds of primary energy will have unlimited supply, such as solar and water and water natural energy. So, these two kinds of natural energy will be also human's future potential electricity market for householder every used essential energy products in possible. In second part , I shall explain whether macro or micro economic method is more easily to predict or measure when and how and why the developing country's consumer shopping desire to be raised or reduced. Can we apply macroeconomic behavioral methods to help developing countries to control current rate of inflation, output or productive rising levels. It is necessary for the developing countries' economy to adjust from its current situation of instability to the target stabilized position.

In fact, any developing countries‘ economic in instability problem is reflecting in high inflation, low output growth and a growing balance of payment deficit. I shall indicate reasons whether we can apply macroeconomic behavioral methods to help developing countries to measure why and how and when consumer behavior or desire to be raised or reduced.

This part researches whether macro economic can measure how social change to influence positive or negative factor will impact any countries' crime rate to be raised or reduced. Has it relationship between global macro economic environment and young unemployed people whose behaviors change, e.g. attempting stealing when they encounter long term unemployment situation or attempting to sell illegal drug to earn income or performing anti-social damage behavior to influence convenient road transportation and working people need catch any public transportation tools etc. traffic jam manual causing anti-social damage behavior? Is poor macro economic environment main factor to influence crime number increases ?

Readers can make more accurate analysis to judge whether macro or micro economic methods can measure when and how and why social crime behaviors occurs as well as social consumer consumption desire why is raised or reduced easily after you read this book.

In the final part, I shall explain whether it is possible to predict how to influence travel behavioural consumption snd energy useful behaviorfrom environment pollution. I shall indicate what factors can influence travel behavioural consumption, such as climate changing, renting travel car tools choice, the country's risk and safety macro economic factor. Then I shall explain how macro economic factor influences traveller psychology to influence travel behavioural consumption, such as: push and pull psychological factor, expectation and motivation and attitude factor. In this part, I shall general investigating methods to predict travel behavioural consumption, such as qualitative of travel behavioural method, advanced traveler information systems (ATIS) method, online tourism sale channel method, actively based patterns of urban population of travel behavioural prediction method, trip based versus activity based approaches of method. In the second part, I shall explain why the future travel age target will be the senior age group and I shall indicate how to use psychological method to predict travel behavioral consumption when environmet pollution occurs.

This part also researches how environment pollution changing factor influences airport how to manage passengers consumption behavior. Nowadays, travellers enjoy to go to different countries to travel. In consumer psychological view, instead of the travelling agents‘ travelling e-ticket cheap and fast seats online booking service or walk in travelling travel agents travelling paper ticket purchase or attractive trip arrangement service to attract travelling consumers’ choice.

In any countries, whether attractive airport appearance design, airport convenient public transportation tools service, e.g. enough airport bus, taxi, train, tram , underground train , ferry etc. number supplying , which can let any foreign travellers find and choose any kinds of public transportation tools to catch to arrive destinations when they arrive any countries‘ airports easily, different kinds of variety of attractive product shops or food courts/shops which can let airport passengers to sit down and choose any kinds of food to eat or they can choose any books, magazines, or stationery or cigarettes, wine, toys , electronic products, e.g. desktop, laptop computers etc. products to consume for reading or using need in the airport’s any restaurants or ships conveniently.

All these airports’ intangible or tangible factors whether they can influence consumers‘ shopping desires in airports, even whether these both factors can attract or persuade many travellers prefer to choose to go to the country to travel and increase the country’s travellers number. Concerning these two questions, my readers can earn more useful opinions to analyze whether any country’s airport’s image will have relationship to influence travellers’ tourism choice and tourism consumption choice behavior , due to the country’s airport’s facility management , service, appearance design , convenient transportation, safety etc. important factors influence in order to assist to develop the country’s tourism industry success in possible.

Does this travelling entertainment activities similar fee comparison factor influence any travellers choose to find the cheaper travelling entertainment activities arrangement provider? If travelling entertainment activities arrangement price is not the main factor to influence traveller individual choice. What other factors can influence traveller individual travelling entertainment activities arrangement choice? I shall explain what the other factors are influenced traveller individual travelling entertainment arrangement choice.

The factors include that the cultural distance on satisfaction and travel intention factor, the lifestyle concept in travel behavioral factor, the business travellers motivation behavioral factor, the impacts of peer-to-peer accommodation use on travel patterns factor, factors influence local tourists decision-making be on choosing a destination factor, transportation, shopping centers, travelling destination facilities supplying factor, social media travelling networking sites promotion factor, traveller’s travelling experience psychological factor, travelling service for disabled people’s travelling need factor, green travel entertainment service for environment protection travelling environment need factor the impact of travel blogging on the tourist, traveller individual vacation destination choice factor, economic impact to the traveller individual sudden changing factor.

In this final part , such as travel entertainment industry, nowadays global travelling entertainment activities are popular, some travellers like domestic travelling or some travellers like to catch airplanes to go to other countries travel. In consumer behavioral view point, when the consumer discovers the product’s price is higher than the another product’s price. Then, he/she will usually to choose to buy the cheaper product, such as travel agent travelling entertainment activities arrangement service case, whether the travelling provider charges higher travelling entertainment activities arrangement service fee to compare the another similar travelling entertainment activities arrangement service provider. Does this travelling entertainment activities similar fee comparison factor influence any travellers choose to find the cheaper travelling entertainment activities arrangement provider? If travelling entertainment activities arrangement price is not the main factor to influence traveller individual choice. What other factors can influence traveller individual travelling entertainment activities arrangement choice? I shall explain what the other factors are influenced traveller individual travelling entertainment arrangement choice.

The factors include that the cultural distance on satisfaction and travel intention factor, the lifestyle concept in travel behavioral factor, the business travellers motivation behavioral factor, the impacts of peer-to-peer accommodation use on travel patterns factor, factors influence local tourists decision-making be on choosing a destination factor, transportation, shopping centers, travelling destination facilities supplying factor, social media travelling networking sites promotion factor, traveller's travelling experience psychological factor, travelling service for disabled people's travelling need factor, green travel entertainment service for environment protection travelling environment need factor the impact of travel blogging on the tourist, traveller individual vacation destination choice factor, economic impact to the traveller individual sudden changing factor.

Therefore, it brings these questions: How any why traveller individual travelling choice won't be influenced by travelling entertainment service price only? Does it mean the travelling entertainment service providers will not reduce their traveller number when they can respect or consider above factors to avoid to bring negative influence to traveller consumers, but they still change higher travelling entertainment arrangement service fee to them? Does this travelling entertainment activities similar fee comparison factor influence any travellers choose to find the cheaper travelling entertainment activities arrangement provider? If travelling entertainment activities arrangement price is not the main factor to influence traveller individual choice. What other factors can influence traveller individual travelling entertainment activities arrangement choice? I shall explain what the other factors are influenced traveller individual travelling entertainment arrangement choice. In my this part, I shall explain above factors how to influence traveller individual behavior to let readers can predict traveller individual behavior more accurately.

In final part concerns how living economy influences our future living experiences and consumption behaviors. It concerns whether wars can impact economy threat to influence consumption behaviors and environment protection countries awareness how influences consumption behaviors. This book is suitable to any readers who have interest to learn whether macro economic methods how can be applied to consumer shopping behaviors in possible.

Prologue

Table of content

Part One
Macro and Micro Economic Strategy measurement consumer behaviors
Chapter 1
Economic environment influences fuel price change p.5-30
● Positive social change influence
Negative social change influence
Terrorisms attack influence
● Is fuel price rising only factor to cause airline risk in short term

● Methods to solve rising air fare prices to decrease travellers' demand
Chapter 2
How applying micro economic method predict future householders accept to use secondary energy useful behaviors p.31-58
reference
Chapter 3
Environment pollution influences householder behaviors change p.59-73
● Environmental impacts of householder greenhouse gas electricity energy consumption activities
● The effect of house space occupancy and building characteristics influences householder electricity energy use
● Solar energy efficient useful characteristics raises secondary energy (human -made

energy) needs or useful desires to be raised.
● Is the low income and rising price of fuels both factors best to influence Nigeria householders choose to use energy efficiently?
● Employment rates or gross domestic product macro economic variation factor, residential space size factor, and the government's implementation of energy labeling schemes provide significant impacts on Taiwan residential electricity consumption .
● Environment scientists' education message how to influence Greece householders home energy consumption behaviors from primary energy to change secondary energy

Part Two Economic methods measure energy consumer behaviors
Chapter 4
The national income measurement behavioral economy method p.74-94
4.1
Industries economic methods p.95-107
Chapter 5
Applied more economic method solves Energy users behavioral challenge
5.1
Behavioral economy consumption desires measurement method p.108-127

Part Three Pollution factor influences traveller behaviors
Chapter 6
Emotional labor factor

6.1Airports service environment
factor p.128-148
6.2Lean maintenance repair
and manual error factor
6.3Influence of airside and off
airport to airport geographical
choice factor
6.4Influencing air connectivity
to service quality factor

6.5How to measure and rise airline
service quality
reference
Chapter 7

Pollution factor influences traveller behavioral
consumption

Prediction travel behavioral consumption
from psychology view and computer
statistic view. p.149--167
Whether climate change can influence
travelling behaviours.

Chapter 8
Pollution influences travel consumption behavior
8.1 What methods predict pollution
influences future travel behavioural
consumption
Individual habitual behaviour can influence travelling behaviour: e.g. renting
travel transportation tools p.168-189
How to determine future travel behavior
from past travel experience and perceptions
of risk and safety for the benefits to travel consumers?

What is push and pull factors to influence
any traveler who chooses where is whose
preferable travelling destination.

Why expectation, motivation and attitude factor
can influence travelling behaviour.
8.2
What methods persuade environment
protection traveller traving desires

How to use qualitative of travel behavioural
method to predict future travel
consumption.
How to apply advanced traveler information
systems (ATIS) to predict future travelling
behaviour.
How does online tourism sale channel can
influence traveling consumption of behaviour.
Actively based patterns of urban population of
travel behavioural prediction method.
What is trip based versus activity based
approaches?
Why senior age will be main travelling target.
Psychological method to predict
travel behavioural consumption.
reference
Chapter 9
Pollution environment influences
travellers self-driving journey choice
9.1 What are usually travel behaviors
and attitudes to disabled tourists p.190-218
9.2 How social internet networking
impacts driving traveler behavior p.219-238
Chapter 10

Informal economic solves pollution influences
poverty tourism industry
development challenge p.239-247
reference
Chapter 11
Living Economy influences our
environment protection awareness
How pollution economic
environment influences
our daily living p.240-269
reference
Chapter 12
Environment impacts
consumption desires
to be changed p.270-288
reference
Chapter 13
GDP measurement to quality
of human life p.289-307
reference
Chapter 14
Behavioral and environmental
economic prediction to
traveler and energy user behavior p.308-327

Macro and Micro Economic Strategy measurement consumer behaviors

CHAPTER ONE

Economic environment influences fuel price change

- Positive social change influence

Negative social change influence

Terrorisms attack influence

What situation is negative social change. I shall indicate globalization society example. We are entering globalization society. For example, air tickets can be bought from internet, so travellers won't need to go to travel agent to buy conveniently. It is due to the global travel industry is increasingly competition. Thus, global travel industry competition will bring negative social change to influences fuel price rising because it will increase traveller numbers and airline flight times to fly. When, traveller's travelling desire demand numbers will be grown up fast, then their online electronic-ticket buying or consumption behaviors will be rise. Thus, it will also cause online e-ticket price is decreased to attract many travellers to choose to buy e-ticket from online channel more than paper-ticket visiting travel agent channel. Thus, it is negative social change influences to cause fuel price rising due to plane flight flying times will increase and airline company will increase demand to buy many fuel to prepare to fly often. When fuel demand will rise, then the fuel sellers will rise fuel price in possible. Thus, airline industry global competition will being negative social change to influence fuel price raising up and air ticket price falling down to attract many traveller numbers to choose to buy among different travel agents.

Negative social change influence

What situation is positive social change. I shall indicate economic growth example. When one country has better economic development in the year. Then, employers will have more effort to do businesses. Then, they will create many jobs to provide to the country citizen to do. When, these unemployed people have jobs to do, they will have extra income to save. They can spend extra to prepare to spend to enjoy their entertainment every year, such as travelling. Thus, the positive social change will influence traveller number increasing, then the plane flight flying times will also increase, it will cause planes need to use much fuel to fly. The result, it will also increase fuel demand, but the fuel natural resource number will decrease , so fuel supply will also decrease. Finally, it will also cause fuel price to be risen.

Also, I shall indicate the financial risk of airline industry evidence from Cathay Pacific airways and China airlines against key determinants of which include interest rate, exchange rate and fuel price risk for the period of January 1996 year to December 2011 year. During this period, these key external factors which were the most serious influence to cause these two airlines choose to change their strategic behaviors.

Due to any these financial risks is difficult to predict and it was also changing often, these factors will also affect any airlines stock returns which arise from changing economic conditions, e.g. fuel price movements and fluctuations in exchange rates. These external unpredicted changing factors will attribute to the air tickets cyclical demand, capital investment, fixed costs of labor and landing rights to this global airline industry.

However, the relationship between fuel price and stock prices varies across economies. The effects of oil price changes in sub-sector indices, such as wood, paper and printing, insurance and electricity. In the past, on global stock exchange market was positively significant in 2011 year. Otherwise, with respect to the U.S.A. aviation industry, some economists suggested that global airlines stock returns were negatively to percentage change in fuel prices related to any airline firm value, e.g. Qantas and Air New Zealand were negatively share price growth to fuel price risk in the short term in the 2011 year.

Thus, it brings this question. Whether positive or negative social change will be one important factor to impact fuel price rising. I feel positive social or negative social change will be one important factor to impact fuel price rising. The reason is such as below:

Nowadays, airline transportation demands are increasing, due to many travelers need to catch planes to travel as well as many cargoes need to be carried to planes to transport to different countries to sell. It seems aviation transportation industry is important to influence the health of the global economy growth nowadays. However, ignorance of internal or external market dynamics, catching travelers business can be detrimental to airline profitability more than carrying cargoes business. Because the demands of travelling different countries' travelers' consumption are still more than the demands of businessmen carrying cargoes in any countries every year. Thus, the travel industry will increase demand to human travelling business more than cargo transportation business. However, the cargo flying transportation demand will rise, due to many global fast speed post businesses are growing. Base on both global cargo flying transportation demand and travellers' flying travelling demand are increasing. Thus, the fuel demand will increase, but the fuel supply will be shortage. So, it will cause fuel price rising consequently.

How can positive or negative social change influence any airlines' air ticket prices to be risen or fallen? In fact, the increase in petroleum price can have chance to affect airlines in a negative manner because increased oil prices have resulted in the reduction of services operations, the number of airline schedules flights, even airline bankruptcies.

Thus, it seems that plan travellers and air flying cargo transportation both demand have been increasing. This social increasing demand change factor, it will be the most influential cause the bad effects to cause airline industry share price reducing or reducing air ticket price or decreasing traveler numbers more than the other factors influence, such as inflation, terrorism, oil shortage, bank interest rate etc. unpredictable external situation factors.

To support this hypotheses, this are my research questions, such as : Does a combination of terrorism and price of petroleum significantly influence airline profit changing mostly? The alternative hypothesis was base on a significant relationship exists between terrorism, price of petroleum and airline profitability more than other factors, such as inflation, bank interest rate or air ticket price changing of these factors influence. I shall indicate that the first assumption was that terrorism has a negative effect on airline profitability and another assumption was that only external factors as oil prices or terrorism affect airline profitability.

Terrorisms attack influence

Whether terrorisms attack will influence fuel price rises up or falls down. I feel terrorisms attack to any country, which will cause plan fuel price falls down. Because travellers will feel dangerous and worry about their life safety when they catch the plan to enter the country if the country has serious terrorisms attack risk to cause plan crash accidently.

However the effects of oil price and terrorism on airline profitability was limited to a regional perspective, e.g. the terrorism attack of plane crash event to USA on 11 Sept. After the terrorism attack happened on USA 11 Sept. incident of terrorism attack was restricted to events of skyjacking, attacks on oil production, refinery and distribution. Thus, USA on 11 Sept. terrorism attack will cause oil price falls down , due to it will influence travellers fear death , so who will reduce times to travel to USA after 11 Sept. date terrorism attack occurrence at the year. The oil sellers will reduce oil sale price to attract many airline companies to buy more supply, due to airlines will decrease demand to buy fuel to provide planes to fly when the traveller numbers has decreasing and flying times will be decrease also. Thus, the fuel price will be decreased consequently after the terrorism attacks to any country.

Other types of terrorist activities, such as attacks on financial targets or senior government officials could have an adverse effect on the petroleum and airline industry. I think the disruption of the production or distribution of petroleum because of incidents of terrorism was costly in terms of loss of business and the inflationary effect on fuel dependent products or services.

In fact, some airlines have adopted more fuel saving technology, so whose fuel consumption would not use more than other non fuel saving technology airlines. So, the owned fuel saving technology airlines which will buy less fuel to use. It means that they won't need fear fuel rising to increase their expenditure because they only need to buy less fuel to use and their fuel demand won't fall , even fuel price has risen.

However, it seems fuel price increasing will not be the only factor to influence the airline industry's traveler numbers decreasing, due it is possible that the airlines need to rise air ticket price to riase their profit, sue to their fuel cost has risen. However, due to some airlines which have fuel saving technology, so which can avoid to use more fuel to provide planes to use and which fuel costs will be reduced, then which can provide cheaper air ticket fare prices to compare the non fuel saving technology airlines. The result will cause some non owned fuel save technological airlines will lose travelling customers in this global airline travelling market, also the non fuel saving technology airlines need to renew their fuel technology if which want to keep their competitive abilities to avoid to close down their businesses.

Can airline fuel self-organization avoid
fuel price rising cost

I feel one airline fuel self-organization can avoid fuel price rising to influence cost rising because it doesn't often buy any fuel from fuel suppliers. However, there are some airlines which are the characteristic of airline fuel self organization and they are present in that both of oil fuel production and providing flights service in airline industry. So, these airline fuel self organizations can control the oil fuel price by themselves. However, one airline fuel self organization is also evident in efforts by businesses acts of terrorism against economic targets by adopting proactive steps, such as airline and airport security. So, it seems airline fuel self organization can reduce the risk to avoid oil price raising and terrorism attacks to raise cost in airline industry risk management sector.

Beside, these airline fuel self organizations which have high technology of fuel efficient aircrafts, the use of one aircraft model, the adoption of direct routes versus customer loyalty programs and other operational cost reductions are strategies for increased profitability. It seems these airline fuel self organizations can solve oil price, terrorism etc. external factor influences to raise cost.

Instead of high technology of fuel efficient aircrafts and airline fuel self organization methods can solve terrorism attacks and oil price rising risks. However, I believe that there are other risks are caused to these airline fuel self organizations to raise their airline cost possibly. The risks include such as user factor, such as culture, tradition, education ; economic factor, such as costs, human resources and macro economic factor, such as political stability, economic development, educational policy, health policy, environmental policy. However, these risks occurrences are resulting in the relationship of cause and effect events. These events are not directly observable. Such as, the complexity of relationship between terrorism and airline profitability. Hence, if global airline industry can predict when those risks occur to do protective strategic behavior. It is possible that which can understand when these risk events will occur and to adopt their protective strategic behaviors to influence their outcomes to be positive to avoid any external risk threats on the long term. However, I think hierarchy, airlines fuel self organization efficiency methods which are as possible predictors of user preferences to avoid risk threat events to cause whose airline businesses cost rising to cause failure occurrences in airline industry.

● Is fuel price rising only factor to
cause airline risk in short term

In my study, I suppose terrorism and the price of petroleum both factors which had properties of distinct and interrelated close relationship to raise airline cost. Moreover, these variables (terrorism and the price of petroleum) displayed differentiation, self replication, efficiency and hierarchy which can cause risk events to airline industry. However, I also think the other internal and external threat factors of airline industry, such as inflation, bank interest rate, business model, service quality, airline fuel or plane engine technology, air ticket pricing, brand loyalty, airline strategic management, government policy and fuel hedging of these factors which can also raise the risks to threaten any airlines existence in airline industry.

There are two basic business models in tourism industry. They are network (full service) and low cost (discount) carriers. The network carrier model employs diversification strategy by increased domestic destinations, serving international routes, providing diverse seating arrangements (business, economy and first class), maintaining a complex system of offering high quality service. Otherwise, low cost (discount) airlines focus on lower air fares. To keep operating costs down, discount airlines offer shorter routes and provide point-to-point destinations rather than through sophisticated flights are primarily in domestic destinations. So, discount airlines operate a common model aircraft fleet, offer a single seating arrangement and cheaper flight services offered to compare network airlines. However, these two basic business models have their unique competitive abilities to provide any airlines existence in tourism industry nowadays.

In fact, natural resource of oil is decreasing in our earth. But as the same time, human demand is increasing and oil supply is decreasing, so it also causes the oil fuel price is increasing to supply to airline industry. It influences not only to airline industry, it also impacts of higher oil fuel price to tourism, such as expansion of airports are made based on expected demand increase.

Tourism has been proven to many adverse events, including terrorism, flight disruptions. Beside, the bad natural climate change influences, such as the volcanic ash cloud event occurred in April 2010 year. So, airline industry need to concern climate change because it will cause high fuel prices indirectly. For example, the event occurred the extreme increase in operating costs for airlines in 2008 year, due to unprecedented prices for aviation fuel also meant, that despite the introduction of fuel charges, so this event causes the global tourism industry recorded losses seriously. Even if alternative fuels become commercially available for airlines which are still likely to be more expensive than present aviation fuel.

Higher airfares in the future are likely to lead to reduction in travel and cause tourists to shift from more distant to closer destination. When some of the economic responses to higher oil prices are obvious assessing the overall economic impacts on tourism is difficult. However, long term changes in global oil price rises will be similar to global changes in other commodity prices, exchange rates and income. It is therefore important to consider the impact of high oil prices on tourism from a general equilibrium perspective rather than relying only on bottom partial equilibrium approaches.

However, I believe tourism and airline industries have close relationship, such as tourism and airline industries are likely to suffer in an environment of high oil prices. Given that tourism destinations receive tourists from a range of origins, it would be useful to understand of some countries are increasing oil prices than others. Such as the net oil importing countries are selling higher oil prices than oil exporting countries generally. For example, New Zealand is an oil import country to provide planes for international visitor arrivals, so its oil fuel price is usually higher to charge to NZ airlines because any NZ airlines need to pay to foreign countries to buy any oil more expensive price. So, NZ airlines usually charge higher airfares to its visitors to compare the other exporting oil countries' airlines. It will impact NZ has negative influence to domestic tourism industry as well as planes need will also be decreased , due to NZ charge high fuel price to cause air ticket price to be raised.

In economic theory, on income effects indicate negative impacts on tourism demand, the exact effects of higher oil fuel prices for specific destinations are far from clear. However, airline industry's different market segments show different sensitivities to air ticket fares changes.

On the first hand, if the visitors are long destinations generally wealthier than average and therefore potentially less affected, as energy costs would be a smaller proportion of their income compared will be those from less wealthy groups. Thus, the more wealthier travelers who won't decrease travelling desire, even the fuel price raises to case the air ticket price to be increased.

On the second hand, oil prices don't translate into higher transport costs especially not on air routes that are highly competitive and that are maintained for strategic reasons. So, non air transportation industry won't influence customer number to be decreased easily.

On the third hand, many other factors shape tourists' decision making, including emotion drivers or those related to images, fashions and perceptions. Increasing environmental protection awareness of tourists could also be an important factor to influence tourism consumption, instead of oil fuel price raising causes air ticket fares raising factor to reduce traveler numbers. However, oil price raising reason causes also due to high use of cars, vans and domestic air transport in some countries, e.g. Hong Kong, China countries, there are many people like to buy cars to drive. So, the private driver numbers are increasing demand to cause these countries' oil fuel prices raise in the short time suddenly. It implies airlines need to consider their country car number whether is increasing or decreasing. If their country car number is increasing, it is possible to cause fuel price to be risen up because car demand is increasing to need to use more fuel and it has less supply of fuel in the year. Otherwise, if their country car number is decreasing, it is possible to cause fuel price to be fallen down because car demand is decreasing to need to use less fuel and it has more supply of fuel in the year.

Is fuel price rising only factor to cause airline risk

in short term

In long run, fuel raising price will not cause risk to airline, due to implications of changes to supply and demand side conditions of oil fuel energy may differ qualitatively. For example, due to investment responses of producers, consumers and governments in alternative energy sources and more energy efficient plants, vehicles are supplied in order to achieve oil fuel price can't be risen seriously.

However, I believe oil fuel rising charge will be an important factor to influence global airline ticket fares to be increased in the short term to cause risk because oil fuel rising charge will be influenced to raise any airlines pressure from other unpredicted factor risk influences.

Firstly, on the bank interest changing factor, e.g. bank interest rate rising which only attract more bank saving. But it can not influence the bank savers who choose to reduce relax time to go to other countries travelling. Otherwise, when the bank savers can save more money to earn higher interest in banks, who will prefer to choose to use their saving to consume travelling. Due to who can earn higher interest rate after a period of saving time. So, I believe who behavioral travelling consumption will be raised when the banks will raise interest rate, then the bank savers won't choose to save more money in banks. So it is possible that who will withdraw more money to consume to go to travelling from banks. It seems bank interest rate changing won't influence bank savers' behavioral travelling consumption to be reduced.

Secondly, on the exchange rate changing factor, although any country's exchange changing will cause other countries' money value to be fallen down or risen up. However, it won't influence any travelers' behavioral consumption to be reduced seriously. Although, it is possible that the traveler won't spend too much to go to shopping when who travel to the another country and arrive the country. But, it is not possible to influence the traveler decides to reduce consumption to buy any air ticket to go to travelling in short time.

Thirdly, any country inflation also can not reduce travelers' travelling consumption easily because inflation can influence consumers who choose to buy cheaper foods and clothing and reduce entertainments in their every day life. But, one country's inflation can not influence it's citizen do not spend much travelling expenditure because travelers only spend one time or two times of travelling every year usually. So, the travelling expenditure rate of any households is not too much to compare daily essential expenditure.

So, it seems that bank interest rate and exchange rate changing and inflation won't influence any travelers' travelling consumption of decisions to be reduced easily in short time. Otherwise, if the oil fuel price raises too much, then global airlines' cost will be raised in long term. So, the airlines only choose to increase their air fare prices to aim to avoid loss possibly in long term. It seems that oil fuel raising price and bank interest rate and exchange rate changing and inflation factors will have direct influence airline income in long term.

Biofuels energy increases supply

I suggest these methods how to avoid the oil raising price factor to cause airline air fare prices to be risen to lead the risk of traveler numbers to be reduced as below:

The first method: Whether aviation fuel markets will have what benefits from biofuels supply to planes. I shall refer the scope includes trends in jet fuel price, airline response to fuel price, increases and volatility and environmental goals for aviation. The aviation fuel supply industry includes production, distribution and consumption of aviation fuel and it outlines players in the aviation fuel supply chain. For example, at each airport, fuel supply chain organization and fuel sourcing could differ with regard to the role of oil companies, airlines, airport owners and operators and airport service companies. However, major jet fuel purchasers are airlines, general aviation operators, corporate aviation and the military, with most of the jet fuel in global different countries demanders being used for domestic commercial and civilian flights carrying passengers, cargos or both.

Commercial aviation fuel efficiency has improved dramatically over time, largely due to aircraft and engine upgrades and operational and air traffic control improvements. So, it seems that fuel supply factor can influence airline fare prices majorly. However, jet fuel prices generally correlate with prices of crude oil and other refined petroleum products, such as diesel. So, increasing prices and the persistent price volatility of jet fuel markets import airline industry finances in any countries.

However, airlines use various strategies to manage aviation fuel price certainty, including financial hedges, increased vertical integration and adjustments in aircraft utilization and size to avoid the jet fuel raising price risk.

Investments in alternative aviation fuel could be a mechanism to diversity expose to the price of petroleum. It seems the use of alternative aviation fuel would serve to diversify the fuel mix to reduce the risk of jet fuel monopoly raising price threat. If a diversified fuel mix were to avoid either fuel raising price in short term or to avoid fuel raising price in long term. Potential benefits include reduced actual fuel costs from only choice of jet fuel supply increased price certainty and lessened fuel costs. This diversify could allow airlines to become more consistently profitable and to make other investments in their businesses.

So, biofuels have potential to meet aviation industry needs, possibly including managing risks of upward fuel price trends and fuel price volatility and avoid risks with greenhouse gas emissions. So, the aviation fuels market could use biofuels to reduce greenhouse gas emission and mitigate long-term upward price trends, fuel price volatility or both.

What are the challenges of high priced oil for aviation? In fact, nowadays not the resources of oil as such, but much more the insecurity of supply, due to geopolitical instability in combination with a tight oil market makes a scenario with much higher oil prices than the world is currently experiencing not unlikely.

Aviation is completely dependent upon oil as its fuel source. Since no practical energy substitute is readily available for commercial aviation, a scarcity of petroleum relative to demand will present a major aviation policy. In addition, efficiency gains, due to operational measures and new aircraft medium term. In particular, it has been demonstrated that the annual reduction rate in fuel consumption traffic unit is not a constant, but is itself also falling, in contrast to past estimates.

So, a high-priced oil scenario will have severe consequences for demand, airline revenues, the competitive position of airports and eventually airline networks, strategies and fleet development. In particular, transfer demand, short-haul and leisure traffic can be expected to be heavily affected by high oil prices, due to their relative high price sensitivity. Also, different countries' governments or/and airlines are valuable to research another new and potential biofuel energy to substitute oil energy to supply our planes to reduce the threat of oil monopoly supply to influence the cause of air fare raising prices. Because the elasticity is very high to travelers, when the travelers feel air fares are rising high or even low level to influence travelers who will choose not to buy the air tickets to go to travel easily.

Whether will the fuel (oil based inputs) risk be high to compare other costs, e.g. engineering maintenance, employees salaries, general cleaning, security office expenses etc. expenditures to airlines? If the probability-weighted upside effect on firm value when a risk is resolved favorably is greater the risk than the probability-weighted downside effect if the risk is resolved badly, then expected value work not be enhanced by hedging. So, the risk will be resolved badly to any commercial airlines.

Airlines are an interesting case because the direct effect of source of risk resides squarely within the no offset in revenue functions (unlike for oil producers, for example), so value effects from costs feed directly into equity value. Most directly, the risk source is fuel costs to commercial airlines. Jet fuel is of course, a mix product of crude oil, so airlines indirectly face oil price risk. There are reasons to expect that airlines' fuel costs might to convex in oil price (i.e. absent any hedging). For example, oil prices, being generally pro-cyclical in recent times, tend to be highest when airline demand is strong.

In conclusion, airlines are therefore apt to use more high priced fuel than low-priced fuel over time. Airlines can raise air fare benefit is limited by the elasticity of demand. Also, cost functions could be influenced from fuel cost corresponds to upturns in economic activity overall (due to demand pressures on oil related prices), so it causes that airline's capacity delivers their services given their level of fixed capital. The essence of airlines basis risk in the case of jet fuel is essentially the time profile of the refining margin between crude and jet fuel, or the time profile of the price differential between other refined distillates and jet fuel. Thus, it is far from clear that risk management with oil is sure to add value to any airlines. It seems the impact of airline energy and any countries' domestic or foreign airline passenger travel numbers which have direct close relationship.

Reducing terrorism occurrence

Can reduce terrorism occur to reduce airline failure risk? It needs to judge to determine if a combination of terrorism and the price of petroleum significantly predicted airline profitability and which variable whether the further period was the most significant between the terrorism occurrence and the price of petroleum influence.

I suggest that different countries' governments or airlines need to collect samples of financial records from which country's any airline commercial passengers and cargo airlines on costs of fuel and any airline profitability. Also, gathering the terrorism data were comparison of terrorist attacks on petroleum in oil-producing nations, and incidents of high jacking aboard any country's aircraft.

When any countries' airlines or governments can judge whether the impact of airline energy and terrorism risk level is high or middle or low level. Then, which can use this sample data to measure how to do positive social change to decide either ought rise or reduce employment in commercial aviation industry, or ought need to invest other higher commercial activity in tourist and other travel related service businesses and when is the most right time to adopt of green technologies by the civil aviation manufacturing industry after the terrorism attacks occurrence to any country. It seems that any countries' governments or airlines which ought concern that the event of when the terrorism attacks will occur and gather past sample data to predict when the next time terrorism attacks event will be occurred and the risk will be high or middle or low level to influence global airline industry development.

● Methods to solve rising air fare

prices to decrease travellers'demand

Will airline industry's ticket price elasticity be influenced by demand and supply factor

In fact, the airline industry is largely dependent on the supply of the oil industry. Otherwise, the oil industry is inelastic. However, the increase or decrease of the price of airfare is directly related to the increase or decrease of the oil's price to fuel the aircrafts because there has no any new energy which can be substituted to oil fuel to airline industry.

So, it seems oil fuel producers are monopolies to control its sale price to be raised easily. Another factor that can affect airline industry to be directly targeted by a tragedy brought about by terrorism. The past four years, from 2001 year to 2005 year, there had been at least $40 billion worth of losses in the airline industry because of the September 11 date terrorism attacks in 2000 year. There had been an expected and significant decrease in the demand for the airline industry services because of the attacks that involved planes hijacking and crashing into key locations like the World Trade Center and the Pentagon in USA. Although, terrorism attacks can bring risk to influence fuel price rising in airline industry. However, this risk occurrence to airline industry is only that after the terrorism attacks occurred. It is possible that terrorism attacks won't occur again in the future.

Otherwise, our concerning ought be the greenhouse emissions and how it affects global warming. The air quality would be better once this new regulations are adopted. However, it would affect large airlines. So, it would increase the price of airfares because of economic fees that airline companies have to cover. Air pollution can give a negative impact on the domestic or oversea owned airline companies for long term. If airlines' planes can use clean fuel to fly, e.g. biofuel, then it will bring benefits to global airlines for long term.

On the positive side, the environment would be healthier as the earth's temperature would rise, and greenhouse effect would be dramatically reduced. This positive effect can come at a cost that is greater than most people perceive. On the psychology view point on travelers, who will be more preferable to catch planes to go to different countries to travel, due to the chance of air pollution and global environmental warm issues will be reduced to low risk to influence our health if planes can use biofuel to be energy to fly in the future one day.

It seems that spending expenditure to research other non polluted biofuel new energy is one solvable method to global airline industry in the future. To solve, any airlines or countries' governments or oil producers ought choose to spend more time to research new biofuel. Otherwise, the predicting when terrorism attacks event will be occurred, it is more difficult to predict the time more than researching to produce new biofuel energy method in the future. So, I recommend that researching the new biofuel energy or other kinds of energy to substitute the oil energy is the urgent behavioral economy which the airlines or oil producers or different countries' governments which need to concern nowadays.

CHAPTER TWO

How applying micro economic method predict future householders accept to use secondary energy useful behaviors

Global energy is facing shortage problem. It is possible that secondary energy or human -made energy can be popular to replace to primary energy to use for global householders at home. How to apply micro economic method to predict this kind of secondary energy will be accepted to consume much than primary energy for global householders energy users in the future?

Global householder energy users and energy manufacturers are considering when earth's primary energy will be all used or energy shortage problem, keeping environment has not been polluted, plays a major role in weather and climate around the world. Several key facts are evident if we follow the flow of energy from the sun through the Earth system. Energy, like sound, travels as invisible waves of different sizes. Essentially, the energy absorbed by the land and oceans is what drives atmospheric and oceanic circulations. Hence, environment pollution issue influences global energy consumers, such as householders and business energy users , they hope to use secondary energy to replace primary energy because they fail primary energy will be used all in future one day. It seems that secondary energy need or demand will increase for global energy users.

Why do energy users and energy manufacturers need to consider earth's energy budget? Because we need to know about how much different kinds of energy can supply enough to us to use for our next generation. If some kinds of energy that we waste to use, then we shall face shortage of supply of the kinds of energy crisis to our next generation

- Global warming and energy shortage challenge influences energy users raising secondary energy need desires

We are facing global warmth and natural resource and energy shortage challenges. Due to our Earth have limited natural resource numbers to supply to us to manufacture energy, but global population has been increasing every year. Thus, it is possible that we have energy shortage crisis. Also, manufactures are spending too much energy to waste to manufacture any products, the energy will cause air or water pollution in manufacturing process or drivers are driving their vehicles to pollute air on the roads. Then it will cause global warmth crisis. Hence, it explains that why householder energy users and business energy users begin to consider whether second energy (man-made energy) can replace primary energy to be used for driving energy, home electrical energy, office electric energy or any property energy used aim. It implies that second energy need or demand ought increase rapidly as well as primary energy need or demand will decrease , due energy consumers are fear primary energy shortage problem and they feel to use less primary energy, their useful behaviors can reduce the energy shortage speed.

- Greenhouse primary gas energy householder users demand number increases

Have you ever seen a greenhouse? A greenhouse can trap heat in the sunlight and keeps the air inside the greenhouse warm enough for plants to grow. The glass roof and walls of a greenhouse let in sunlight but prevent heat from escape, this makes the greenhouse warm inside. Similarly, some gases in the Earth's atmosphere can trap heat from the sun and keep the Earth warm. This is called the greenhouse effect. The gases energy that can trap heat from the sun are called greenhouse gases. It is future one kind of potential primary energy to reduce environmental pollution new energy products for human consuming.

- Underwater primary water energy householder users demand number increases

The world's underwater meeting took place around a table about five meters underwater. Many scientists believe that due to melting of ice caused by global warming, the sea level will rise by as much as 1 m by the end of this century. If the level of the sea rises in the future, most regions of the country will be underwater.

Questions
What impact of global warming is mentioned by underground water?
Can human apply underwater water technology to explore natural underground water energy to avoid global warming threat?

Why do safety in using fuel and handle gas leaks factor can influence fuel energy users' demand number to be decreased? Why can town gas smell influence town gas energy buyers' demand number to be decreased ? How is electricity located at electric station far away from town area? How to solve problems caused by the use of fossil fuels? How to reduce the use of fossil fuels? All of these fuel related matters which will bring poor emotion to influence fuel energy users's demand to be decreased if second energy (man-made energy) can be invented to replace this kind of fuel energy to use in future one day.

This fuel energy consumers will feel how to solve the problems, the best way is to reduce their used of fossil fuel. This helps prevent fossil fuels form being used up too quickly. Also, it helps us to reduce environmental problems because fewer pollutants are given out when less fossil fuels are used. Can human help to reduce the use of fossil fuels? Fossil fuels are mainly in power station. Although we use some fossil fuels for our gas cooker and car, it won't make much difference if I use less. So, if fuel manufacturers can not solve any one of above bad emotion feeling to any one fuel users, I believe that fuel energy users number will decrease, if one day second energy (man-made energy) is invented to replace any one kind of primary energy to use in success.

- Why does fossil fuel will not be one kind of popular energy to be used by householders?

Fossil fuel is not used renew primary energy. Most of energy we use come from fossil fuels, for example, the electricity we use is generated in power stations by burning fossil fuels. The buses we ride use diesel oil. Therefore, we can help reduce the use of fossil fuels by saving energy in our daily lives. The actions that we can take such as: setting the air-conditioner to a higher temperature, walking instead of using lift, taking a short shower instead of a bath. This reduces the use of the hot water and thus the energy needed to heat the water. Thus, many people can help a lot to reduce our use of fossil fuels to avoid fossil fuel shortage risk occurrence.

For Hong Kong people energy consumption case, how much energy is used when a person travels from Hong Kong to Beijing by airplane? (The distance between Hong Kong and Beijing is about 2000 km). How much energy is used when Hong Kong people take a bus form Tai PO city to Central city? How much energy is used if Hong Kong people drive a car instead? (The driving distance between Tai Po city and Central city is 10Km).

Science explorer, we can visit the England website. Find ways to reduce energy usage from UK people energy using methods. Energy is very important to us. We need energy to walk and carry on any actions. We need energy to grow. We also need energy from food to survive. Without energy, we will die. All machines we use need energy. Without energy the electrical appliances in our homes won't work, the machines in factories will stop.

There are different forms of energy, e.g. light, heat, sound, wind, water, electrical kinetic, chemical and potential energy. Some form energy is primary energy and it can not renew to use, e.g. light, sound, wind, water, fossil fuel etc. Some form energy is secondary energy and it can renew to use in possible, e.g. nuclear, electric charge battery etc. Why does human need to concern how to manufacture secondary energy? Because it is possible that our natural resource will be consumed all, thus we will face primary energy shortage risk. If human can invent any new form of man-made secondary energy to renew to use in order to avoid primary energy shortage to supply to use to use, then human won't only depend on our Earth natural resource energy supply numbers. Hence, energy manufacturers can invent any new secondary energy to renew to use again either replaces primary energy or instead of primary energy limit number supply.

What is energy change? For television energy change power case. Firstly, electrical energy changes to television power to be used by television itself, then it changes to light power, next it changes to light power. How to choose fuel form to use? Due to energy can change to different form of powers to supply different form of power advantages to supply to human to use, so it is possible that we can also invent any secondary man made renew used energy to change different form powers to supply us to use, e.g. nuclear energy changes to light or sound or heat form of powers ; electrical charge batteries changes to light or sound or heat form powers to satisfy our daily life needs. For primary natural resource fuel energy example, different fuel has different feature, e.g. easy to burn, safe to use, gives out a lot of energy, inexpensive, produces little air pollution, easy to transport and store. How can we use in different channels, such as heating food, hot pat, driving vehicles. For example, although coal is not expensive to cause electricity energy for past transportation tool, e.g. traditional coal energy train or our daily home cooking, but it has negative influence to environment air pollution. Hence, we ought to follow the primary natural resource energy's feature to decide how to apply what aspects of our life needs. For example, if the country's people hope to reduce pollution when who use any kind of energy, e.g. US , Europe energy markets. The energy entrepreneur ought concentrate on manufacturing the kind of energy which can reduce environment pollution to be the least level to supply the country people to use, e.g. electric charge battery supplies to these countries' drivers to drive their vehicles on the roads, wind energy or water energy to manufacture electricity power supply to reduce air or water pollution ; or if the country people hope to buy the inexpensive energy to use, even the energy's quality and performance is worse, e.g. China, India, Hong Kong markets. The energy entrepreneur ought concentrate on manufacturing the lowest cost and enough supply of natural resource to manufacture the kind of energy to sell cheap price to these countries to use, e.g. China, Africa can accept to use e.g. gas, coal, fuel energy to use to compare developed countries people, e.g. UK, US; or if the countries people who hope to use energy which can easy to transport and store, e.g. light coal. The energy entrepreneur can choose to concentrate on manufacturing much coal to supply to the countries people to use, e.g. China, Arica Thus, to choose to manufacture which kinds of energy supply to the countries market people to use, the energy entrepreneur how decides to manufacture which kind of energy, it depends on which kinds of fuel advantages of the countries people most concerning.

Hence, when human feel energy shortage will come soon, energy users will reduce to use more energy to avoid energy shortage occurs in possible. It means that energy consumption number will be influenced to reduced or energy consumption buyers will reduce much expenditure to buy energy products for driving use or home use or office , warehouse working places to use. Energy needs or demand will reduce, due to environment pollution problem and energy shortage problem can influence global energy consumers' useful behaviors to be reduced in the future.

Why does secondary energy demand increase?

What is energy meaning? It is defined a dynamic quality, it is a fundamental entity of nature that is transferred between parts of a system in the production of physical change within the system, and it is usually regarded as the capacity for doing work, and it is usable power (such as heat or electricity) or the resources for producing such power. Why does secondary energy own investment worth? Because the different forms of primary natural resource energy will have supply shortage crisis, such as natural resources coal, gas, solar, wind, water, geothermal, biomass(organic material) etc. However, human can attempt to explore any undiscovered Earth or Space resource to manufacture any kinds of secondary energies, e.g. nuclear energy, electric recharge battery energy to supply to electric vehicle or space robots transportation tools to use or satisfy our daily life needs in future one day. So any kind of undiscovered secondary man-made renewed used energy resources have potential commercial worth to any energy entrepreneurs, it is possible that they can replace traditional primary energy to supply to human to use for our different aspects of life needs. In the future, the secondary energy demand will increase, when primary energy supply number has decreased form natural exploration. So, it will cause the effect of any demand of secondary energy product to be raised and prices to be increased in possible. Due to global population has been growing up, considerably China and India both countries populations have been increasing rapidly. Scientists predict there are more than 1.2 billion people worldwide will lack access to electricity, and more than 2.5 billion still use wood, charcoal to cook and heat in the future when primary energy has no enough number to supply to us to use. Hence, the fact that demand is this much greater than supply to make energy a prime market for further growth.

● Secondary energy can reduce investment risks

Although, secondary energy will have much investment worth, but energy like all other investments will carry risks. The internal and external risk factors include such as: policy is always changing to prohibit which do energy trading more easily between the energy exporting and importing countries, the secondary energy manufacturer itself own abilities to invent and to manufacture any kinds of secondary energy, improved technology can quickly make an technology obsolete, geopolitical rifts can happen overnight, the country's energy consumer (user)'s preferable choice to use which either kinds of secondary energy or secondary energy. So, it seems that (man-made) renewed used secondary energy industry can provide above-average returns, but it can also bring high risk commercial investment.

● Second energy solves energy exploration challenge

Traditionally, energy supply companies will apply those methods to operate energy providing businesses. For Shell,. Exxon examples, which had own gas stations, explore and drill for gas on their own. Other companies specialize in a part of the energy market, e.g. leasing oil rigs for example, or operating a pipeline. Energy supplying companies can choose to manufacture any kinds of energy to supply, e.g. trade oil, gas, coal, uranium, electricity etc. Any energy price and supply is demanded on the countries energy users' which kinds of energy most choice need or certain energy commodities to be chose to use popularly. For example, if US most people prefer to use secondary man-made renew used energy more than primary energy. Then, US energy manufacturers ought concentrate on manufacturing much different kinds of secondary man-made renew used energy to prepare to supply to its domestic US market in order to raise secondary energy price to sell in its country. So, the energy manufacturer's energy manufacturing choice, it is depend on which the country's people prefer to use which kinds of energy for their daily life needs.

However, scientists predict secondary energy market will have large market share, due to primary energy will have shortage to explore to supply in our earth and future energy consumers(users) prefer to choose to use more efficiency, less energy consumption, none environment pollution cause, cost effectiveness, renew to use of any kinds of energy. For example, the electricity recharge battery secondary man-made renew used energy is one kind of reducing air pollution power to push any electric battery vehicles to be driven to compare gas energy during drivers are driving their cars on the roads. They can reduce noise and air pollution and drivers can drive safely, who only need to buy one electric recharge battery to recharge in any electric recharge battery stations on streets when the electric recharge battery has no enough power to push their cars and they need to recharge their electric recharge battery drive when they had driven between one to two days. Due to primary energy, e.g. fuel , gas, the kinds of primary energies will have shortage to supply to global drivers to drive their traditional cars. Thus, the electric recharge battery or any undiscovered secondary energy will be future driving market needs. So, man-made renew used secondary energy, e.g. biofuel, hydro-electric, nuclear, will be one kind of efficient, clean, less pollution cause, cost-effective of energy to supply to our global vehicle market, even any other undiscovered new markets. Supposing they are popular to be used for electric vehicle market globally in future one day, then their prices will be decreased and constructed to average car requires up to 1,700 gallons of oil. Also supposing that making average computer requires more than ten times or weight to fossil fuels, every calories of food eaten in the US requires roughly then calories of fossil fuels. Hence, cheap energy will be one successful factor to influence future potential energy consumer (user) individual choice needs. Conversely, ion good economic times, people are more willing to travel, to buy products, and all of which success demand and low process for energy.

● Food production industry needs secondary energy useful number increasing

In the future, secondary energy will be the best choice to food production market. The modern food production system is essentially a success of changing fossil fuels into food. So, raising energy prices are almost higher food costs and even shortage for fossil fuels energy. If one day, one kind of discovered secondary man-made renew used energy can supply to any restaurants or homes to be used to cook at the cheap price, then the profit is very high for this kind of food production energy. Thus, future food production secondary energy consumption market is large and because the primary energy inputs for agriculture are higher than the energy outputs of the food. However, future secondary man-made renew used energy for food production system is only one part of whole energy consumer in food industry. The food production is related to whole food consumption market which includes: household cooking energy market, agriculture or vegetable, rice, fruit etc. foods farming machines energy market, food manufacturing factories market, food machine package market, transportation food delivery market, supermarket or fruit/food sale stores market. They must need any energy inputs to achieve the food production or food transportation or warehouse / stores electricity supply or cooking energy needs. Hence, these food suppliers relate to any whole food factory manufacturers, food retailers, food wholesalers, farmers and home/restaurant cookers, all of them must need to use energy to carry on their food producing or food cooking or food transportation activities every day in overall food industry. Thus, it seems that undiscovered any second energy demand will be increased, when the primary energy supply number is decreasing. Also, when people can accept to use secondary energy to replace primary energy to be used for any cooking, transporting food, manufacturing food, food retail stores or warehouse food delivery energy need activities. Then, the secondary energy price will be fall down to attract many food energy consumers.

Nowadays, the food industry energy may includes primary nature resource gas energy or electricity energy for house families or restaurants cooking needs, food delivering lorry drivers driving needs usually. If future second man made renew used energy is invented successful popular to be used, e.g. hydrogen, electric recharged battery energy for electric vehicles or restaurant/home families cooking needs or food factories machine manufacture energy needs. Then, the secondary energy will have possible to replace primary energy to be food industry energy market.

Wiley, composition services graphics indicated that global primary energy consumption had been increasing 30 billion tons from 1830 year to 510 billion tons in 2010 year as well as global population size had been increasing from 70 billion 1830 year to 510 billion in 2010 year. Thus, it seems that global primary energy consumption will be needed largely after 2010 year. If future global nature resource primary energy is explored full number and it had not enough energy number to supply global human to use. Then, it will being many people feel uncomfortable and inconvenience ,e.g. Some countries won't have enough energy to supply transportation tools to be driven, some homes and restaurants won't have enough energy to supply to cook to eat or to provide restaurant clients to eat etc. daily activities, due to human's much activities which are needs energy supply. Thus, it seems that global primary energy consumption will be needed largely after 2010 year.

- Primary energy faces shortage challenge influences energy users' useful desires to be reduced

Wiley, composition services graphics also explains that why the primary energy consumption demand can be needed to achieve the same level to the global population size increasing in 2010 year. The graph showed these reasons why cause the same level of global population size and global primary energy consumption demand which may include: The graph showed that after a nation is developed, its per-person energy use high to level off. In North America and Europe, where energy demand has remained flat, or fallen sight, in each of the past few years. But the 1.3 billion people on those two continents are far out weighted by the 5 billion people in Asia and Africa, e.g. Chinese and Indian. who currently have more energy need to compare average per man to North America and Europe per man, ensuring that overall energy demand will rise for years to come.

Wiley, composition services graphics also predicted that the growth in primary energy demand. China will have 4,500 million tons in 2035 year. India will have 3,000 million tons in 2035 year. Other developing Asia will have 2,000 million tons in 2035 year. Russia will have 1,500 million tons in 2035, Middle East will have 1,300 million tons in 2035, other rest of world will have 1,000 million tons in 2035. Hence, it implied that China will be the largest primary energy need country in the future.

China will be future the primary potential energy consumer market. The primary energy includes water, coal, wind, fossil oil, gas ,solar, geothermal energy, biomass (organiz material) etc. different natural resource primary energy. Otherwise, US, UK, Europe will be secondary energy potential need market. For example, electrical recharge battery energy will be raised demand to supply to any future new design electrical charge battery vehicles in US, Europe, UK markets.

Due to US, Europe, UK people concern environment protection, so they will invent many electric charge battery vehicles to consume electrical charge battery to replace polluted gas energy to avoid air pollution when the drivers are driving cars on themselves countries‘ roads. For example, second man-made renew used nuclear energy can be applied to rockets to push them to leave our earth to fly to other space far away and consuming nuclear energy will be cost efficient, and nuclear energy saving will be more when nuclear to spend long time to be used in any long time space journey. Hence, nuclear energy and electric charge battery secondary energy will be popular to be applied to vehicles and rockets energy needs in US, Europe, potential markets, even our daily energy needs in global second energy market.

● Law and policies in energy supply industry influences primary energy price rises and energy users' useful desires to be reduced both effect. They have cause effect relationship.

Every energy entrepreneur needs to consider how whose government implement law and policies to prohibit whose energy consumption, energy distribution and energy production behavior in order to protect energy consumers can have fair price energy purchase from the country's energy suppliers between themselves. For US energy law and policy example, the energy independence and security Act of 2007 year. It's major provisions include: Accelerated research of clean energy technologies Act, energy savings in building and industry Act, improved standards for appliances and lighting Act, improved vehicle fuel economy Act and increased production of biofuel Act. It aims to prohibit any US energy manufacturing suppliers do any unfair energy trading transaction behavior to its domestic or foreign energy consumers immortally.

● Energy entrepreneur's business strategy influences different kinds of energy users' demand desire to be controlled to increase or decrease

Before you decide to operate either any kinds of secondary energy or primary energy supply business or both kinds of energy supply business. I recommend that you need to consider how to solve these questions before choosing which kind of energy product to manufacture. The questions may include as below:

Who are your energy business's competitors (peers)? How do they compare? How have your energy business company performed cyclically? How to choose to manufacture to sell which kinds of primary or secondary energy product(s), either manufactures only primary energy product(s) or manufactures only secondary energy products or both? Which countries do you plan to sell your energy product?

Illustration by Wilsey, composition services graphs showed that these natural resources to energy product the world's electricity percentage, such as below:

41% of coal, 5% of oil, 21% of gas, 13% of nuclear, 16% of Hydro, 3% other renewable secondary man-made energy.

Hence, coal will be future the major natural resource to produce electricity. The energy entrepreneur ought attempt to explore any coal resources, when who choose to supply electricity power to consumers for future energy consumption country markets.

Wiley, composition services also predicted that the expectation is that North America coal will supply the expectation is that North America coal will supply Asian demand, Us export terminals have a total capacity of 173 million ton output. China will drive 16% of the nations total output. China will drive the sea-born demand for coal over for the predictive future. Chinese energy consumption will grow more than 12 % between 1980 and 2009 years.

Though, China heads global demand, India is growing faster in terms of coal imports. Much of the global coal demand will be supplied by Indonesia and Australia. Colombia, Russia, South Africa and Mongolia are also players in global export coal energy resources.

Consequently, I believe that secondary energy will be one kind of new energy product to replace traditional primary energy product for human energy consumption market global needs. Hence, it is right time any energy entrepreneur needs to research how to explore any undiscovered man-made renew used secondary energy products to avoid primary energy shortage crisis occurrence.

- Solar energy efficient useful characteristics raises secondary energy (human -made energy) needs or useful desires to be raised.

What is solar energy? Every day, the sun radiates (send out) and enormous amount of energy, called solar energy. It radiates more energy in one day. Then, the world uses in one year. This energy comes from within the sun itself. The sun makes energy in its inner core in a process called nuclear fusion.

Only a small part of the visible radiant energy (light) that the sun emits into space ever reaches the earth enough to supply all our energy needs. Every hour enough solar energy reaches the earth to supply our nation's energy is considered a renewable energy source due to this fact. Today, people use solar energy to heat buildings and water t generate electricity. Solar energy accounts for a very small percentage of U.S. energy less than one percent. Solar energy is used by residences and to generate mostly electricity.

Method to gather solar: A solar collector is one way to capture sunlight and change it into usable clean energy. A closed car on a sunny day is like a solar collector. As sunlight passes through the car's windows, is it absorbed by the seat covers, walls, and floor of the car. The absorbed light changed into heat. The car's windows let light in, but they don't let all the heat out. A closed car can get very hot!

Which is space heating? It means heating the space inside a building. Today, many homes use solar energy for space heating. A passive solar home is designed to let in as much sunlight as possible. It is like a big solar collector. For example, a passive solar home doesn't depend on mechanical equipment, such as pumps and blowers to heat the house, whereas active solar homes do. It seems that future human can attempt to apply solar energy to use in home conveniently.

How can apply solar energy? Solar energy can be used to heat water. Heating water for bathing, dishwashing and clothes washing is the second largest have energy cost. Installing a solar water heater can reduce home water heating bill be as much as 50 percent. A solar water heater works a lot like solar space heating. For example, installing a solar collector on a house roof where it can capture sunlight. The sunlight heats water in a tank. The hot water is piped to faucets throughout a house, as it would be with an ordinary water heater.

Solar energy can also be used to produce electricity. Two ways to make electricity from solar energy are photovoltaics and solar thermal systems both. However, compared to other ways of making electricity photo voltic systems are expensive. It can cost to 30 cents per kilo hour to produce efficient from solar cells. Similar to solar cells, solar systems also celled solar power, use solar energy to produce electricity, but in a different way, most solar thermal systems use a solar collector with a mirrored surface to focus sunlight onto a receiver that heats a liquid. However, solar energy has great potential for the future. Solar energy is free, and its supplies are unlimited. It doesn't pollute or otherwise damage the environment. It can't be controlled by any one nation or industry. IF we can improve the technology to harness the sun's power, we may never face energy shortages again.

For active solar home example, passive homes can get 30 to 80 percent of the heat, they need from the sun. They store their heat energy by using think walls and building materials that retain heat well like concrete, stone and even water. For sole water heating another example, solar energy can also be used to heat water for household use. Heating water for bathing and washing is the second largest home energy cost. Installing a solar water heater can cut that cost in half. A solar water heater works a lot like solar space heating. The sunlight heats water and stores it in tank. The hot water is piped to faucets throughout a house, such as it would be with an ordinary water heater. Finally radiant energy to electricity example, solar energy can be used to produce electricity, e.g. solar-powered toys, calculators, many lighted roadside signs all use solar cells to covert sunlight into electricity.

Next kind of solar electricity manufacturing method is solar power tower. At full peak, estimated electricity generation each year is 155,000 megawatt-hours, enough to power 11,000 homes. This makes the Martin Next generation solar energy center the largest solar thermals power plant in the Eastern United States.

In conclusion, human can earn benefits of solar energy include: Solar electric systems are safe, clean and quiet to operate. Solar systems are highly reliable, solar systems are cost-effective in remote areas and for some residential and commercial applications, solar systems are flexible and can be expanded to meet increasing electrical needs for homes and businesses, solar systems can provide independence from the grid on backing during outages, the fuel is renewable and free and domestically produced, harnessing solar energy spurs economic development, using solar energy to generate electricity produces no greenhouse gases. Hence, future solar energy will be a kind of renewable and reused and recycled natural resource energy to be provided to human to use.

- Water energy efficient useful characteristics raises

energy users' demand number increases

The efforts to improve water and efficiency from both the supply and the demand sides would allow countries to reduce resource scarcity and maximize water energy benefits. However, water efficiency is a concept, it means " doing more and better with less by obtaining more value with the available resources by reducing the resource consumption and reducing the pollution and environmental impact of water use for the stage of the value chain and of water service provision."

Improving water efficiency means increasing water productivity, reducing the intensity of water use for, and pollution from socio-economic activities through maximizing. The value of the uses of water, improving the allocation of water greater socio-economic value per drop of water in order to achieve aim to ensure environmental flows, and improving technical efficiency of water services and the management efficiency of their provision over the complete life cycles.

How to enable water and energy efficiency? Water thirsty energy demonstrates the importance of combined energy and water management approaches through demand-based work in several countries. In order to ensure water energy users to earn water energy efficient benefits.

How to make the right choice among water resource efficient technologies? These include recycling and reuse of water, low water using appliances, efficient irrigation systems, decentralized sewerage systems, information and communication technologies, rainwater cater and reclamation of nutrients and creating new opportunities to water renewable energy potential and the need of innovation and development and serves to solve energy shortage from water renewable and reused resource energy invention.

Water energy efficient production method includes, it will allow differentiating between water withdrawal, water consumption and net water consumption and calculating different kinds of interactions between the activity and its water environment. With an annual investment of US$198 billion on average over the next forty years, water use can be made more efficient, enabling increased agricultural, biofuels, and industrial production (UNEP, 2011).

Investing US$170 billion annual in energy efficiency worldwide could produce energy savings of up to US$900 billion per year (SE4ALL, 2012) and each additional US$1 spent on energy efficiency in electrical equipment, appliances and buildings avoids more than US$2 on average in energy supply investments (IEA, 2012).

How can water energy distribution solution? The facilitate greater operational efficiency including energy-efficient water supply operation systems and water distribution control systems that help in ways that include reducing electricity costs as well as the load on the environment. For one example to water distribution solution for more efficient operation of water supply and individual technologies. The water distribution system will consist first stage is component technology to (linear programming and modeling). Second stage is solution: water supply, it is operation and planning techniques that works with electronic power demand response. The final stage is water source, water will be in taken to adequate them to deliver water treatment plant. Next step, the water treatment plant water will be delivered to main water pipe. Final stage, water will be delivered to water distribution network from water distribution network to this whole water distribution process. It depends on the time of day. Incentive schemes, such as load control programs request users to reduce their power use at times when the supply of electric power is constrained and pay them for doing so in the form of a bonus from water power station suppliers. So, nowadays, some countries' water power station supplies have developed a water supply operation technique that reduces electricity costs by earning these incentives.

What is water supply operation technique? The water supply operation technique consists of operation mode that seeks to smooth electric power use in ways that cut the basic tariff by smoothing demand across the course of day and a demand response operation mood that earns incentives by reducing demand in response to requests. Water supply surplus uses a large number of distribution reservoirs to buffer the gap between demand for water and the supply from the water treatment plants.

Furthermore, falling demand in recent years means there are a significant number of distribution reservoirs with excess capacity. This means that peaks in electricity demand can be shifted or cut by taking advantage of this unused water storage capacity to shift the timing of conveying pump operation. Minimizing electric power consumption as far as possible during demand peaks or during time periods specific in demand response requires. But, it also requires risk management to ensure that the water levels in distribution reservoirs don't full below their lower limits. Consequently, water supply will be another kind of reused energy resource to provide to human to use.

● What is future household energy consumption trend?

In general, household energy consumption includes , i.e. for lighting, cooking, heating etc. The household sector is responsible for about 15 to 25 percent of primary energy use for a higher share in many developing countries. Average per capita household energy use in developed countries is about nine time higher than in developing countries, even though in developing countries a large share of household energy is provided by non-commercial fuels are historical trends in per capita household energy consumption by these kinds of energy, i.e. fuel, coal, petroleum, natural gas and electricity etc. energy.

Some scientists indicate Asia and South America have consequently lower energy efficiency. However, the major factors contributing to countries which lower and higher energy efficiency differences include, such as levels of urbanization, economic development and living standards. Other factors are country or region specific, such as climate or cultural practices. However, energy efficiency depends both in the types of fuel used and on the characteristics of particular appliances.

Consequently, future trend of energy will be renewable, reused, cheap more efficient and productive secondary energy for human to use.

● The reasons why water and solar energy users number will increase

In our earth, we own much natural resource supply, some natural resource has shortage crisis, e.g. gas, coal, fuel etc. But, some natural resource which still have unlimited supply and we shall have enough energy supply to solve our energy shortage crisis if we can invent them to change to electricity or any power successfully, e.g. wind, solar, water natural resource.

However, I believe that wind and water and solar nature resource will be another kind of potential energy supply to solve our energy shortage crisis. I shall indicate the reasons as below:

First, on wind nature energy supply aspect, human can apply wind power to change to be electricity energy. So, I recommend human can seek any places which can have much wind natural resource to attempt to produce wind energy. For New Zealand country, Auckland and Wellington cities which own much wind natural resource power. Hence, this countries are suitable to invent any wind electricity manufacturing factories to manufacture wind electricity to solve our electricity shortage crisis.

Second, on water natural energy supply aspect, New Zealand is one country which own clean water place. It's water can even to be driven and it does not need to heat to supply to us to drink fresh water. So, New Zealand own much clean water supply, we can attempt to use this country extra water natural resource to manufacture water electricity when New Zealand has many water manufacturing factories, then we shall have much water electricity to prepare our future use.

Third, on solar natural energy supply aspect, our sun will have unlimited natural heat supply. Hence, solar natural resource will be our future one kind of energy supply source. I shall recommend Africa country will be one good location choice to build solar factories because Africa is one hot and much sun natural resource country. Hence, if scientists can attempt to build solar power factories to manufacture solar energy. Then, we shall have one country which can concentrate on manufacturing solar energy to supply to us to use.

Consequently, New Zealand and Africa will be the suitable countries to build solar, wind and water factories to manufacture solar, wind and water energy to prepare to us to use as well as natural resource solar and wind and water will be our future reused and recycle energy to solve our electricity needs for our next generation. So, nowadays, it is right time that energy scientists ought attempt to build energy factories on these both countries to invent any one kind of these three kinds of natural resources to solve energy shortage crisis.

Reference

Sustainable energy for ALL (SE4ALL) initiative, United Nations secretary. http://www.sustainableenergyforall.org

Towards a green economy pathways to sustainable development and poverty eradication. Unites Nations Environment program (UNEP), 2011
http://www.unep.org/greeneconomy

World energy outlook, executive summary, p.7 IEA , 2012

CHAPTER THREE

Environment pollution influences householder behaviors change

Can economic environment influences householder electricity energy consumption or useful activities to be more or less? In general, house owners have both intentions for whose property. One intention is living the house by householder himself or herself or householder with families themselves. Another intention is that renting to others to receive rent income (landlord). So, in the housing market, the housing consumer includes either the property owner intents to rent to others to live for rent income aim or the property buyers intents to buy the house to be house owner to live. Does these both different property purchase intentions, which will influence the householder's attitude to use electricity energy consumption desire to be more or less, due to the householder's demand to whose house quality factor influence? This is one interesting question concerns the householder electricity energy consumption desire change to the householder, due to house's investment or house's living intention influences to house quality factor.

How does house quality factor influence to householder electricity energy consumption desire to be more or less? Has it relationship between house quality and house investment or living intention to cause house quality demand to influence the householder electricity energy consumption desire change or demand to be more or less? Has it relationship between regional housing market living or rent investment intentions, housing quality and electricity energy consumption more or less desire? I suppose that the determinants of the residential electricity energy demand form space-heating and cooking, due to the property quality demand influence and the householder's living or rent investment intention influence both, which will influence the householder's electricity energy consumption or useful behavior when he/she/they is/are living in the house.

I argue that rent properties are not only consumer goods, but it also constitute financial market assets. It is therefore reasonable to assume that rational (rent income investment intention) investors choose to raise housing quality (e.g. thermal insulation technological installing at home, heating or cooling technology or artificial intelligent window, lighting, door opening or closing) in order to attract many people choose to rent whose house to live. The householder's aim is to achieve an acceptable return on investment (ROI) or raising rent income aim when he/she rents whose house to anyone, it is easy to attract many people to choose to pay higher rent his/her house to live in the property rent market. Moreover, the another important factor is that rents and future house sale prices of properties differ regionally (or even locally), and largely depend on housing market fundamentals, such as either the house living buyer's income levels or the house rent buyer's income levels, vacancy rates, and/or householder investor's expectations.

Thus, if the householder expects to rent whose house and raises rent to attract many people choose to rent whose house to live, who will attempt to install many new technology in order to satisfy their high quality of life need when they can pay higher rent to rent to choose to rent whose houses to live. Their aim only achieves to raise housing quality, but any new technology will lead to increase electricity energy consumption or use in the house.

Hence, any high quality of houses will influence the householder to use or consume more electricity energy at home. It means that the householder will choose to consume or use more electricity energy at home, if he/she or the family householder demands to live more comfortable house and he/she/they can have high quality of living life at home. This comfortable living demand to the householder (property renter or property buyer) view point can explain why the better quality of house factor will influence the electricity energy consumption desire to the householder also to be more daily.

I shall indicate one home electricity energy consumption experiment, it indicated that utilizing aggregate data on regional space-heating energy consumption form over 300,000 apartment buildings in 97 German planning regions. The study applies structural equation modelling to estimate the influence of housing market fundamentals on the level of housing quality, and subsequently on regional electricity energy consumption. Consequently, it suggests that housing market fundamental explain regional differences in the housing quality.

In particular, findings show that the level of per capita income, investor' expectations about future housing market development as well as vacancy all explain regional differences in housing quality has a significant impact on electricity energy consumption.

In the way, this experiment can indicate evidence that regional housing market fundamental have a substantial influence on regional levels of housing quality and energy consumption desires to the German regional householders. This Germany regional householder experiment found important implications for high or low housing quality of the regional property building and householders either property living or property rent intention of comfortable living feeling need factor which will influence the regional property householder electricity energy consumption desire to be raised or reduced. These factors will influence the consequence of electricity energy demand to be increased or decreased needs every day for the regional householder as well as the country's electricity energy supplier(s) can gather the regional properties whether they are high or low quality to predict the regional properties householders' electricity energy consumption supply budget more accurate. It implies that an important determinant of residential housing quality will have possible to influence electricity energy demand to be more or less for long term. IN particular, this Germany regional residential experiment can explain and find an important role in formulating assumptions about the quality factor has chance to influence the regional residential future levels of electricity energy efficiency and consumption in the country. Hence, housing developments and electricity energy firms can follow this regional residential housing quality factor to evaluate whether the regional housing market is the corresponding investment patterns as well as the energy researchers can follow the regional residential housing quality whether it is high or low housing quality factor to evaluate the more accurate models of regional electricity energy demand to any regional residential householders' houses in the country.

In consumer behavioral view point, it explains that if the country government expected many householders feel to need to spend much electricity energy or have much electricity energy useful demand or desire at home. The country government ought to encourage the country residential property or house developers choose to build many houses which have technological product installed to satisfy the regional householders' residential comfortable living need when they choose the regions to build the high quality houses to let them to live. Then, the regional householders will be influenced to consume or use much electricity energy at homes, due to they feel that they are living at high quality and comfortable and high building technological installed apartments in the country's regions. Then, the country's government and electricity energy provider(s) may be raise much electricity energy efficiency and supply and profit , due to the regional residential householders' electricity energy consumption or useful desire need is therefore influenced to be more by the regional high quality of residential houses factor. So, the regional high quality of residential house factor will have relationship to the regional electricity energy consumption and efficiency to the regional householder's houses.

Otherwise, if the country government felt electricity energy is shortage, it ought encourage the property developers build many low quality and low building technological houses to let householders to live themselves or rent to others to live in the country's different regional residential development market. Due to the low quality of properties and low technological installed to properties factor which will influence any these different regional residential householders to choose method to solve shortage of electricity energy challenge to the country.

In conclusion, to apply consumer behavioral economic theory to property development market, if property quality factor can really influence the householder's electricity energy consumption desire to be used more or less at home daily. The country's property developers can apply this factor to predict property consumer individual property buying consumption behaviors more accurate. For example, if the US property developer planned to build low quality and low technological design buildings and lesser comfortable residential houses in the region in US. Then, its residential householder target will be trended the less acceptable of electricity energy consumption property buyers to choose to buy these regional properties to live in the US region because they can only accept to spend less electricity energy to use when they are living in the houses in order to save money daily. SO, the low quality , less comfortable and low technological installed design residential houses will satisfy their living needs. Otherwise, if the US property developer planned to build high quality and high technological installed design buildings and more comfortable residential houses in the region in US. Then, its residential householder target will be trended to the more acceptable of electricity energy consumption property buyers to choose to buy these regional properties to live in the US region because they can accept to spend more electricity energy to use when they are living in the houses in order to improve their living of quality. So, they wont's consider to spend more expenditure to use electricity energy for any technological products are installed in their properties in order to satisfy their comfortable living needs at their homes every day.

Consequently, property developers can attempt to gather marketing research concerns whether how many people who accept to use more electricity energy or use less electricity energy in order to predict they ought build how many high quality or low quality houses number in different regions more accurate in themselves countries or overseas countries property development market.

- Environmental impacts of householder greenhouse gas electricity energy consumption activities

Has environment factor relationship to influence householder electricity energy consumption behaviors? Socially, householder electricity energy consumption provides us with sources of living satisfaction , but if any sudden environment factor changes, whether it will influence householder consume or use more or less electricity energy decision at home. However, I assume householder electricity energy consumption will have a considerable proportion of the environmental impacts be influenced by our way of life and our economic decision of electricity energy consumption behavior.

What different environmental factors will influence householder electricity energy consumption decision? The external environmental factors include, for example, the country's electricity firms or government changes to electricity energy regulations, electricity energy production technologies change and business practices and government policies changing etc. different external environmental factors will influence any country's electricity energy consumption to householders' consumption desire to be more or less. It will also require changes to influence the householders to consume which kinds of electric products which are needed to be used in different electricity energy natural manufacturing resources.

Why does these external environmental factors impact householders' any behaviors to influence them to concern to use more or less electricity energy power or which kinds of electricity energy products choice at homes. How any why environmental factors impact will influence householder activities at home, such as electricity energy consumption and choice? What are the key components of external environmental factors influence householders' electricity energy consumption behaviors. I shall explain as below:

Firstly, we need to know whether what external environments are which can influence why and how householders need to change their activities to choose more or less or which kinds of energy power to be provided to them to use at home. Who is householder? Householder is an individual, family, or group of individuals living together as unit in a home. Consumption of electricity energy at home may be cooking food needs, needing have colder feeling to turn on fan or air condition at home in summer or needing have warm feeling to turn on heater at home in winter, watching television programs or listening music , playing computer games or used computers activities , reading activities and applying artificial intelligent technological tools to help householders to open or close homes' windows, doors etc. different home equipment which need to use electricity energy provisions. SO, their home activities need to turn on lighting electric tools , televisions, music machines, radios etc. different equipment which need to use electricity energy provision at home. SO, the purpose of householder consumption means consumption by individuals living in a household and it includes consumption both in and outside the home. Why does environmental impacts link to householders' electricity energy consumption? I shall focus on discussing of greenhouse gases (GHGS) energy product how any why it can influenced to householders to use.

The environmental impacts will influence this kind of greenhouse gases (GHGS) energy in the product lifecycle or delivery of the service to link the householder's energy consumption at home such as these several aspects:

Extraction and greenhouse gases production (supply number), physical distribution (delivery far long or close near short distance between the greenhouse gases manufacturing factory and the greenhouse gases supplier), resources consumed by marketing and retail activities (householder's needs to use the quantity of the greenhouse gases energy product), the greenhouse gases consumers search and purchasing activities(e.g. travel to shops, internet purchasing channel, , finding the which kinds of greenhouse gases products from internet, magazines, newspapers, radio advertisements etc. different medias,) , post-use greenhouse gases energy disposal (resale, reused or rubbish). The householder's physical behavioral impact environmental factor will influence how and why he/she chooses to consume greenhouse gases energy daily , e.g. impacts of a housing development, or a wind –farm that supplies greenhouse gases with power. So, the householder's greenhouse gases energy consumption behavior which will depend upon individual personal and subjective perspectives and value.

So, the householder's useful behavior or attitude of greenhouse gases energy product which will influence how he/she/ the family use or consume greenhouse gases energy, such as the householder individual environmental protection attitude which can impact how he/she/the family spends the quantity of greenhouse gases energy every day at home, if the householder does not expect our air or water or land is polluted , due to extraction of any natural gas resources to be manufactured any kinds of greenhouse gases products. Then, this environmental pollution issue will influence some householders choose to reduce to use more quantity of greenhouse gases products every day. Another environmental factors include the bio relates the (unsustainable) use of resources to avoid wasting much greenhouse gases energy to cause greenhouse gases energy supply shortage, avoiding the cause negative impacts of quality life , e.g. noise causing when the extraction of any natural resource from lands to the householder's house is near to the natural resource extraction land and health impacts, e.g. when the greenhouse gas householder user who often use the kind of greenhouse gas product when it is used to cook or heat any equipment to cause they to breathe dirty air at home often. These impacts can be measured in different ways include: monetary costs or loss, physical quantities of resources used or waste or pollution produced and the burden the greenhouse gases energy place on environmental resources. All of these external environment factors will impact the householder individual attitude or behavior how to use or consume greenhouse gases energy product at home.

All these environmental factors concern householder greenhouse gases energy consumer individual consumption attitude is influenced by environment pollution, greenhouse resource supply shortage challenge, greenhouse gases influence the householder's negative quality of life, negative health impacts, noise, waste money , raising economic cost to the householder which will impact whether how the householder choose to use the quantity of greenhouse

gases product or the kinds of greenhouse gases products or other kinds of electricity energy products.
However, these are other external environmental factors which can impact how the householder decides to use greenhouse gas product at home. They include: the changes of energy regulation, e.g. the country government has quota number implementation to prohibit to import above the limited quantities of any kinds of greenhouse gas products to any countries. So, when the greenhouse gas energy supplying quantity is decreased, but if the country has may householders who need to buy different kinds of greenhouse gases products to be used at home. Then, the different kinds of import greenhouse gases energy products prices will be raised in possible, due to demand is more than supply in the country's greenhouse gas energy product market. Consequently, if the greenhouse gas energy price us risen above the general social acceptable level to the home greenhouse gas energy product householder consumers. Finally, it will influence them to choose to buy other kinds of gas energy products to replace the greenhouse gas energy product to use at home.
Another side, if the country's greenhouse gas energy manufacturing supplier sudden changes its greenhouse gas energy production technologies to choose to concentrate on manufacturing other kinds of energy products. Then, the greenhouse gas energy supply quantities will be only decreased, even future one day , it will cause greenhouse gas supply shortage challenge to let the country's home greenhouse gas householder consumers who can not buy enough quantity of any kinds of greenhouse gas energy products to satisfy their electricity needs at home every day. Consequently, when future on day , the country greenhouse gas energy manufacturer has none any quantity of greenhouse energy products to supply to the country's greenhouse energy householders to use at home. The, they must only choose other kinds of new energy products to replace the traditional useful greenhouse gas energy products to be used at homes.
In conclusions, these non-controlled external environmental factors can impact and influence the country's every householder consumer individual attitude or consumption behavioral change to how any why the country's householders either choose to buy much or less quantity of greenhouse gas products to use at home.

- The effect of house space occupancy and building characteristics influences householder electricity energy use

Can economic factors measure how much space occupancy is the suitable size as well as what the most suitable building characteristics influence each householder electricity energy useful activities or behaviours? In general, society believes large space size occupancy house building characteristics factor which will influence householder use more energy at home, e.g. in summer, when the householder is living at the large space size occupancy house, who ought turn on all air conditions or fans at sleeping rooms or eating room or studying room. So, if the householder's house has two to three or more sleeping rooms. Then, he / she needs to buy more air conditions or fans in order to let all rooms' temperature to be fallen down to let he /she feel more cool comfortable feeling when the temperature is above 30 degree or more extreme hot in summer weather. Otherwise, when the temperature is low, e.g. between 0 degree to 10 degree or below 0 degree in winter weather. When the householder is living in one large space size occupancy apartment, which has thee to five sleeping rooms , even more and two studying rooms and one eating room, even more as well as every room has one heater. Then, he / she must turn on all heaters to let who to feel warm feeling when he / she is staying in the house. It brings these interesting questions.

Will large or small size space occupancy housing characteristics influence any householder often turn on heater or air condition or fan in whole house space occupancy area in order to the householder feels warmer or cooler feeling when he /she is staying in the house?

Has any space occupancy housing characteristics relationship to influence any householder to turn on heater or air condition or fan in whole house space occupancy area in order to the householder feels warmer or cooler feeling when he /she is staying in the house?

Does it bring positive relationship between turning on long time fan or air condition or heater and the house occupancy space characteristics is large or small size?

I shall attempt to give psychological evidences to explain the householder's house space occupancy area large or small size factor whether it can influence the householder choose to do long time or short time turning on heater or air condition or fan behavior in order to let he/she/the family to feel more cooler or warmer comfortable feeling when he/she/the family is staying in the house in summer or winter weather.

Does the house occupancy space size characteristics factor is the only one or important factor to influence the householder choose to turn on long or short time fan or air condition or heater in the house to let him/her/the family to feel more cooler or warmer comfortable feeling in summer or winter weather?

I feel that it is not exact right , due to the householder's house space occupancy size whether it is large or small characteristics to influence the householder choose to turn on long time or short time fan or air condition or heater time to let him /her/ the family to feel more cooler or warmer when he / she / the family is staying at home in summer or winter weather. The reason is because that the lifestyle of living quality need is different between developed countries and developing countries. The lifestyle of living quality factor will change the country's householder's expectation about the quality of living life. For example, for Africa, Korea, China , Japan, Hong Kong etc. developing countries. On the lifestyle of living quality need to these developing countries' householders aspect, that will cause a high environmental burden when they need to often turn on air conditions to satisfy more cooler feeling when they are staying at homes in summer or they need often to turn on heaters to satisfy more warmer feeling when they are staying at home in winter. Due to if their houses are large size space occupancy characteristics and they have more than at least two sleeping rooms and studying rooms and eating rooms and toilets number. Then, these householders who are developing countries' large space occupancy size characteristics houses, they won't like often turn on heaters long time to keep more warmer in their indoor whole space area in winter or they won't like often turn on air conditions or fans long time to keep more cooler in the their indoor whole space area house environment in summer .

The reason is possible because that the developing countries' householder chooses often to turn on their heaters or air conditions or fans long time in their houses when they are staying long time in their houses and their houses space occupancy sizes are very large, it will bring the electricity energy to be used more to these developing countries' householders' large space occupancy size characteristic houses. It means that the electricity fee will be also increased due to they often turn on heaters or air conditions or fans long time to keep their indoor temperature to be more cooler in summer or more warmer in winter. So, it seems that the developing countries' householders are living in the house whose space occupancy have very large size characteristics and more than two rooms house characteristics in the developing countries as above. Then, they won't often choose to turn on heaters or air conditions or fans long time to keep more cooler or warmer feeling in their house whole indoor space occupancy environment when they are often staying at home long time.

Their lifestyle of living comfortable feeling are lesser than the developed countries householders. Consequently, their lesser cooling or warming comfortable demand of living lifestyle factor will change their attitudes to use air conditions or fans or heaters turning on time in order to limit heaters or air conditions or fans turning on time to be shorter than the developed countries householders' heaters or air conditions or fans turning on time at homes. Due to the long time turn on air conditions, fans , heaters at the developing countries' householders' homes, it will cause to spend much electricity energy to lead electricity fee charges to be raised to the developing countries' householders ' homes when they are often staying at homes in summer or winter weather. Hence, the house space occupancy large size characteristics ought not influence the developing countries householders choose to turn on air conditions , fans or heaters long time in order to let them to feel more cooler or warmer at homes in summer or winter weather.

So, the developing countries' house space occupancy large size characteristics householders won't be more acceptable to pay higher electricity energy fee when they are staying at homes at summer or winter weather. Due to they do not often choose to turn on heaters, air conditions or fans long time during they are staying at homes. Otherwise, the developed countries, e.g. UK, UK , France, Germany, Swiss, Singapore, Italy etc. countries. In general, these developed countries' householders' living lifestyle quality needs are higher than the developing countries. So, when the summer or winter weather is coming, if the temperature is extreme cold, e.g. below than 0 degree or it is extreme hot, e.g. higher than 30 degree.

Then these developed countries' householders will easy accept to turn on air conditions or fans or heaters long time at home in order to keep their apartment in door temperature to be more cooler in extreme hot in door environment or more warmer in extreme cold in door environment when these developed countries' householders are often staying at homes long time at night after their day time working time or schooling time. Because these developed counties' householders' quality of living lifestyle needs or demands are higher than the developing countries' householders. So, they won't consider that they will pay more electricity fee , due to they often turn on air conditions, fans or heaters long time to let them to feel more comfortable in cooler or warmer indoor large size space occupancy environment. So, it seems that the electricity energy efficiency will be raised to the developed countries' householders who are living in the house space occupancy large size characteristics and they will be possible to pay more electricity fees during they are often staying at home in extreme hot summer or extreme cold winter weather.

In conclusion, due to the living lifestyle quality need (demand) is different between the developed countries' householders and the developing countries' householders. It will influence the householders' long time or short time spending time on air conditions or fans or heaters indoor space occupancy size characteristics environment in order to achieve more cooler or more warmer feeling in their houses. Consequently, the long or short time of turning on air conditions, fans, heaters for the developed or developing countries householders‘ activities factor will be more influential to compare the house space occupancy large or small size characteristics factor to influence their cooler or warmer feeling in their houses. SO, the house indoor environment electricity energy consumption efficiency degree to the developing or developed countries' every householder house in summer or winter to the developing or developed householders in summer or winter weather , which is more influenced by the living lifestyle qualty factor to the either developed countries or developing countries householders. Hence, any developed or developing countries‘ electricity suppliers need to consider the building areas of property development market buyers their living style quality demands (needs) whether their living style quality demands are higher or lesser than the other building areas of property development market, they ought not consider whether the building locations of the houses' space occupation sizes whether they are large or small sizes in order to evaluate the householders will live at the building areas of property development locations ,whose electricity energy spending efficiency more accurate.

- How economic factor influences low income household earners to reduce not essential electricity energy expenditure spending at homes

Has it relationship between the householder income and the electricity energy needs? How to evaluate the subsidies and social tariffs to assist lower income earners to analyze household energy consumption more accurate? Electricity energy is essential needs for every householder at home, e.g. lighting, cooking power, healthcare, sanitation, cooler or warmer temperature indoor control at home. However, for lower income household earners, it its burden when they need often to use electricity energy to supply power to any home electricity tools to do any activities at homes. If any these countries‘ lower income householder earner target can not get the reasonable subsidies to assist them to solve any electricity energy tools' electricity energy needs. Due to their lower income level, it is possible that to influence them have enough electricity supply to help them to use to cook rice and food and vegetables to eat, boil water to drink, turning on light tools to help them to read, watch TV, listen radio, music any entertainment or essential needs at homes at night or morning afternoon time. These lower income household earners will be easy to sick , due to they have no enough electricity supply to help them to use electric bottles to boil water or cook food to eat. Then they only drink not boiled water or not cooked food to eat at homes in possible, due to they have no enough income to pay electricity fees every month.

Hence, how to evaluate the lower income household earners‘ electricity fee need (demand) level in order to provide the reasonable subsidies amount to assist every country's low income household earner to help them to pay the reasonable electricity fee which is one important issue to every country's government today. It brings this question: How to evaluate or analyze or predict every lower income household individual or family earner's every month electricity energy demand (need) more accurate?

It is one essential issue to be value to consider to every country's government. Moreover, to the extent that energy subsidies must be essential to be provided by public sources to all low income household earners or that a social tariff may be designed for improving access to energy for certain low income social earner groups. Hence, how to structure the energy subsidies between energy and income levels to be better target, such public mechanisms, and to avoid regressive subsidies unfairly. For example, India and China these both countries ' income poverty and energy poverty population are the large number. So , these both countries' governments need to focus on more aggregated effects and analyze the effects of rural electrification at the local level on the decrease in energy poverty in rural low income poverty and energy poverty householders. Therefore, every country government needs to point regressive of the subsidy for electricity. There is room to analyze to what extent low income household earners along the income distribution demand some forms of energy, and to suggest better and fair low income targeting household earners energy subsidies supply policies.

Each government does not only consider energy issues from a social point of view, it also needs have a manner to consider a possible link between energy, hunger reduction, and food security for each country's low income household earners group. So, every government has responsibility to calculate the determinants of different sources of energy consumption at the low income household earner level for urban and rural both populations in order to evaluate the electricity subsidies and to test whether every low income householder earner characteristics plays a role in determining energy consumption.

In general, in the use of energy measured as that for cooking, such as LPG reduces the exposure of households to hazardous, increases the consumption of different types of foods and medicines, improves the distribution of time between household members, enables studies with more light, reduces the use of digital computer entertainment tools at home, and moderates the use of wood as fuel, preventing deforestation. These methods are the best suggestions to help low income householder earner groups to reduce time to use electricity at homes. When they spend less time to use electricity to do any not essential activities, e.g. watching television, playing electric games from home computers, listening music. They only use electricity to turn on light read, to turn on rice cooker to cook, when they feel hungry to eat. Then, I believe that these social low income household earner groups will reduce to pay much not essential electricity energy expenditure at homes. Hence, every country government ought need to persuade low income household earners to avoid to use electricity to do any not essential activities in order to raise electricity energy consumption in long term time.

It will bring less amount of energy subsidies expenditure benefits to every country's government. Hence, the success to persuade any countries' low income household earners to reduce to spend much time to do any electric entertainment activities of consumption behaviors at homes often. This is the most efficient and the most successful energy subsidiary method to help them to reduce electricity energy expenditure when they are staying at homes. Hence, if any country government expected the low income household earners can continue really reduce electricity energy expenditure, they need to learn to do the meaning essential activities which are needed to use electricity at home in habit. Then, they can change their electricity useful entertainment living habit, e.g. using computers to play games, listening music, watching television entertainment habits at homes to cause essential daily needs of electricity useful living habit, e.g. using cookers to cook rice or cook food to eat, turning on lights to read , turning on heaters to bath, turning on air conditions to keep cool temperature or turning on heaters to keep warm temperature at homes. Consequently, they won't need to pay much electricity expenditure at home, due to their waste useful electricity entertainment living habits have changed to do any essential useful electricity activities at homes.

Another kind of method to reduce the determinants of energy demand to the low income householder earners. The governments can persuade them to consider the variation factor can influence their electricity energy expenditure are increased or decreased at homes. It is not the electricity or gas price is increased from the electricity suppliers. It is that their bad living habits of waste electricity or gas to do any not essential activities at homes. e.g. the householder often turn on light tools to read or listen music or watch television in whole night, he/she ought need to sleep at night, but he/she does not go to bed to sleep in whole night. He/she chooses to turn on light to do these activities. Then, he/she will waste much electricity at whole night. Also, some householders like to bath more than half hour, even one hour, when it is winter, they need to turn on heaters to provide electricity to cause the bath room has warm water to provide to them to bath, Their long time bathing behaviors will be also waste electricity or gas energy from long time heating in bath rooms. So, they need to change their waste electricity consumption living behaviors at homes.

So, I suggest that some low income household earners will need to be taught to change their bad using electricity energy living habits from governments' public relation promotion in order to change the low income household earners' bad or incorrected useful electricity or gas living attitude to achieve and to avoid them often to do electricity or gas energy waste behaviors at homes. So, different countries' governments need to teach them how to do the correct or right electricity or gas useful activities (living habits) or let them know or feel how to use their electricity or gas which can help them to reduce to waste the not essential extra electricity or gas energy. Consequently, they must reduce electricity or gas expenditure as well as electricity or gas shortage challenge won't be caused by their electricity or gas useful waste behaviors (activities) at homes.

In conclusion, energy subsidies method is not the best solution to help low income household earners to reduce to use electricity or gas energy. Because it is only short term benefit to reduce their electricity or gas expenditure at homes. The best solution is that to let them to know or feel why and how they have responsibilities to change their incorrent or wrong electricity or gas consumption bad habits in order to avoid global electricity or gas energy is waste to be used, even it is caused shortage from householders' energy waste behaviors.

● Factors influence householder energy efficient consumption behaviors at homes

What factors can influence householders how to use energy in efficient way at homes? It depends on different countries householders' living habits to cause their choices to use energy efficiently at homes. In general, global householders energy every day consumption or use aims include cooking, heating, and cooling or warming rooms, lighting , water-boiled use and computer playing games entertainment etc. activities at homes every day. Some activities are often essential at homes, e.g. cooking, cooling or warming temperature in rooms, lighting , water-boiled use. So, their activities must not avoid to use energy at homes often. Otherwise, some activities are not essential at homes, e.g. playing entertainment games from computers, cooling rooms in summer, listening music, watching television etc. these activities. The householder can choose either to use energy to turn on these equipment tools or not to do these non essential activities at homes often. In general, householders rely on energy to make ourselves lives comfortable, productive and enjoyable. However, global householders need to learn how we can use energy resources wisely because global every householder has responsibility to manage resources includes: reducing total energy use and using energy more efficiently in order to avoid energy shortage crisis occurrence. The choices are make about how we use energy, e.g. turning machines off when not in use of choosing to buy energy efficient appliances will have increasing impacts on the quality of our environment and lives.

Energy conservation includes any behavior that results in the use of less energy. Energy efficiency involves the use of technology that requires less energy to perform the same function. For example, a compact fluorescent light build that uses less energy to produce the same amount of light as an incandescent light bulb is an example of energy efficiency. So, a householder's decision to place an incanadescent light bulb with compact fluorescent is an example of energy conservation. So, as individuals, every countries' householder choices and actions can result in a significant reduction in the amount of energy used in each sector of the economy.

So, I bring this interesting question: What factors can influence householder to choose to do any efficient energy consumption or useful behaviors at homes? I believe every countries‘ householders will have their different living attitudes and their living attitudes can influence their behaviors or activities to choose how to use energy at home. I shall indicate some countries' householders‘ living attitudes to explain the factors can influence them to use energy efficiency at homes as below:

- Is the low income and rising price of modern fuels both factors best to influence Nigeria householders choose to use energy efficiently?

Firstly, for Nigeria householders energy consumption habit at homes example, it is richly with natural resources, modern energy resources which provide many householders with biomass (mostly firewood) and some other householders modern energy sources, such as kevosene, liquefied, petroleum, gas and electricity for their use. So, it is one country which can manufacture to provide energy for itself to use. It doesn't need to depend on other countries to import any kinds of energy to householders to buy to use at homes. But, it has social challenge, the poverty problem in Nigeria goes beyond low income, savings and growth rate, due to its low level of education, poor governance, high level of unemployment factors influence.

It is important to know how Nigeria householders meet their basic energy needs between poverty and energy can be described in terms of quality and quantity of energy used. Generally, most poor householders use biomass fuels because of affordability and they (householders) do not have energy equipment (such as, gas cookers, electric cookers etc.) . So, it seems Nigeria householders won't demand their living quality to be improved. It implies that they will use any kinds of energy efficiently at homes, e.g. gas, electricity, due to they find themselves in energy poverty. Although, this country has enough nature resources to manufacture energy to provide to householders to use, but due to many people are low income group, so they won't spend too much expenditure to buy much energy to use at homes. So, the rising prices of modern fuels, such as liquefied, petroleum , gas (LPG) and electricity and their erratic supply have made many householders revert to the use of traditional fuel, such as firewood and charcoal.

It brings this questions: Is the low income and rising price of modern fuels both factors best to influence Nigeria householders choose to use energy efficiently?

The hypothesis is predicated on the economic theory of consumer behavior. However, when income increases, householders not only consume more of the same goods, they also need higher quality . So, it applies economic theory to householder's energy consumption behavior at home. It explains why low living standards induce greater dependence on firewood and other biomass fuels owing to a combination of income and substitution effects, such as Nigeria low income household energy home users case. it explains why Nigeria householders can accept to use firewood and charaval traditional energy to replace liquefied, petroleum , gas (LPG) and electricity modern energy . So, economic theory explains the Nigeria household energy users why they can accept to use traditional energy to replace modern energy and their energy useful or consumption behaviors are efficient at homes. Although, Nigeria has enough natural resource to manufacture modern energy to supply to householders to use at homes. But, due to these modern energy products prices are raised to the price level of householders who can not accept. it causes to Nigeria householders only choose to buy the cheap biomass, fire woods to replace high price of modern energy products to use at home often. So, they can accept their quality of living to be fallen down. So, expensive modern energy product price is one factor to influence some countries' householders to choose to buy cheap traditional poor quality of nature energy, e.g. firewood or biomass, to use at homes. Hence, they can raise energy efficiency to use when they choose to use traditional nature energy to replace modern nature energy at homes.

- Does season factor influence New Zealand householders' energy consumption behaviors at homes?

Secondly, for New Zealand householders energy consumption habits at homes , for example, their living quality needs are general comfortable need feeling. Their countries' houses of space heating was found to average 34% of total householder energy use. The relation to space heating includes low indirect temperature are associated with persistent under-heating , whether some space heating sources tend to be higher or lower in winter indoor temperature than others and winter indoor temperatures are compared to international benchmarks and established healthy temperature ranges. So, New Zealand occupant's perceptions of winter indoor temperature conditions are presented and explored in relation to heating patterns and houschold energy consumption. So, it seems that NZ winter temperature is low. Moreover, it will influence householders need to turn on heaters to keep more warmer feeling indoor. Then, they will use more electricity energy. In special, if the householders' houses spaces are large sizes . Hence, their heaters need long time to keep whole houses' areas or spaces or rooms temperature to be risen up in order to let they do not feel very cold in winter. So, NZ's winter extreme cold weather will influence householders' energy use or consumption to be increased in winter.

The electricity efficiency to every NZ householder is very high in winter to compare spring, summer, autumn seasons. Hence, if NZ electricity suppliers expected to forecast electricity consumption more accurate in NZ. In order to ease the life for both electric net designers and electricity suppliers, it was decided to find out, how the

NZ weather conditions and every householder's house space size factors to influence the power consumption to NZ householders. If there is a clear trend observed , then this relation can be used for power consumption forecasts to NZ householders.

Why does NZ weather condition factor and householder's house space size factor can predict householders' electricity consumption at homes. Due to geographic location on the global the lowest south sets specific conditions for weather, such as NZ's south island geographic location is near to south ocean in our earth. It is a country where average annual temperatures are well between 10 degree to below 10 degree at NZ south island special geographic location to near to the South ocean in our earth at the same time.

However, large part of mankind is living in the conditions where there are four different seasons in NZ geographic location, dark winter, which is cold and snowy, spring with rising temperature and high precipitation, sunny , dry and rather hot summer, and windy and wet autumn. These conditions lead to different patterns in electric appliances use in NZ householders, in special, in NZ south island householders. If trends in electric energy use have substantial correlation with weather conditions, this can help NZ electric energy suppliers and producers to forecast electricity consumption and thus organize and manage production of electric energy.

Consequently, it will lead to much more stability in energy supply to NZ every householder. For example, when the NZ energy supplier gathers data concerns every householder's house space size data, e.g. the house has how many sleeping rooms, toilets, bath rooms, eating rooms and reading rooms number, even the house has how many family members are living in every NZ geographical location. Then if it can follow different location of NZ houses spaces sizes whether they are large or small space size as well as whether every house has how many family members are living to evaluate whether how much electricity efficiency can satisfy their comfortable living needs in winter. Then, it can evaluate whether they will use how much electricity efficiency for their needs in different seasons. If in winter, many householders are living in the large space size house in the geographic location. Then, it is possible that the geographic location is householders will use much electricity efficiency and where geographic location householder who will be possible to pay the most highest electricity fee to compare the other geographic location of small space size of house householders. Hence, weather factor is the most influential to change NZ householders ' electricity energy consumption behaviors at homes.

● Urbanization level and income per capita both tangible factors as well as temperature (weather variation factor) will have close relationship to influence China householder energy consumption or useful needs at home every day

For China householder energy consumption habit example, what factors can determine to impact this country's householders energy useful behavior at homes? Can the impacts of these factors be quantified? What are China householder energy consumption trends and characteristics? I shall explain as below:

I believe the influential factors include these three aspects to China householder energy users: Income per capita, urbanization level an annual average temperature (weather). These factors will influence any China householder energy useful or consumption behavior at homes.

Temperature (weather variation factor) is intangible from eastern region to western region of Chin, variances largely depend upon economic level and the provincial level. So, some regions were warmer and cooler temperature will influence the regional China householder how to use electricity. In addition, the influence of urbanization level varies according to income level as well as the urbanization level has more significant impact on the structure and efficiency of China householder energy consumption that on its quantity. So, the urbanization level and income per capita both tangible factors will have close relationship to influence China householder energy consumption or useful needs at home every day. Moreover, these two tangible factors (urbanization level and income per capita both factors) have the more influential to impact China any one of household family energy consumption or useful habit to compare temperature factor at home. Because temperature can only influence than to choose to turn on heaters to keep more cooler in summer or turn on air conditions (fans) to keep more warmer in winter.

The electricity energy needs for these equipment tools which will be influenced less. Otherwise, the urbanization level and income per family householder how to choose to spend more or less electricity or gas etc. energy at homes. Because in behavioral economy view point, when individual householder has more income and the urban in the China geographic location is rising many high income and high household families members to every house. Then, the urbanization household energy household energy useful or consumption level will be raised. Such as China household electricity users case, e.g. large cities have many high income and many houses have more than four families members to live on one house together. Then, the electricity or gas energy efficiency will be influenced to rise. The city urbanization and per capita income level is high to these large cities have high to income population, who are living in these cities in China.

Moreover, the impact of lifestyle on energy use mainly reflects types and purposes of fuels are chosen by different China households factor which will influence the urbanization level of energy choice use. China is a country with typical binary economics and social diversity and these is significant difference in the consumption pattern between urban and rural regions. Urban residents consume high-quality energy, such as electricity, natural gas , heating power, solar energy and gasoline. For rural residents, usually use coal, and biomass energy because they are cheaper price energy products which requires much time and labor and are heavy indoor pollutants . The difference in energy consumption pattern between urban and rural China residents is closely related to living of quality needs, building structure, e.g. steel or stone etc. different materials, manufacture, easily access clean and effective feels through the electric grid, natural gas network and district heating systems.

Therefore, it explains why urbanization level is as an integrated variable reflecting social progress situation to influence urban and rural regions, such as large cities , small cities and rural countryside regions' household energy consumption or useful behaviors which have different kinds of fuel useful demands and energy efficiencies qualify and quantity demand, or needs at homes. Consequently, it explains, urbanization level and income per capital level both factors are more influential to China household energy consumption at home to compare temperature (weather , seasonal) factor.

● Employment rates or gross domestic product macro economic variation factor, residential space size factor, and the government's implementation of energy labeling schemes provide significant impacts on Taiwan residential electricity consumption .

For Taiwan householder electricity consumption characteristics in the residential sector, which has different factors and pattern to compare China householder electricity householder electricity consumption habit at home. Although, they are the same Asia country. I shall explain these reasons as below:

For Taiwan electricity householder factors influence their energy useful or consumption behaviors at homes. The main factors can influence their electricity energy useful patterns include: employment rates or gross domestic product macro economic variation factor, residential space size factor, and the government's implementation of energy labeling schemes provide significant impacts on Taiwan residential electricity consumption . However, the impacts of electricity raising price and the energy supply reducing shortage efficiency standards do not significant to influence the Taiwan residential electricity consumption behavior at sources.

It means that it won't influence Taiwan householders to use electricity or gas or any kinds of energy number to be reduced, even the Taiwan government energy suppliers sudden raise, any kinds of energy price and reduce to supply energy to satisfy Taiwan householders daily essential needs at homes.

In fact, Taiwan had improved gross domestic product (GDP) and it had raised employment rates recently. So, many Taiwanese has jobs to work, due to Taiwan economy had improved to be better. So, growth had also raised. The economy improvement causes many Taiwanese had enough jobs to work, due to new businesses are set up. Many consumers excite any kinds of businesses are invested to Taiwan from overseas or local investors. So, consumption is grown, the electricity consuming appliance are selected, as the household consumer focus group number if also influenced to be increased. So, Taiwan economy had improved to be better, it will encourage many electricity consuming appliances products are encouraged to excited to be selected to sell in Taiwan. Due to many different kinds of electricity consuming appliances are supplied to attract Taiwanese to choose to buy to bring to their homes for cooking, boiling water, or keeping rooms to be cooler or warmer temperature comfortable feeling intention in winter or summer seasons. So, these electricity consuming appliances, e.g. rice cookers, heaters, air conditions, fans, bathing gas heaters etc. different home electricity consuming appliances will be increased to supply to satisfy Taiwan householders' needs. When they decide to buy any news electricity consuming appliances to bring to homes to use.

- Environment scientists' education message how to influence Greece householders home energy consumption behaviors from primary energy to change secondary energy

Finally , I shall indicate Greece, this western which will influence this country's householders have desires to do household energy conservation patterns or conservation energy consumption behaviors or energy conservation activities at homes. I shall explain the social economic variable, such as consumers' income and family size variation factor which can influence the different Greece family household members differences towards energy conservation preferences. IN addition, the variable, such as environmental information feedback and consciousness of energy problems are characteristics of the energy saver consumer.

Why and how can environmental pollution , environmental protection, energy conservation information message can influence Greece householders to choose to do energy use consumption conservation or less energy useful behaviors at homes. It is one interesting energy efficient use behaviors , due to Greece householders are influenced by energy conservation or environmental protection message.

In fact, scientists agree overconsumption of natural resources is a major threat to our lives in earth. Environmental problems like greenhouse effect, ozone layer depletion, and acid rain effect are not any more problems of a specific region or environmental problem. Also, economic theory is indicated that in order to gain comfort and time households are becoming excessive energy users, neglecting the environmental impact of their choices.

Environment scientists bring these environment pollution message to influence Greeks (Greece householders) to change their energy consumption behaviors at homes. The environment scientists' message indicate that we are facing global warmth and natural resource and energy shortage challenges. Due to our Earth have limited natural resource numbers to supply to us to manufacture energy, but global population has been increasing every year. Thus, it is possible that we have energy shortage crisis. Also, manufactures are spending too much energy to waste to manufacture any products, the energy will cause air or water pollution in manufacturing process or drivers are driving their vehicles to pollute air on the roads.

Hence, environment scientists' message influence Greece householders began to consider these questions concern to reduce fossil fuel energy. Why do we need to Safety in using fuel and handle gas leaks? Why do we feel town gas smell? How is electricity located at electric station far away from town area? How to solve problems caused by the use of fossil fuels? How to reduce the use of fossil fuels?

Greece householders consider to solve the problems, the best way is to reduce their used of fossil fuel. This helps prevent fossil fuels form being used up too quickly. Also, it helps them to reduce environmental problems because fewer pollutants are given out when less fossil fuels are used. Can human help to reduce the use of fossil fuels? Fossil fuels are mainly in power station. Although they use some fossil fuels for our gas cooker and car, it won't make much difference if I use less. Fossil fuel is not used renew primary energy. Most of energy Greece householders use come from fossil fuels, for example, the electricity we use is generated in power stations by burning fossil fuels. The buses they ride use diesel oil. Therefore, they can help reduce the use of fossil fuels by saving energy in Greece daily lives.

The actions that Greece householders can take such as: setting the air-conditioner to a higher temperature, walking instead of using lift, taking a short shower instead of a bath. This reduces the use of the hot water and thus the energy needed to heat the water. Thus, many people can help a lot to reduce our use of fossil fuels to avoid fossil fuel shortage risk occurrence.

Greeks (Greece householders) had been beginning to concern that they will face energy shortage challenge if they can not adopt more energy conservation actions. Because the Greece government began to bring negative environmental pollution and energy shortage challenge message if they often waste to use any kinds of energy, e.g. electricity , gas excessive number efficiency at homes. Then, they will be possible to face energy shortage and environmental pollution challenge to their country in future one day. So, this energy shortage and environment pollution message has bring predictive negative worries to influence many Greece householder energy home users choose to reduce to avoid the waste of any kinds of energy use at homes.

So, their reducing energy use actions that had encouraged them to cause habits to avoid to waste excess energy to do any non essential electric appliances useful or consumption activities at homes often. Moreover, the environment protection and energy conservation message has changed many Greece householder to make decision and activities to change their lifestyle to b low living quality from high living quality. So, the environment protection and energy conservation message factor has much influential to change Greece household energy users' daily energy conservation or less energy use consumption activities at homes.

Greeks feel greenhouse energy can be environmental protection energy. A greenhouse can trap heat in the sunlight and keeps the air inside the greenhouse warm enough for plants to grow. The glass roof and walls of a greenhouse let in sunlight but prevent heat from escape, this makes the greenhouse warm inside. Similarly, some gases in the Earth's atmosphere can trap heat from the sun and keep the Earth warm. This is called the greenhouse effect. The gases energy that can trap heat from the sun are called greenhouse gases. It is future one kind of potential primary energy to reduce environmental pollution new energy products for human consuming. So, environmental protection message influence them to consume greenhouse energy at homes.

So, environment scientists‘ environment pollution message had influence Greece householders concern to apply secondary energy (environment protection) to replace electricity energy to use at home. They will change energy to use at home. The scientists' messages have more influential Greece householders energy change consumption behaviors at homes. The messages are as below:

There are different forms of energy, e.g. light, heat, sound, wind, water, electrical kinetic, chemical and potential energy. Some form energy is primary energy and it can not renew to use, e.g. light, sound, wind, water, fossil fuel etc. Some form energy is secondary energy and it can renew to use in possible, e.g. nuclear, electric charge battery etc. Why does human need to concern how to manufacture secondary energy? Because it is possible that our natural resource will be consumed all, thus we will face primary energy shortage risk. If human can invent any new form of man-made secondary energy to renew to use in order to avoid primary energy shortage to supply to use to use, then human won't only depend on our Earth natural resource energy supply numbers. We can invent any new secondary energy to renew to use again either replaces primary energy or instead of primary energy limit number supply.

What is energy change? For television energy change power case. Firstly, electrical energy changes to television power to be used by television itself, then it changes to light power, next it changes to light power. How to choose fuel form to use? Due to energy can change to different form of powers to supply different form of power advantages to supply to human to use, so it is possible that we can also invent any secondary man made renew used energy to change different form powers to supply us to use, e.g. nuclear energy changes to light or sound or heat form of powers ; electrical charge batteries changes to light or sound or heat form powers to satisfy our daily life needs.

The environment scientists‘ energy consumption education influence Greece householders concern how to change to use secondary energy to replace primary energy at homes as below:

For primary natural resource fuel energy example, different fuel has different feature, e.g. easy to burn, safe to use, gives out a lot of energy, inexpensive, produces little air pollution, easy to transport and store. How can we use in different channels, such as heating food, hot pat, driving vehicles.

For example, although coal is not expensive to cause electricity energy for past transportation tool, e.g. traditional coal energy train or our daily home cooking, but it has negative influence to environment air pollution. Hence, we ought to follow the primary natural resource energy's feature to decide how to apply what aspects of our life needs.

For example, if the country's people hope to reduce pollution when who use any kind of energy, e.g. US , Europe energy markets. The energy entrepreneur ought concentrate on manufacturing the kind of energy which can reduce environment pollution to be the least level to supply the country people to use, e.g. electric charge battery supplies to these countries' drivers to drive their vehicles on the roads, wind energy or water energy to manufacture electricity power supply to reduce air or water pollution ; or if the country people hope to buy the inexpensive energy to use, even the energy's quality and performance is worse, e.g. China, India, Hong Kong markets. The energy entrepreneur ought concentrate on manufacturing the lowest cost and enough supply of natural resource to manufacture the kind of energy to sell cheap price to these countries to use, e.g. China, Africa can accept to use e.g. gas, coal, fuel energy to use to compare developed countries people, e.g. UK, US; or if the countries people who hope to use energy which can easy to transport and store, e.g. light coal. The energy entrepreneur can choose to concentrate on manufacturing much coal to supply to the countries people to use, e.g. China, Arica Thus, to choose to manufacture which kinds of energy supply to the countries market people to use, the energy entrepreneur how decides to manufacture which kind of energy, it depends on which kinds of fuel advantages of the countries people most concerning.

What is energy meaning? It is defined a dynamic quality, it is a fundamental entity of nature that is transferred between parts of a system in the production of physical change within the system, and it is usually regarded as the capacity for doing work, and it is usable power (such as heat or electricity) or the resources for producing such power.

Why does secondary energy own investment worth? Because the different forms of primary natural resource energy will have supply shortage crisis, such as natural resources coal, gas, solar, wind, water, geothermal, biomass(organic material) etc. However, human can attempt to explore any undiscovered Earth or Space resource to manufacture any kinds of secondary energies, e.g. nuclear energy, electric recharge battery energy to supply to electric vehicle or space robots transportation tools to use or satisfy our daily life needs in future one day. So any kind of undiscovered secondary man-made renewed used energy resources have potential commercial worth to any energy entrepreneurs, it is possible that they can replace traditional primary energy to supply to human to use for our different aspects of life needs. In the future, the secondary energy demand will increase, when primary energy supply number has decreased form natural exploration. So, it will cause the effect of any demand of secondary energy product to be raised and prices to be increased in possible. Due to global population has been growing up, considerably China and India both countries populations have been increasing rapidly. Scientists predict there are more than 1.2 billion people worldwide will lack access to electricity, and more than 2.5 billion still use wood, charcoal to cook and heat in the future when primary energy has no enough number to supply to us to use. Hence, the fact that demand is this much greater than supply to make energy a prime market for further growth.

Although, secondary energy will have much investment worth, but energy like all other investments will carry risks. The internal and external risk factors include such as: policy is always changing to prohibit which do energy trading more easily between the energy exporting and importing countries, the secondary energy manufacturer itself own abilities to invent and to manufacture any kinds of secondary energy, improved technology can quickly make an technology obsolete, geopolitical rifts can happen overnight, the country's energy consumer (user)'s preferable choice to use which either kinds of secondary energy or secondary energy. So, it seems that (man-made) renewed used secondary energy industry can provide above-average returns, but it can also bring high risk commercial investment.

Traditionally, energy supply companies will apply those methods to operate energy providing businesses. For Shell,. Exxon examples, which had own gas stations, explore and drill for gas on their own. Other companies specialize in a part of the energy market, e.g. leasing oil rigs for example, or operating a pipeline. Energy supplying companies can choose to manufacture any kinds of energy to supply, e.g. trade oil, gas, coal, uranium, electricity etc. Any energy price and supply is demanded on the countries energy users' which kinds of energy most choice need or certain energy commodities to be chose to use popularly. For example, if US most people prefer to use secondary man-made renew used energy more than primary energy. Then, US energy manufacturers ought concentrate on manufacturing much different kinds of secondary man-made renew used energy to prepare to supply to its domestic US market in order to raise secondary energy price to sell in its country. So, the energy manufacturer's energy manufacturing choice, it is depend on which the country's people prefer to use which kinds of energy for their daily life needs.

However, scientists predict secondary energy market will have large market share, due to primary energy will have shortage to explore to supply in our earth and future energy consumers(users) prefer to choose to use more efficiency, less energy consumption, none environment pollution cause, cost effectiveness, renew to use of any kinds of energy. For example, the electricity recharge battery secondary man-made renew used energy is one kind of reducing air pollution power to push any electric battery vehicles to be driven to compare gas energy during drivers are driving their cars on the roads. They can reduce noise and air pollution and drivers can drive safely, who only need to buy one electric recharge battery to recharge in any electric recharge battery stations on streets when the electric recharge battery has no enough power to push their cars and they need to recharge their electric recharge battery drive when they had driven between one to two days. Due to primary energy, e.g. fuel , gas, the kinds of primary energies will have shortage to supply to global drivers to drive their traditional cars. Thus, the electric recharge battery or any undiscovered secondary energy will be future driving market needs. So, man-made renew used secondary energy, e.g. biofuel, hydro-electric, nuclear, will be one kind of efficient, clean, less pollution cause, cost-effective of energy to supply to our global vehicle market, even any other undiscovered new markets. Supposing they are popular to be used for electric vehicle market globally in future one day, then their prices will be decreased and constructed to average car requires up to 1,700 gallons of oil. Also supposing that making average computer requires more than ten times or weight to fossil fuels, every calories of food eaten in the US requires roughly then calories of fossil fuels. Hence, cheap energy will be one successful factor to influence future potential energy consumer (user) individual choice needs. Conversely, ion good economic times, people are more willing to travel, to buy products, and all of which success demand and low process for energy.

In the future, secondary energy will be the best choice to food production market. The modern food production system is essentially a success of changing fossil fuels into food. So, raising energy prices are almost higher food costs and even shortage for fossil fuels energy. If one day, one kind of discovered secondary man-made renew used energy can supply to any restaurants or homes to be used to cook at the cheap price, then the profit is very high for this kind of food production energy. Thus, future food production secondary energy consumption market is large and because the primary energy inputs for agriculture are higher than the energy outputs of the food. However, future secondary man-made renew used energy for food production system is only one part of whole energy consumer in food industry. The food production is related to whole food consumption market which includes: household cooking energy market, agriculture or vegetable, rice, fruit etc. foods farming machines energy market, food manufacturing factories market, food machine package market, transportation food delivery market, supermarket or fruit/food sale stores market. They must need any energy inputs to achieve the food production or food transportation or warehouse / stores electricity supply or cooking energy needs. Hence, these food suppliers relate to any whole food factory manufacturers, food retailers, food wholesalers, farmers and home/restaurant cookers, all of them must need to use energy to carry on their food producing or food cooking or food transportation activities every day in overall food industry. Thus, it seems that undiscovered any second energy demand will be increased, when the primary energy supply number is decreasing. Also, when people can accept to use secondary energy to replace primary energy to be used for any cooking, transporting food, manufacturing food, food retail stores or warehouse food delivery energy need activities. Then, the secondary energy price will be fall down to attract many food energy consumers.

Nowadays, the food industry energy may includes primary nature resource gas energy or electricity energy for house families or restaurants cooking needs, food delivering lorry drivers driving needs usually. If future second man made renew used energy is invented successful popular to be used, e.g. hydrogen, electric recharged battery energy for electric vehicles or restaurant/home families cooking needs or food factories machine manufacture energy needs. Then, the secondary energy will have possible to replace primary energy to be food industry energy market.

Wiley, composition services graphics indicated that global primary energy consumption had been increasing 30 billion tons from 1830 year to 510 billion tons in 2010 year as well as global population size had been increasing from 70 billion 1830 year to 510 billion in 2010 year. Thus, it seems that global primary energy consumption will be needed largely after 2010 year. If future global nature resource primary energy is explored full number and it had not enough energy number to supply global human to use. Then, it will being many people feel uncomfortable and inconvenient ,e.g. Some countries won't have enough energy to supply transportation tools to be driven, some homes and restaurants won't have enough energy to supply to cook to eat or to provide restaurant clients to eat etc. daily activities, due to human's much activities which are needs energy supply. Thus, it seems that global primary energy consumption will be needed largely after 2010 year.

Wiley, composition services graphics also explained that why the primary energy consumption demand can be needed to achieve the same level to the global population size increasing in 2010 year. The graph showed these reasons why cause the same level of global population size and global primary energy consumption demand which may include: The graph showed that after a nation is developed, its per-person energy use begins to level off. In North America and Europe, where energy demand has remained flat, or fallen, in each of the past few years. But the 1.3 billion people on those two continents are far outweighed by the 5 billion people in Asia and Africa, e.g. Chinese and Indian. who currently have more energy need to compare average per man to North America and Europe per man, ensuring that overall energy demand will rise for years to come.

Wiley, composition services graphics also predicted that the growth in primary energy demand. China will have 4,500 million tons in 2035 year. India will have 3,000 million tons in 2035 year. Other developing Asia will have 2,000 million tons in 2035 year. Russia will have 1,500 million tons in 2035, Middle East will have 1,300 million tons in 2035, other rest of world will have 1,000 million tons in 2035. Hence, it implied that China will be the largest primary energy need country in the future.

China will be future the primary potential energy consumer market. The primary energy includes water, coal, wind, fossil oil, gas ,solar, geothermal energy, biomass (organize material) etc. different natural resource primary energy. Otherwise, US, UK, Europe will be secondary energy potential need market. For example, electrical recharge battery energy will be raised demand to supply to any future new design electrical charge battery vehicles in US, Europe, UK markets.

Due to US, Europe, UK people concern environment protection, so they will invent many electric charge battery vehicles to consume electrical charge battery to replace polluted gas energy to avoid air pollution when the drivers are driving cars on themselves countries' roads. For example, second man-made renew used nuclear energy can be applied to rockets to push them to leave our earth to fly to other space far away and consuming nuclear energy will be cost efficient, and nuclear energy saving will be more when nuclear to spend long time to be used in any long time space journey. Hence, nuclear energy and electric charge battery secondary energy will be popular to be applied to vehicles and rockets energy needs in US, Europe, potential markets, even our daily energy needs in global second energy market.

Who are your energy business's competitors (peers)? How do they compare? How have your energy business company performed cyclically? How to choose to manufacture to sell which kinds of primary or secondary energy product(s), either manufactures only primary energy product(s) or manufactures only secondary energy products or both? Which countries do you plan to sell your energy product?

Illustration by Wilsey, composition services graph showed that these natural resources to energy product the world's electricity percentage, such as below:

41% of coal, 5% of oil, 21% of gas, 13% of nuclear, 16% of Hydro, 3% other renewable secondary man-made energy.

Hence, coal will be future the major natural resource to produce electricity. The energy entrepreneur ought attempt to explore any coal resources, when who choose to supply electricity power to consumers for future energy consumption country markets.

Wiley, composition services also predicted that the expectation is that North America coal will supply the expectation is that North America coal will supply Asian demand, Us export terminals have a total capacity of 173 million tomes output. China will drive 16% of the nations total output. China will drive the sea-born demand for coal over for the future. Chinese energy consumption will grow more than 12 % between 1980 and 2009 years. Though, China heads global demand, India is growing faster in terms of coal imports. Much of the global coal demand will be supplied by Indonesia and Australia. Colombia, Russia, South Africa and Mongolia are also players in global export coal energy resources.

Hence, environment scientists‘ education messages influence Greece householders believe that secondary energy will be one kind of new energy product to replace traditional primary energy product for human energy consumption market global needs. Hence, it is right time any energy entrepreneur needs to research how to explore any undiscovered man-made renew used secondary energy products to avoid primary energy shortage crisis occurrence. Greece householders will be the highest population number to choose secondary energy to replace primary energy to use at homes. it means that environment scientists had changed Greece householders’ energy consumption behaviors at homes.

In conclusion, different countries will have different factors influence how the country’s householders energy consumption behavioral changes. Hence, it seems that any country’s householders‘ energy use of consumption behaviors will be possible influenced by exteral environment factors influence. Also, every country’s energy providers can attempt to find whether the country has what kinds of unique factors to influence its householders’ energy consumption efficiency to increase or decrease in order to find the methods to solve the energy efficiency demand reducing challenges successfully.

Economic methods measure energy consumer shopping behaviors

CHAPTER FOUR

The national income measurement behavioral economy method

The national income accounting measurement is one good method to help any development countries to research whether what issues are their weaknesses or strengths is order to improve their economic development challenge. The central concept in national accounting is to measure the total output of products or services of the country's economy over a given time period.

The measure is known or gross domestic product (GDP). Output is produced by employing various factors of production (mainly labor and capital), and the revenue from sale of output of used to make payments to these factors of production. The value of output is identified, to the value of income paid out, or what is known as national income. Since the output produced is sold (or added to stocks), the value of output is also equal to the value of expenditure. Hence, GDP can be regarded as the value of output produced (aggregate supply), the total value of expenditure on output (aggregate demand) or the total value of income in producing the output (real income). So, any developing countries can find whether how much or amount different industries value of output produced from and the real aggregate demand from consumers for different industries' products sale number or services demand in order find whether what factors cause the kind of industry's total GDP product sale number and real income reduction amount. For example, last year, the developing country's cloth industry sale number has 600,000 pieces and real GDP income has US$5 million. But, this year, its cloth industry sale number has 400,000 pieces and real GDP income has US$ 2 million. Hence, the developing countries can know its current year overall cloth industry sale number and GDP real income must reduce. Then, this country can attempt to find any factors had influenced itself cloth industry why this country itself cloth buyers number and their wearing demand has reduced. the reasons may include overall cloths price is exceed the normal price level or too high to compare its other foreign cloth sellers (overall local cloths price is exceed foreign cloth sellers' price extremely, or overall cloth fashion is not update or not attractive or quality is poor, or import cloth material producing price is too high to cause overall cloth sellers' cloth sale prices are needed to rise in order to earn balance profit or avoid reducing profit, or this developing country's cloth sellers' loyalties or brands are not famous to influence overall local cloth buyers know to choose to buy in itself country. Hence, this developing country can attempt to apply macroeconomic behavioral method to find whether what it/are the main factor(s) to cause its overall cloth industry's real GDP income and sale number is influenced to fall down suddenly in this year.

This macroeconomic country income measurement method can also measure why or what factors cause its any industries' overall supply and demand imbalance problem existence or cause. The reader will notice that the aggregate supply curve (AS) is drawn with an upward slope from left or right. So that at higher price levels more output is provided obviously, there will be a point when, given fixed amount of capital, labor and technology, output can not be increased in the short term.

This represents the full employment level, and at this point, the aggregate supply curve will become vertical. The aggregate demand curve simply shows the relationship between the total amount of products and services consumers desire and the price level. For one developing country's overall computer industry example, if it had overall aggregate supply of computer manufacturing number is one million pieces last year, but this year, it's aggregate supply of computer supply of computer manufacturing number is only five hundred thousand pieces. Hence, its overall computer aggregate manufacturing number fell down half pieces in this year.

But if it's overall computer buyers aggregate demand number climbed up from last year one million number to two million number this year. It means that this developing country has overall computer manufacturing number shortage problem to any local computer sellers in this year. Why does it encounter computer manufacturing number shortage problem? The reasons may include: lacking high technological material supplies to manufacture any laptops or desktops for itself country's computer manufacturers, lacking technician labors to manufacture computers , it is possible due to many technicians choose to go to overseas to seek new computer manufacturing jobs, because they feel salaries are low or poor welfare from local computer employers, or computer manufacturers number decreases or close their businesses number increase, dismissing many computer technician labors , they are replaced by artificial intelligence or manufacturing machines, which are used to manufacture any computer products, or the country's overall computer manufacturing technology is not advanced to adapt to manufacture nowadays computer products.

On conclusion, any developing countries can apply national income measurement method to attempt to find what factor(s) cause(S) its aggregate supply and demand imbalance problem existence. Hence, national income measurement method is one kind of good macroeconomic behavioral method to measure or find why what reasons cause its some industries' products supply and demand number is imbalance or sale number and real GDP income decreases suddenly. Hence, any developing countries can apply macroeconomic analysis to find any factors to cause their any industries' development challenges in possible.

1.1 Industries economic methods

Industries economic theory explains how share the common feature of objectives for the firms (whether profit maximisation, growth of sales maximisation, satisfying etc.) and investigate the consequences of the pursuit of these objectives. Hence, industries economic theory can be attempted to find why the firm's customer number reduces, profit level is felt sudden higher to consumers, why customer's satisfactory level is low to the company's products. Due to the conduct of any firms covers the objectives, price-setting behavior, and attitudes to rivals (actual and potential). For example, if the country's publishing industry's competition rivals are more, due to it permits many overseas publishers enter to itself domestic publishing market. So, its local publishers will feel more pressure to attract its readers to choose its local any publishers' books to buy because they have different countries' publishers choices to buy any books in their country.

Hence, the country's local publishing industry structural features of perfect different countries; publishers' competitions are a large number of overseas publishing firms of roughly equal size with free entry into this country's publishing industry suddenly. Even, this country's publishing industry book sellers does not plan to reduce their books sales prices or their books sale prices are not higher to compare their any one overseas publishers' books sale prices.

I believe that this country's local publishing firms readers number can not increase easy immediately because it is not the main reason of this country's overall local publishers' books sale prices are higher issue. It is due to its government permits many different overseas countries' publishers free enter to itself local publishing market raise itself county's overall books sale effort for its local publishers. So, it is unfair to this country's local all publishers as well as free entry publishing market structure influences its all publishers' sale performance to improve easily. It ensures that a free entry market structure challenge to cause this country's publishers feel book sale difficult challenge.

The another case is that when many firms are grouped together as an industry and as firms which sell in the same market, e.g. perfect competition, homogenous, oligopoly and monopoly. In these causes, an industry's defined in terms of a product and the products of that product are members of the industry. Market and industry are very closely related in the case of homogenous products. It is assumed that each firm produces only one of a particular form to a specific industry in terms. If the nature of the firm's output and product which defined the industry.

What happens when a world of differentiated products and of multiproduct firms is considered? the existence of differentiated products can avoid these products which are close substitutes in demand. More formal, a group of products (or services) is considered as close substitutes for each other when the cross or services is greater than some others. For example, if the country's computer industry has many similar laptop or desktop computer products are selling in itself country. When each grouping the country's any computer brands products are close substitutes, but between any two kinds either desktop or laptop computer products in different computer brands grouping , the degree of substitution is low.

In this approach, the country's computer industry is defined in terms of high demand conditions to any brands of computer firms in this country and it would be expected that the size of this country's computer industry would depend on the degree of substitutability used. Hence, it implies this country's computer industry is very suitable to produce a homegeneous computer product under similar or identical cost conditions, due to itself country's computer buyers won't easy to change their computer purchase choices, when they feel another brand computer firm (later another brand computer product choice) which can provide the similar computer brand product feature or function to replace their the early or prior computer brand product choice easily.

CHAPTER FIVE

Applied more economic method solves energy user behavioral challenge

Can apply macro economic method to predict consumer variable behavior to any country? For example, when and how and why do the country consumers , they reduce shopping times or consumption desires in the country. For production and the labor market concept, production is integrated into the general equilibrium framework by firms. Firms utilize capital and labor to produce output and maximize the wealth of the agents who own them.

Households (house consumers) now maximize their utility through the consumption of commodities and leisure in themselves country. Households provide labor inputs to firms in return for wages in order to be able to obtain commodities. There are now markets for factor of production , capital and labor, in addition to commodity market.

In short run, the marginal product of labor (the extra amount of output obtained by adding another unit of labor) full as a firm takes on more employees. Profit-maximizing firms will increase employment to the level at which the revenue resulting from employment an additional employee equals the marginal cost of an extra employee. Thus, the lower the real wage, the higher the demand for labor. Individual workers maximize utility by choosing the combinations of work and leisure and the supply of labor's defined as the level of employment forthcoming at a given real wage rate.

Hence, all who desire to find employment at the existing level of real wages will do so , when the country's employment condition and product sale number both are in equilibrium , due to the country's businessmen must have enough buyers number as well as their demands are still increasing. Then , the country's employers will choose to increase employees number or increase wage to attract them to help their businesses to increase more productivities.

So, it explains when on developing country has high unemployment ratio to compare other general developing countries . It implies that itself country's consumers' shopping desires will reduce or their shopping times will reduce, because their shopping desires reduce,, it influences the country's businessmen products sale number will also reduce. Then, they will choose to reduce employees number or reduce their wages to compensate their sale loss in possible.

On conclusion, in macro economic view, it proves that it has direct or indirect case and effect relationship between the country itself employment rate and the year consumers overall shopping times or consumption desires level and overall market GDP (consumer expenditure overall amount in the year. It can apply the year employment rate number to measure whether the country's consumer shopping desires had been reducing or had been raising in the country in possible. Hence, any country's difference between the year employment ratio and last year employment ratio which can explain why it's the year overall consumption market GDP amount had risen up or has fallen down in possible in order to predict what reasons cause this country's consumer shopping desires to be increase or decrease.

5.1 Behavioral economy consumption
desires measurement method

How to apply behavioral economic theory to measure consumption level or consumption desire to the country? I shall assume that consumption is to be measured by private and public expenditures at constant prices at conventionally defined and all money prices are assumed constant. How to measure real consumption?

In fact, consumer behavior has relationship to any country, itself economic growth or recession in any economic and consumption environment . The purpose of income calculations in practiced affairs to give consumers an indication of the amount which they can consume. It would seem that we ought to define a man's income as the maximum value, which he can consume during a week, and still expect to be well at the end of week as he has at the beginning. An economy which uses money , but uses it is as a neutral link between transactions in real things and real assets and does not want of a better , a real exchange economy with an economy in which money plays a part of its own and affects motives and decisions and as , in short, one of the operative factors in the situation. So that the course of events can not be predicted either in the long period or in the short period, without knowledge of the behavior of money between the first state and last. It is a monetary economy means to influence any country itself consumer behavioral consumption desires change to more or less shopping times.

Hence, money matters in both the long and short run. Money affects real decision making and employment and output outcomes to any countries. The economic system is moving through calendar time from an irrevocable past to an uncertain and statistically unpredictable future.

Any country's past and present consumption market data do not necessary provide correct signals regarding future outcomes. This means that economic data are not necessarily generated by a process. Denominated in money terms are a human in an entrepreneurial economy. It helps humans efficiently organize time-consuming production and exchange processes in a world of uncertainty.

In any money using entrepreneurial economy, entrepreneurs' decisions regarding production and hiring depend on expectations of receiving contractual sales revenues (cash inflows) in excess of the contractual money costs of production (cash outflows). Since, the money wage contract is the most efficient oriented contracts, modern economies can be characterized as money-wage contract-based systems.

Hence, money processes two essential elasticity that differentiate is from the products of industry. These describe why (a) money does not grow on trees (money's elasticity of production is zero)and (b) why producible products are not good liquid stores of value (the elasticity of substitution between liquid assets , such as money and producible products is zero).

If money has these elasticity , then unemployment develops, that is to say, because people can not be employed, when the object of desire (i.e. money, good useful product or good quality product , even shopping enjoyable feeling,) is something which can not produced and the demand of shopping desires are reduced to the country's people.

Hence, unemployment rather than full employment is a normal outcome in any entrepreneurial, market oriented, money-contract-using system in a free competition market environment to the country. So, when the country's people consumption desires are reduced in possible , because unemployment rare rises or living of cost rises, general products prices rise, a spot or commodity price inflation etc. different factors. Then, they will influence the country's economic recession occurrence more easily.

Thus, any countries leaders can not neglect the relationship between unemployment and consumption desire and economic growth or recession relationship. Because in long term, unemployment ratio rises, it has possible to bring many consumers their shopping desires to be reduced as well as economic recession effect to the country.

It implies that any countries' consumers desires, which has relationship to whether themselves jobs supplying number is enough to let themselves countries' people to work. However, labor shortage issue must be better to compare job supplying shortage issue to any country, because labor shortage won't influence consumers' shopping desires to be reduced absolute. It will influence any businesses' productivities are less or reaching the low productive level. Otherwise, jobs supplying shortage will influence consumers' shopping desires to be reduced in the country. It is possible due to the country has many people lose their jobs suddenly. Then, they can not accept to spend money to buy too much any things in their countries easily.

On conclusion, any countries' consumer behaviors or consumption desires must have relationship to themselves countries' jobs supplying number. Hence, any countries leaders need to concern whether themselves countries have enough jobs supply to let low education or high education people to work in order to satisfy their living needs in nowadays societies.

Pollution factor influences traveller behaviors

CHAPTER SIX

Emotion Labor Factor

Airline service industry, front line travelling passengers service workers' emotional challenge concerns cabin crew and airline ground service employee whose service quality or performance how to serve travelling passengers in order to reach service level or satisfy their service performance needs to be accepted. So, how to influence airline service labour individual emotional matter which will be one major factor to let travelling passengers how they feel satisfactory to the airline service.

The question concerns how to let airline service cabin crews and air ground service employees build long term good emotion to serve their airline travelling passengers. Because
bad emotional airline service labors will damage the whole airline employers' loyalty as well as reducing travelling passengers number in possible.

Will a lot stresses at work cause bad emotion to airline ground service employees? The hospitality industry comprises of travel and tourism and the major segments include lodgings and cuisines (hotels, restaurants), transport(airlines, rentals, cruise and railway companies), travel and tour operators. All of these related travelling industries' employees , they are emotional labor, whose service performance or service attitude will influence future potential travelling passengers' airline choices to the airline operating servicer again. Any airline service employees in these service sector industries, have to interact with their travelling clients, be its customers on a regular emotion reflecting basis. So, they must be patient to listen any travelling passengers' enquires in order to help them to solve any problems considerably.

Emotional labor is managing one's feelings to generate a publicly accepted facial and bodily display of emotion. Emotional labor is an expression of emotion for a wage. Jobs involve face to face or voice to voice interactions with clients (travelling passengers), jobs demanding the employee to produce and alter an emotional state in other person, and jobs allowing the employer to implement certain amount of control over the emotional activities of the employees, produce or create emotional labor among the employees.

Thus, long time bad emotional airline front labors number increasing, it will influence the airline whole service member performance to be its airline passengers. However, many airline organizations have their owning set of norms or policies that determine these feeling rules. These are specially seen in customer service industries. IN long term, these strict policies will let airline front service staffs feel stress or pressure, because they won't feel to be punished in possible, e.g. without salary continue increasing, dismissal (lose jobs), changing to another position to do more simple or boring job duties, if they are discovered that their working service performances are not satisfied to their airline employers in any time.

So, strict airline organizational policies will be one strict or pressure emotional regulation to any airline front service staffs. This emotional regulation refers to a person's capability to accept and understand his or her experience of emotions to get involved in healthy strategies in managing emotions which are uncomfortable whenever required, when they need to contact their airline passengers every day. In fact, it has possible that they will accept unreasonable complaint from their airline passengers, even they perform very good or they have help their airline passengers to solve any enquiries when they feel any needs, they stay in airports any time. So, it has close relationship among airline front service staffs' emotions and the airline's policy as well as their service attitude. Thus, good airline policy will build good airline service staffs' emotions and good service attitude or service behaviour to serve their airline passengers every day in possible.

Any airline organizations can not neglect to consider how to build (keep) good airline front labor emotion issue. Because they are any airlines' representatives, if they can build good

images to let the airline the airline passengers to feel. Then, it will influence many airline passengers to choose to buy the airline tickets to replace other airlines because they like its front airline front staffs' services. SO, any airline organizations need to consider front service staffs' health status and definite psychological or mental diseases more than physical diseases, because many airline front service staffs only need to serve their airline passengers and they do not need to move any heavy things in airports in general. They need to spend more time to contract their passengers more than any things. When their passengers give their passports or/and any related travelling documents, e.g. air tickets to them to check in to find whether they can allow to enter airport restrict areas, and if they give their luggage to them, they also need to help them to measure its size and weight heavy to decide whether they need to pay extra fee and their luggage are permitted either to keep to them together to enter the air planes to fly or separate air planes to fly to destination. So, they need to make accurate judgement need to avoid any error occurrence. They do not allow to do any wrong judgement or error in order to be complain by their airline passengers often. Hence, any airline organizations need have good method to help their airline front service staffs to avoid to do any wrong judgements in order to influence any flights delay or customers' complaints , due to their personal wrong judgement to their passengers cause in possible.

Thus, any airline organizations require to enquire themselves these questions: Is there any influence of emotional labor (surface acting and deep acting) on the general mental health or psychological disease of airline employees? Is these any difference in the experience of emotional labor across demographics (age/gender/mental status/work experience of airline employees influence their service performance? Because above any one factors , such as every airline front service staff individual age, airline service experience, marital status of these factors will influence their emotions to be good or bad to serve their airline passengers every day. Hence , any airline organizations need to investigate every airline front service employee individual background in order to arrange the most suitable policy to train their front line or ground airline service staffs' skill in order to let them to feel less stress or pressure or they can feel happy to enjoy to serve their airline passengers.

On conclusion, reducing airline front or ground service staffs' psychological stress or mental pressure issue which will be the most effective or the best solution to assist them to raise confidence to serve their airline passengers in airports in long time. I believe that it is the most rapid psychological solution method to assist any one airline front or ground service staff to raise service level in short time.

6.1

Airports service environment factor

The environment of airports service environment for the airline services, which will also influence travelling passengers' travelling destinations and travelling frequent times choices. The airport price factor includes income growth, aviation technology and local economic / geographical features of the country's domestic or overseas airports both. IN fact, airports, airports are indeed two sides businesses, it has commercial relationship between both airlines and passengers. So, airports' pricing will influence passengers' travelling demands to the airlines in the country. Any countries' airport(s) need(s) to respond how to help themselves country airlines how to increase passengers number and airlines choices in order to achieve attracting traffic on frequent air planes flying aim. Because the country's travelling passengers number increases , it will influence the country's airport(s) ' income increases indirectly, instead of the countries' any airlines themselves incomes.

Hence, any country's airport(s) will be one good platform to let travelling passengers to stay in the country's airport(s). It means that id the country's airport(s) can build good service image and reasonable products sale price and comfortable shopping environment to attract any countries' passengers feel comfortable and worth to stay in themselves countries' airport(s), when they need to transfer air planes to stay in the country's airport, e.g. one hour to five hours short time, even overnight long time staying. However, if they feel the country's airport(s) are(is) more comfortable and clean to stay, less noise, as well as they have enough chairs to let them to sit or sleep and large area to let them to work in the airport ground floor.

Moreover, the country's airport(s) can have enough restaurants , bookshops, any electronic or other kinds product shop[s, even cinema etc. shopping or entertainment services to satisfy the passengers whose eating needs, entertainment needs, shopping needs in the airport. Then, I believe that the country's airport(s) can help itself airlines to attract many passengers to choose to increase travelling times to the country frequently. For example, when the country's airport passengers feel that the airport restaurant food concessionaires will probably provide enjoy positive external gains from having more flights at the airports, additional or better eating facilities are unlikely to provide external benefits to the airlines by stimulating many more passengers with local origins or destinations to use the airport. I believe these airport restaurants can influence the choices of transit passengers whether which country will be their transfer

air plane's short journey staying airport destination to fly to their final destinations. Although, transit passengers usually stay to the transfer air plane airport in short time, but they hope that these any one transit staying airport can have any restaurants to provide good taste food to them to eat when they feel hungry, if the transfer air plane country's airport can provide enough restaurants and they can have different food taste choice and reasonable price. Then, the airport's restaurants may attract many short time transit passengers to choose to eat their food, even many passengers will like to choose the country's airline to buy tickets to stay short time to wait to
transfer another air plane to fly to their final destination to replace another country's airport to stay short time.

Hence, it seems that any countries' airports' entertainment, eating and shopping service environment will influence any countries transit passengers whether they ought either choose to stay short time this country's airport in prefer or another country's airport to stay short time in prefer in order to decide to buy the country's airline air ticket for transfer airplane to another destination. Hence, any airports service environment will influence any countries passengers how to make transit airport destination short time staying choice.

However, I also suggest that an airport will place a lower revenue -over cost burden on that side of the travelling market that benefits the other the most. Assuming one passenger can earn benefit enjoyed by airlines from an extra-passenger using the airport, the airlines will be willing to pay up to this amount to increase passenger enjoyed benefit feeling.

The airport can extract rent from the airlines up to above their allocated costs for providing the airport short time staying platform (transfer air plane short time staying airport) for eating, entertainment, shopping need service of increasing their destination arriving passengers or transfer another air plane passengers number base. This involves transferring the external benefits derived by airlines from additional passengers using the transfer airport to the another destination airport.

On the another view, from a airport location choice perspective, locating or expanding an airport near a city center can reduce or at least contain passenger access costs . But, because land is like to be more expensive, the airside costs to airlines are serious higher and if the various other external costs of aviation are included. Hence, countryside or the airport is built far away from city center in the country. This location is one reasonable location choice, because it can reduce noise to influence people who are living when air planes are often flying or landing on the airport and the rent cost to the airport's any business renters will be influenced to reduce. Then, their food , product or entertainment service prices charge to the airport consumers will also be reduced. Thus, any airports ought nor neglect their building location choices in any countries because they will influence airport business renters sale prices.

6.2
Lean maintenance repair and manual error factor

Any airlines must need air plans to catch passengers to fly to travel. So, any air plans will need often to fly. Every flight will need long time to fly, e.g. short trip needs to fly less than five hours, even long trip needs to fly more than five hours, even ten hours. If many passengers choose the country to travel, the air plan needs to fly frequently to catch every flight passengers to go to the travelling destination frequently. So, any airlines air plans often need to check whether they have any engine machines has broken, need to be repaired in possible in order to let passengers feel the airline air plans are safe. If the airline's any air plans have occurred any accidents when they are flying, even the accidents cause any one passengers hurt, even death. Then, these flying accidents will let passengers feel life risk to choose this airline's any air plans to catch to fly. IN special, long time trip(s) flight(s). So, lean maintenance and engine check is needed to consider for any one airplane to any airline in order to improve efficiencies and minimize costs, maintenance, repair,

and overhaul services in the aviation industry sector, even avoiding any flying accident occurrence or reducing serious flying accidents occurrence chance to bring any one passenger

hurt, even death when they are catching any one of the airline air plans to travel. Thus, any one of airline safety is one important successful factor to any airlines.

Instead of passenger safety aspect, the flying logistics safety factor is also important. The central tenet of the lean to a flying process can mainfest in a variety of ways , as over stalled and underused inventory and misallocated labour, time transportation and logistics. From a customer's perspective, value-added activities are necessary and customers are willing to pay for activities(Bamber, 2000, Glass, 2016). For example, improvements caused by lean introduction in aviation industry in order to avoid misallocated labour time, increasing number of old broken tools, and obsolute jigs and fixtures. Aviation MRO services have been reported by the MIT Lean Aerospace Initiative (2005) to result in:

(1) Set up time: 17 to 85 percent improvement.
(2) Lead time: 16 to 50 percent improvement.
(3) Labour hours: 10 to 71 percent improvement.
(4) Cost: 11 to 50 percent improvement.
(5) Productivity: 27 to 100 percent improvement.
(6) Cycle time: 20 to 97 percent improvement.
(7) Airline airplane manufacturing factory floor space: 25 to 81 percent improvement.
(8) Travel distance (people and products): 42 to 95 percent improvement.
(9) Airplanes engine inventory or work in progress: 31 to 98 percent improvement.
(10) Scape, rework , deflects or inspection: 20 to 80 percent improvement.

Hence, any airlines' airplanes need to be achieve any one of above improvement at least percent level in order to keep airplane's accident occurrence chance to the least level.

Moreover, airplanes' pilot employees their flying experiences or flight numbers factor is also important to influence airplane safe flying issue. Because if the pilot has less flying

experience or he is not proficient pilot, or his flight number is less. This pilot's individual flying factor will also influence the air plan's safety when he is driving the airplane. So, any airlines need to consider how to train any one of pilot to be one proficient pilot, because id less experienced pilot , he/she is not proficient to drive any one airplane to fly. Then, the flying accident occurrence chance will also raise. It is one critical successful factor to influence passengers' confidence to choose the airline's airplanes to catch, instead of maintenance repair and checking engines factor.

On conclusion, raising travelling passengers‘ safe confidences factor will be one critical successful factor to influence any airlines' services level, because flying safety issue
must be one important matter to be considered to any passengers when they decide to choose the airline's airplane to catch to fly to any destinations. If one airline can not guarantee any flying accidents won't occur, to cause any passengers hurt or death. Then, any passengers won't have confidence to feel its others services level can satisfy their basic flying enjoyment needs. Due to passengers‘ life cost must be no worth calculation more than other service cost. When they choose to catch the airlines' any one airplane to fly to the another destination form the country's airport. Hence, the influence of human factor in airport maintenance factor will influence any airlines‘ services feeling level to their passengers because human factor is one of the safety barrier which is used in order to prevent accidents or incidents of aircraft.

Therefore, the question is to which extent the error caused by human factor is included into the share of errors that are made during aircraft maintenance, such as flying
accidents, incidents, injuries, death, damages related to aircraft operation and maintenance. More airlines' detailed analyses have led to the knowledge that it is necessary to study the interrelation of repair people, machines, airline factory maintenance and manufacturing working environment, and the air planes production processes. Human is the key factor production process and in the process of operation of technical means since gives new value to the object of any one airplane manufacturing process.

As a factor, the human is not perfect and introduces unintentional error in the system. It is important to develop a system of ever identification and to work constantly on error prevention. The works and activities on aircraft maintenance can produce hidden and active errors on the aircraft. Hidden errors are a type of errors that are seemingly invisible during aircraft flying. Active errors are errors that occur immediately and result in immediate aircraft damage or injury , even death to any travelling passengers.

Hence, non human or without human factors will be less number to compare human factors to cause any flying incidents or accidents occurrence easily, e.g. damaging engine, old engine (no renew engine), fire, crash etc. different kinds of causes. However, the main causes of human errors to cause any flying accidents may include: lack of communication between the pilot(s)and airport airplane landing staffs, complacency (assessment of work according to previous working experience), lacking of flying knowledge to the pilot, distraction, lack of team work, fatigue, lack of materials and technological support), pressure on the work performer, lack of assertiveness (lack of self-confidence or technical approach to work),stress (working under pressure), lack of awareness etc. different human factors. Any one of above human factors will influence any flying accidents cause.

Moreover, instead of human factor, the flying working environment which refers to the space and place for work as well as the conditions of work factor will also influence human
error occurrence increasing chance, e.g. time pressure, equipment and tools enough number supplies, night shift, all of any one work environment factor will also influence human error
occurrence increasing chance in any flight flying. However, the factors that lead to cause of maintenance error may be caused from wrong information system supplies of equipment , aircraft manufacturer, wrong working equipment and tools, wrong design of aircraft equipment and parts, incorrect working task arrangement, lacking technical education to the aircraft maintenance
workers, employee's bad personality, poor aircraft factory manufacturing working environment, poor airline company organization structure, working management and control and poor communication etc. different manual or non manual factors.

Hence, all of above any one non manual factors will also raise manual error factor to cause any flying accidents occurrence chances. However, if any airlines hope to satisfy their passengers' flying service level. They must consider non manual and manual both factors for aircraft lean maintenance repair service aspect.

6.3

Influence of airside and off airport to airport geographical choice factor

What does airport airside means ? It includes a system of three components: runways, taxiways and agron-gate areas, on which aircraft and aircraft support vehicles operate. It brings this questions: Why can airport airside operation influence passengers feeling to the country's airport and airline services? How does it influence airport ground service staffs' service performance?

In fact, this airside airport physical area choice has direct relationship between aircraft and apron gate areas of the terminal processing of passenger and cargo. They are major factors to influence operations on runway component. It means that airport ground service staffs' service efficiency, used for the passengers and air fright catching any airplanes processing.

Hence, in a geographical sense, landside and airside capacity on how designing and building og geographical area can bring indirect influence to passengers. They need to enter or indirect influence the airport , in special, many flights are staying on the airport runway as well as many passengers need to leave from the airplanes or enter to the airplanes in the same time on the airport boundary. Hence, if the airport has good airside design , then many passengers will feel convenient to leave or enter the airport from the airside areas.

Airports are perhaps truly inter model terminals in the transportation system. They provide an inter safe among air highway, rail and even water way travel. They are an important part of the medium and long distance intercity transportation system in our future transportation tools. Hence, it has enough reasons to support airside geographical airside and off airport factors can influence an airport and its airline flying service providers on its capacity as well as how it's capacity can influence passengers' satisfactory level when they arrive the country's airport. Hence, airport's congestion growth problem that is needed to consider to any airports because when one airport 's congestion is growing.

It will influence passengers service satisfactory level to be fallen down in possible, e.g. capacity is increased by the addition of a new access road, such as additions provide a major increase. Thus, the stair step growth, it will cause congestion growth because if the airport had used many areas for stair step growth and passengers will have less space to let them to walk on the ground and their airport congestion feeling will also increase when passengers are staying to leave the airport or waiting for check in or check out or waiting to transfer another airplane in the country's airport. The major airside factors to influence travelling passengers whose airport service feeling may include as below:

Availability of enough land for expansion for runways, availability of aids to navigation and air traffic control techniques that could result in reduction of separation between aircraft , noise, aircraft mix, load factor, exclusive use and use of gates , enough airside and outside facilities, availability of airspace, whether aircraft large size is enough capacity and where is location of gates, staffing, equipment freight, environmental protection regulation, and community attitudes toward airside operation.

Thus, whether the airport has enough facilities to satisfy passengers staying in its airport service need, it will have indirect influence further passengers increasing or decreasing
number problem. For example, if the airport terminal functions are spread over a large geographic area, access and facilities have to be expanded to accommodate the spread-out configuration of the terminal or if terminal facilities are grouped together, the access facilities can be congregated into a smaller geographical area.

The capacity of the landside is a function of the terminal design , which has a major influence on the relative to between airside and landside capacity. Also, these off airport factors can also
influence landside capacity, they may include: off airport parking, off airport terminals, urban development pattern, multiple jurisdiction, financial resources etc. issues. The sub factors of the off-airport access functions , they can influence passengers' services feeling to the airport. They may include: user and vehicle characteristics, e.g. occupants per vehicle, separate and preferential guide way subsystems, roadway traffic management, access link to major transportation , transportation connections. All of these airside and off-airport facilities will influence passengers' servicing feeling when they arrive any countries' airports. Hence, any countries' airports ought not neglect any one of these minor airside facilities of inside airports to outside airports both.

The another geographical choice airport building issue, it is also one critical factor for how the development of airport cities. It will influence passengers' service feeling to any country airport. The questions may include: Why may any country need to develop an airport city? Can it bring economic benefit and attract many passengers to choose to travel the country? Can the airport city reform to raise airport service performance or service level? Airports have become new dynamic centers of economic activity, incorporating several commercial and
entertainment services inside passenger terminals, when developing a hotels and accommodations , office complexes, conference and exhibition centers or leisure facilities choices for leisure passengers and business

passengers both.

Airport-centered development may occur at different spatial scales (from the micro scale of the passenger terminal to the regional or metropolitan scale), thus assuming different shapes and mainfestations. Different concepts to address these developments can be found in the " airport city", airport corridor, and aerotopolis (Guller, M. & Guller, M, 2003).

I shall explain how airport city concept can help to raise passenger service performance feeling in airports and airlines as below:

In general, airport passengers hope airports ought provide these different kinds service and achievement the lowest satisfactory service quality or performance level to let
them to feel, such as air transport needs have complex airport -neighborhood interactions (in what concerns an eventual development towards the concept of airport city) requires the identification of thes takeholders involved and an awareness of the relationships between them. Any airport's main task needs to provide traveling, air transport, shipping, entertainment services to
the dual market of airlines and travelers. As such, its primary interaction consists of the supply and demand relationship with the users stakeholder group (passengers and airlines), which results in broad terms in the airports aeronautical revenues. Furthermore, non-aeronautical (commercial) revenues also result from the interactions between airport and users, namely from agents such as cargo and passengers oriented organizations who pay rents or concession feeling to the airport authority, depending on the commercial arrangements binding these agents.

Thus, one successful airport city, it ought provide good neighborhood transport service to travelling passengers, e.g. bus, taxi, ferry etc. public transportation service. It aims to avail any airport passengers can catch any one of these public transportation tools to arrive airport or leave the airport easily. It also needs to provide hotel, conference service for business visitors as well as retail shops, cinemas for shopping visitors or entertainment visitors when they are staying in the country's airport(s). Also, it ought provide facilities to any cargo -oriented
organizations to deliver any cargo in short time rapidly. So, one airport's any neighborhood facilities have relationship to influence any passengers and airport organizations' service performance feeling between different user agents including: service provision (e.g. between passengers and businesses), business transactions, supply and demand (e.g. between public transport providers and passengers and passengers or visitors) and employer-employee relationships (businesses and workforce , such as airport airline ground service workers). Because if they feel that they can work in one comfortable airport working environment, they will feel happy and enjoyable to serve their passengers more everyday. It means that any airports' facilities will have indirect relationship to influence airport ground service workers' psychology to feel either enjoyable or hate to work in the airport environment often.

On conclusion, airports ought need to consider themselves airside and off airport facilities whether they have enough supplies and innovate their facilities to be better , even perfect in order to satisfy any airport visitors, travelers, user organizations and airport ground service employees to enjoy to work and use their services if they hope their service level or performance is satisfied to their service needs for long term.

6.4

Influencing air connectivity to service quality factor

Can air connectivity growth decreases travel costs for attracting travelling passengers, consumers and businesses and facilities global productive growth? This seems to be particularly an issue when airport capacity is scare or when new airports are added to an existing airport system. What is air connectivity ?

Why does air connectivity raise passengers services? How to measure air connective service?

When direct and indirect connectivity relate to the airport connectivity available to local travelling passengers, any airports ought need to raise extra

airline services to raise service quality , e.g. cheaper air ticket price, in-flight service extra service provision, e.g. comfortable and clean and quiet air port waiting environment

service provision and feeling. However, passengers will generally prefer direct, non-stop connections over indirect air connectivity service.

Air connectivity service can assist airlines to raise competitive effort an offer and they provide access to the many destinations with too little demand for a direct flight, such as minimum connecting time differs in quality , due to in-flight time differences, the inconvenience and risk of missing a connection and transfer time for direct or indirect flights. Hence, any airlines can reduce passengers indirect or direct flight in-flight time to wait airplanes arrive to catch when they arrive any airports. This air inflight waiting time shorten service will attract many passengers to choose the airline to catch airplanes if its inflight waiting time to airport passengers is lesser than other airlines‘ in-flight waiting time in any airports. It can raise airline service quality, due to the airline has many passengers feel in-flight waiting time is shorten than other airlines often.

In fact, airport connectivity is one good concept method to raise passengers' satisfactory service level. One of the important factors for the connectivity of airports may include: The size and economic strength of the local catchment area how drives outbound demand, size and economic activities as well as tourism attractiveness are an important carry factor in explaining

inbound demand (including the propensity to flying demand), landside accessibility drives the size of the catchment area that airlines can serve from a particular airport within a certain landside travel time, apart from the socio-economic variables factor, also cultural , political and the historical ties play a role in explaining demand the origin-destination level factor. All of the research on the factors that explain air level, demand at the origin-destination or airport level is widespread, including gravity modelling (e.g. a bed at al., 2001) and regressions on aggregate

airport demand (Dobruszkes, 2011). All of any one factors may be airport connectivity service to influence passengers‘ service feeling level in airports and airlines both service quality.

ON airport visit costs aspect, airlines also need to consider airport visit costs in their route development strategy. Visit costs may also influence passenger choice behavior when airlines pass on higher/lower charges to the passenger through air fares. Although, airport visit costs generally represent a limited share of an airline's total operational costs, this share can be more significant for short haul flights as well as fair airlines. All of any one these airport charges and passenger fees variable may influence passengers airlines choice. They may include:

Fees variable, landing charge, parking charge for their vehicles or aircraft, passenger luggage charge, security charge, boarding bridge charge, noise charge, emission charge, airport development service increasing charge, check -in charge, terminal charge, cargo charge. So, if any one of these charges influence the airline ticket price rises, it will influence passengers' air ticket purchase choice to the airline in possible.

On airport service levels aspect, for keeping and attracting passengers, airlines and airports need to compete with services that improve the passengers experience. Such service
factors concern for immigration and luggage, but also relate to the terminals, waiting transfer another air plane time, shopping facilities, toilets, atmosphere and space cleaniness, friendliness of staff and availability of delicated lounges. Together they determine the image of an airport and its perceived value by passengers and airlines.

On airline routes development aspect, it can also influence passengers choices to the airline, e.g. Australia airline had developed long route to England destination. Any Australia passengers can fly to England route directly. They do not need to transfer another air plane to go to England. Although, flying time is above 12 hours long time, but it can bring available to
passengers. They do not need to spend time to wait another air plane to transfer to go England in Australia any airports. Thus, airline route development strategy airline planners require detailed, accurate information to make new route decisions, but airlines usually do not have the resources to fully evaluate every new route market. So, they need a sound well articulated business case, can convince airlines to introduce new air services, as well as airport / destinations can influence the airline planning process.

For example, Interviewer indicates that new routes are a huge investment and risk to an airline in airline economic view point, if the airline had not gathered any data to evaluate
whether the new route is worth to develop and predict passengers' new route choice behavior. It assumed 75% lead factor will influence any new route development in success. It indicates these different aircraft type and seats per flight, annual passenger requirements data for these aircrafts: Boeing 747 aircraft needs to satisfy 400 at least seats per flight and annual passenger requirement need 219, 000, aircraft airbus A340 aircraft needs 280 at least seats per flight and annual passenger requirements need 153,300 , Boeing 767 to 300 aircraft needs 220 at least seats per flight and annual passenger requirements need 120, 450 . Boeing 737 to 700 aircraft needs 76,650 and regional Jet aircraft needs 100 at least seats per flight and annual passenger requirements need 54,750.

Hence, any airlines need have route priorities strategy before they decide which new flight route(s) will be developed , in order to achieve airlines add service in order of expected profitability, different airlines have pursued different strategies, destinations can move up the priority board with: solid research and analysis (always) and incentives (sometimes).However, any airline questions for new routes may include as below:

What is the current, actual market for a potential route?
How much can my airline stimulate the flight flying market?

How will the competition react?
How much market share will achieve?
How will be the connectivity contribution?
Will the new route be a financial success?

Hence, any airlines need to reduce uncertainty and risk, before they decide to develop any new route market.

The air service development process may include as below:

Step one: market assessment, required a quantify the time size of the existing air travel market

step two: strategy, deficiency analysis and detailed route analysis

step three: business case analysis, packaging and presenting the information to airlines

step fourth: evaluate and negotiate airline incentives

It is the final steps an appropriate incentive, in certain circumstances, helps airlines commit to new air service to satisfy any new route passengers' more satisfactory flying needs.

Similarly, the strategy steps follow: benchmark air services, identify deficiencies, identify new route opportunities, identify potential air service providers, assess viability of potential air services and prioritize route opportunities and target carriers.

Any airlines may find any information concerns new route business cases to decide their countries flying new routes choice , such as: catchment area profile: demographics, economy, tourist etc. information, airport profile : traffic and facilities information market profile; market sizes , top city pairs, traffic leakage etc. information, suggested service : frequency , schedule, airport routing information, route analysis: market share, load factor, stimulation potential, self-diversion etc. information, any airlines' past flying routes strategic considerations etc. information in order to predict and evaluate whether how many further passenger number is flying that they accept to choose the new flying routes travelling needs.

Hence, how to design to impact either the supply or demand for any new flight routes that is only important because of the country has less number of passengers accept to choose the new flying route to fly. Then, the new flying route does not needed to be design to supply to the country's travelling passengers because their acceptance to this new flying route ends are very less. However, the demand level is low new flying route needs to satisfy these three qualifying services criteria, such as: Are new routes only? Increase on existing routes? Does it work service rent incentives? Will the new flying route be satisfied to air service to the airline passengers and airport waiting passengers, e.g. strategically important? Marginally (unprofitable) self-sustaining in the short term? New flying routes only? Increase an existing routes? Service rent incentives?

How can airports afford aggressive airline incentive / fee discounts and still fund route development marketing in a difficult economy? I recommend that the solution method may include new flying route design and developing and maximizing non-aeronautical revenue streams both, such as retail and duty free, food and beverage, parking , loyalty and premium programs and land development to airport building. Marketing funding strategy may be an ineffective incentive for travelling destinations. However, it may not differentiate a market, as route marketing incentives are used by over 80% of communities in the U.S. marketing incentives can be: Unilateral airport pays 100% or cooperative airlines matches some portion, funding amounts are often tied on the capacity of inbound seats to be available on the new flight (flying) route. By calculating the economic impact of new visitors (spend at the destination), a destination can calculate the return on investment in cooperative new flight (flying) route market.

On conclusion, air connectivity is one important factor to influence any country's travelling passengers to the airline's service quality or service level in order to achieve new flying (flight) route design , reducing inflight transfer another airplane waiting time in airport, or marketing development in success. So, any airlines can not neglect this air connectivity will influence their passengers' service quality.Hence, air connectivity factor is also very important to influence any travelling passengers' service satisfactory level.

6.5 How to measure and rise airline service quality

How are airline performing ? Nowadays, the rise of the low cost airlines' competition is serious, due to airlines hope to rise themselves attractions to influence passengers to choose to use their travelling services. So, different airlines have spend long time to build their unique person-to-person passenger services, which passengers use of different airlines, e.g. digital electronic air tickets purchase method. Any airlines hope to make each journey personalized to the individual will gain market share and improve its service quality to be more unique in order to reach the efforts of airlines to build high levels of customer service appears to have been generally noticed by passengers, when they choose to buy the airline's digital electronic ticket or paper air ticket to use its flying service.

Hence, improvement their digital e-ticket purchase experience and communications factor, for example, if any passengers can enter the airline's air ticket purchase website to buy electronic ticket to pre-book seats in the short time rapidly as well as there are enough seats number to supply to them to pre-book. So, they do not need to worry about without any seats to supply to them to catch the airline's flight to fly to anywhere in any time available conveniently. So, it seems that there is plenty of space for airlines to grow and improve their digital experience and communication method to let any passengers to feel, if the airline hopes to let its passengers to feel that it has unique service to compare others airlines.

The aviation industry plays a major role in the aspect of work and leisure to passengers around the global. So, nowadays passengers' demands to any airlines' service quality had been raised. Hence, any airline service industry messengers are under pressure to prove their services are customers oriented service improvement of performance that guarantees competitive advantages to the global travelling marketplace. So, it also implies that any airlines' services performance will be influenced to cause many passengers feel more poor and let passengers dissatisfy the airline's service performance. The, the airline will possible lose many passengers, due to passengers have many airlines choices, they can find any airlines to replace which any one airline to buy air ticket from internet at home immediately.

However, airlines' comfortable seats arrangement service provision feeling factor is still important in preferable to compare other factors, because passengers must need to sit any seats in any air planes. So, whether the air plane can provide new comfortable seats to let passengers to feel this factor is still the most important factor to influence any passengers to choose to the airline's air plane to catch. For example, service comfortability is how passengers observed the quality of service offered them by the airline's cleanliness, quiet zone, shops, restaurants and business pavilion in functioning like staffs, information desk, and in flight announcement are included as tangible features by the passengers (Geraldine et a.,2013). All of these factors are needed often to measure whether their service performances are satisfactory to themselves passengers service needs.

Moreover, the other factors may include service affordability , it can be regarded as given passenger the opportunity to select from inclusive air ticket prices made available to the different group of passengers by the airlines, as a gesture of goodwill , to establish and reinforce customer loyalty and repeat purchases essential for the airline continuity as well as service reliability. it is the probability that airline will carry out its expected function satisfactory as stated in the flight schedule. Hence, there is a strong link between different airlines‘ service quality variables, airline image and repeat patronage from the passengers.

Service quality is a measure of how well the service level delivered matches passengers expectations to measure service quality based on input from focus groups. It consists of five factors (tangibles, reliability, responsiveness, assurance and empathy). All of these factors will be identifies that how the airline service quality can be satisfactory to its passengers ' psychological and emotion enjoyable service needs.

Any one of these any five service factors will be important to influence the airline's passengers service feeling level to the airline. It means that the passenger will have more chance to choose the airline's service again (repeating purchase its air ticket). Hence, any airlines can not neglect any one of service feeling to its passengers. It needs often to enquire questionnaires to evaluate whether its these five aspects of service quality , if it discovered any of these five aspects of service level is poor, e.g. 5 scale is the best service performance level, then it can attempt to find its error whether which aspects, it needs to very need to reach the 5 scale , the best service performance level when many passengers feel, e.g. enquiring 100 passengers who give 5 scale to reliability service aspect, before reliability service aspect has less than 50% passengers from 100 passengers who feel the airlines concerns this reliable service level aspect questions to be the best. It is one kind of measurement service quality method to any airlines.

Other service performance evaluation factor is satisfaction in the job to every airline front service or ground service staffs to the airline. Job satisfaction describes how content an employee is with his or her job. It is how the employee responses to a job. It can be considered as a part of life satisfaction to one organization, when the employee is working in the organization. Hence, if one airline front service as ground service staff who can feel more job satisfaction to compare his/her prior airline employer. Then, he/she won't be easy to change his/her present airline employer.

However, some factors can influence job satisfaction are pay and benefit, fair performance appraisal, career and promotional opportunities, proper reward and recognition, work-family life balance, the job itself, proper working conditions, leadership chance, autonomy in work.

Job satisfaction can also involve complex number of variables, circumstances, opinions and behavioral tendencies and a variety of work related outcomes, such as commitment, involvement, motivation, satisfaction, attendance. Hence, any airlines also need to concern how let their employees feel job satisfaction issue in order to avoid their leaving turnover number increases, due to job satisfaction and dissatisfaction depend on the expectations what the job supplies for an employee not the nature of the job.

Finally, instead of concerning employees job satisfaction issue, any airlines also need to concern passengers satisfaction issue because it will have any passengers will choose the airline, if it can bring more service satisfaction to let them to feel , then they will become repeat passengers to the airline.

What kinds of factors passengers were looking for and what were the reasons of choosing a specific airline? When one airline often is complained from its passengers. It will have more mistakes to let them to feel or dissatisfy its service. Hence the airlines needs to find which are its mistakes and improve in order to satisfy its passengers' expectations, e.g. finding what are the mistakes to the airlines' serious concern regarding passenger complaints and complaint satisfaction in order to make the airline more likely to meet its passengers' expectation in case of a problem. Hence, any airlines need to concern how to improve its employees' satisfactory service as well as its passengers' satisfactory service both issues as well as how to measure their service quality whether is enough to achieve general service acceptable performance to its passengers.

Reference

A bed, S. Y. A.O. Ba-Fail and S.M. Jasimuddin (2001), " An economatic analysis of international air travel demand in Saudi Arabia". Journal of air transport managmement, vol. 7, pp.143-148.

Bamber, L., & Dale, B.G. Lean production : a study of application in a traditoinal manufacturing environment. Production planning & control, 11 (3), 291-298, 2000.

Dobruszkes, F.M. Lennert and G. Van Hamme (2011). " An analysis of the determinants of air traffic volume for European metropolitan area". Journal of transport geographyy, vol. 19/4/pp.755-762.

Gealdine, O., & David , U.C. (2013). effects of airline service quality on airline image and passengers' loyalty: Findings from Arill Air Nigeria passengers, Journal of hospitality and management tourism, 4(2), 19-28. doi: http://dx.doi: 10.5897/HMT 2013, 0089.

Glass, R., Seifermann, S., & Metternich, J. The spread of lean production in the assembly, Process and maching industry. Procedia CIRP, 55, 278-283, 2016.

Guller, M. & Guller, M. (2003) From Airport to airport city. Editional Gustavo , Gili, Barcel on a.

Intervistas Consulting Inc.

Massachusetts Institute Of Technology (MIT), Lean Aerospace Initiative, Available: www.lean.mit.edu, 2005.

CHAPTER SEVEN

Pollution factor influences travel behavioural consumption

Prediction travel behavioral consumption from psychology view and computer statistic view.
How to predict travel consumption? It is one question to any travel agents concern to use what methods which can predict how many numbers of travelers where who will choose to go to travel more accurately. I think that who can consider how to predict travel behavioral consumption from psychology view and computer science view both.

On the psychology view, It has evidence to support the relationship between self-identify threat and resistance to change travel behavior to any travelers, controlling for whose past travelling behavior, resistance to change if a psychological phenomenon of long standing interest in many applied branches of psychology. Past travelling behavior has been acknowledged as a predictor of future action. Such as travelling behavior that is experienced as successful is likely to be repeated and may lead to habitual patterns. Some psychologists differentiate habit between two concepts, such as goal oriented and automatic oriented both. Although repeated past travelling behavior is addition goal oriented and automatic oriented. Further non-deliberative nature of habit may make appeals to judge and to predict future individual traveler's behaviour accrately. However, repeated travelling behavior without a necessary constraint of goal orientation and automatic oriented both. So, it seems that psychological factor can influence any individual traveler why and how who choose to decide whose travelling behaviour.

On the computer statistic view, structural equation modeling is an extremely flexible linear-in-parameters multivariate statistical modeling technique. It has been used in modeling travel behavior and values since about 1980 year. It is a software method to handle a large number of variables, as well as unobserved variables specified as linear combinations (weighted averages) of the observed variable.

Whether climate change can influence travelling behaviours.

The flexibility of human travelling behavior is at least the result of one such mechanism, our ability to travel mentally in time and entertain potential future. Understanding of the impacts is holidays, particularly those involving travel. Using focus groups research to explores tourists‘ awareness of the impacts of travel own climate change, examines the extent to which climate change features in holiday travel decisions and identifies some of the barriers to the adoption of less carbon intensive tourism practices. The findings suggest many tourists don't consider climate change when planning their holidays. The failure of tourists to engage with the climate change to impact of holidays, combined with significant barriers to behavioral change, presents a considerable challenge in the tourism industry.

Tourism is a highly energy intensive industry and has only recently attracted attention as an important contributions to climate change through greenhouse gas emissions. It has been estimated that tourism contributes 5% of global carbon dioxide emissions. There have been a number of potential changes proposed for reducing the impact of air travel on climate change. These include technological changes, market based changes and behavioral changes. However, the role that climate change plays in the holiday and travel decisions of global tourists. How the global tourists of the impacts travel has on climate change to establish the extent to which climate change, considerations features in holiday travel decision making processes and to investigate the major barriers to global tourists adopting less carbon intensive travel practices. Whether tourists will aware the impacts that their holidays and travel have on climate changes.

When, it comes to understand indvidual traveler's behavioral change, wide range of conceptual theories have been developed, utilizing various social, psychological, subjective and objective variables in order to model travel consumption behavior. These theories of travel behavioral change operate at a number of different levels, including the individual level, the interpersonal level and community level. Whether pro-environmental behavior can be used to predict travel consumption behavior in a climate change. However, the question of what determines pro-environmental behavior in such a complex one that it can not be visualized through one single framework or diagram.

Despite the potentially high risk scenario for the tourism industry and the global environment, the tourism and climate change ought have close relationship. Whether what are the important factors and variables which can limit tourism? e.g. money, time, family problem, extreme hot or cold weather change, air ticket price, journey attraction etc. variable factors. Mention of holidays and travel were deliberately avoided in the recruitment process, so as not to create a connection factor to influence traveler's individual mind. However, the dismissal of alternative transportation modes can be conceived as either a structural barrier, in the sense that flying is perhaps the only realistic option to reach long-haul holiday destination, or a perceived behavioral control barriers in that an individual perceives flying as the only option open to whom. The transportation tool factor will be depend to extent on the distance to the destination. This can also be interpreted in a social perspective as an intention with the resources available where much international tourism is structured around flying. To increase the availability of different transportation modes, tourists could choose holiday destination closer to home.

Finally, also how to predict future travel behavioural consumption. I feel that travel agents need to predict whether any country's random daily variation of weather factor is also important to influence travel behaviour. e.g. in weather, temperature, rainfall adn snowfall with traffic accidents factors will have relationship to cause travel demand. Some scientists estimate suggest that when warmed temperatures and reduced snowfall are associated with a moderate decline in non-fatal accidents, they are also associated with a significant increase in fatal accidents. Thus increase in fatalities and temperature. Half of the estimated effect of temperature on fatalities is due to changes in the exposure to pedestrians, bicyclists and motorcyclists as temperature increase. So, if any countries have rainfall, snowfall and low temperature to cause traffic accidents, whether this accident occurrence will influence the travelers who liking climb snow hills, riding bicycle, running sports who will avoid to travel to these countries' bad weather after occurs. So, why I feel that this natural climate factor will also be one serious factor to influence travel behavioral consumption.

11.1 Whether individual habitual behaviour can influence travelling behaviour : e.g. renting travel transportation tools

Whether habit can be intended to predict of future travel behavior to people are creatures of habits. Many of human's everyday goal-directed behaviors are performed in a habitual fashion, the transportation made and route one takes to work, one's choice of breakfast. Habits are formed when using the some behavior frequently and a similar consistency in a similar context for the some purpose whether the individual past travel consumption model will be caused a habit to whom. e.g. choosing whom travel agent to buy air ticket or traveling package; choosing the same or similar countries' destinations to go to travel ; choosing the business class or normal (general) class of quality airlines to catch planes. Does habitual rent traveling car tools use not lead to more resistance to change of travel mode? It has been argued that past behavior is the best predictor of future behavior to travel consumption. If individual traveler's past consumption behavior was always reasoned, then frequency of prior travel consumption behavior should only have an indirect link to the individual traveler's behavior. It seems that renting travel car tools to use is a habit example. So, a strong rent traveling car tools useful habit makes traveling mode choice. People with a strong renting of traveling car tools of habit should have low motivation to attend to gather any information about public transportation in their choice of travelling country for individual or family or friends members during their traveling journeys.

Even when persuasive communication changes the traveler whose attitudes and intention, in the case of individual traveler or family travelers with a strong renting travel car tools habit. It is difficult to change whose travel behaviors to choose to catch public transportation in whose any trips in any countries. However, understanding of travel behavior and the reasons for choosing one mode of transportation over another. The arguments for rent traveling car tools to use, including convenience, speed, comfort and individual freedom and well known. Increasingly, psychological factors include such as, perceptions, identity, social norms and habit are being used to understand travel mode choice. Whether how many travel consumers will choose to rent traveling car tools during their trips in any countries. It is difficult to estimate the numbers. As the average level of renting travel car tools of dependence or attitudes to certain travel package policies from travel agents. Instead different people must be treated in different ways because who are motivated in different ways and who are motivated by different travel package policies ways from travel agents.

In conclusion, the factors influence whose traveler's individual behavior either who chooses to rent traveling car tools or who chooses to catch public transportation when who individual goes to travel in alone trip or family trip. It include influence mode choice factors, such as social psychology factor and marketing on segmentation factor both to influence whose transportation choice of behavior in whose trip.

How to determine future travel behavior from past travel experience and perceptions of risk and safety for the benefits to travel consumers?

How to determine future travel behavior from past travel experience and perceptions of risk and safety for the benefits to travel consumers? Why does individual traveler avoid certain destination(s) is(are) as relevant to tourist decision making as why who chooses to travel to others. Perceptions of risk and safety and travel experience are likely to influence travel decisions. If travel agents had efforts to predict future travel behavior to guess whether travelers will feel where is(are) risk and unsafe to cause who does not choose to go to the country to travel. Then, the travel agents will avoid to choose to spend much time to design the different traveling package to attract their potential travel consumers to choose to travel. The reason is because in the case of individual traveler's tourism experience, the traveler whose past disappointment travel experience (psychological risk) will be a serious threat to the traveler's health or life (health, physical or terrorism risk). The past safety or unhealthy risk to the country(countries) will influence the traveler decides to choose not to go to the countries(country) to travel again in the future.

What is push and pull factors to influence any
traveler who chooses where is whose preferable travelling destination

How to predict individual traveler's behavioral intention of choosing a travel destination. Understanding why people travel and what factors influence their behavioral intention of choosing a travel destination is beneficial to tourism planning and marketing. In general, an individual's choice of a travel destination into two forces. The first force is the push factor that pushes an individual away from home and attempt to develop a general desire to go somewhere, without specifying where that may be. The other force is the pull factor that pull an individual toward in destination, due to a region-specific or perceived attractiveness of a destination. The respective push and pull factors illustrate that people travel because who are pushed by whose internal motives and pulled by external forced of a destination. However, the decision making process leading to the choice of a travel destination is a very complex process. For example, a Taiwanese traveler who might either choose new travel destination of Hong Kong or another old travel Asia destinations again or who also might choose any one of Western country, as a new travel destination. The travel agents can predict where who will have intention to choose to travel from whose past behavior and attitude, subjective and perceived behavioral control model.

The factors influence where is the traveler choice, include personal safety, scenic beauty, cultural interest, climate changing, transportation tools, friendliness of local people, price of trip, trip package service in hotels and restaurants, quality and variety of food and shopping facilities and services etc. needs. So, whose factors will influence where is the individual travel's choice. It seems every traveler whose choice of travel process, will include past behavior. e.g. travelling experience, travelling habit, then to choose the best seasoned travelling action to satisfy whose travel needs. This process is the individual traveler's psychological choice process, who must need time to gather information to compare concerning of different travel packages, destination scene, climate change, transportation tools available to the destination, air ticket price etc. these factors, then to judge where is the best right destination to travel in the right time.

Why expectation, motivation and attitude factor can influence travelling behaviour.

Social psychology is concerned with gaining insight into the psychological of socially relevant behaviors and the processes. For instance, on a global level bad influence to global warming, it influences some countries extreme cold or hot bad climate changing occurrence, then it ought influence some travelers' behavioral decision to change their mind to choose some countries to go to travel at the moment which do not occur extreme hot or cold climate (temperature). e.g. above than 40 degree in summer or below than 0 degree in winter. Due to the extreme climate changing environment in the countries, it will cause them to feel uncomfortable to play during their trips. So, the global warming causes to climate changing factor will influence the numbers of travel consumption to be reduced possibly. This is global climate changing environment factor influences to bad or uncomfortable social psychological feeling to global travelers' mind of traveling decision. What is individual traveler expectation, motivation and attitude? Tourism sector includes inbound (domestic) tourism and outbound (overseas) tourism both incomes to any countries. According to recent article, a tourist behavior model has been developed, called the expectation, motivation and attitude (EMA) model (Hsu et al., 2010).

This model focuses on the pre-visit stage of tourists by modeling the behavioral process by incorporating expectation, motivation and attitude. Travel motivation is considered as an essential component of the behavioral process, which has been increasing attention from the travel; industry. The economic approach defines "tourism" is an identifiable nationally important industry. It includes the component activities of transportation, accommodation, recreation, food and related service. So, tourism behavioral consumption is concerned the individual tourist's usual habituate of the industry which responds to whose needs, and of the impacts that both the tourist and the tourism industry have on the socio-cultural, economic and physical environment.

However, travel motivation means how to understand and predict factors that influence travel decision making. According to Backman and others (1995, p.15), motivation is conceptually viewed as " a state of need, a condition that services as a driving force to display different kind of behavior toward certain types of activities, developing preferences, arriving at some expected satisfactory outcome." So, motivation and expectancy which has close relationship to any tourist before who decided to do any tourism of behavior. Some economists confirmed motivation and expectancy which has relations, such as expectation of visiting an outbound destination has a direct effect on motivation to visit the destination; motivation has a direct effect on attitude toward visiting the destination; expectation of visiting the outbound destination has a direct affect on attitude toward visiting the destination and motivation has a mediating effect on the relationship in between expectation and attitude.

CHAPTER EIGHT

Pollution influences traveler behavior

What methods predict pollution influences future travel behavioural consumption

How to use qualitative of travel behavioural method to predict future travel consumption.

I also suggest to use qualitative of travel behavioural method to predict future travel consumption. Methods such as focus groups interviews and participant observer techniques can be used with quantitative approaches on their own to fill the gaps left by quantitative techniques. These insights have contributed to the development of increasingly sophisticated models to forecast travel behavior and predict changes in behavior in response to change in the transportation system. First, survey methods restrict not only the question frame but the answer frame as well, anticipating the important issues and questions and the responses. However, these surveys methods are not well suited to exploratory areas of research where issues remain unidentified and the researched seek to answer the question "why?". Second, data collection methods using traditional travel diaries or telephone recruitment can under represent certain segments of the population, particularly the older persons with little education, minorities and the poor. Before the survey, focus group for example can be used to identify what socio-demographic variables to include in the survey, how best to structure the diary, even what incentives will be most effective in increasing the response rate. After the survey, focus, focus groups can be used to build explanations for the survey results to identify the "why" of the results as well as the implications. One Asia Pacific survey research result was made by tourism market investigation before. It indicated the travel in Asia Pacific market in the past, had often been undertaken in large groups through leisure package sold in bulk, or in large organized business groups, future travelers will be in smaller groups or alone, and for a much wider range of reasons. Significant new traveler segments, such as female business traveler. The small business traveler and the senior traveler, all of which have different aspirations and requirements from the travel experience.

Moreover, Asia tourism market will start to exist behaviors in the adoption of newer technologies, a giving the traveler new ways to manage the travel experience, creating new behaviors. This with provide new opportunities for travel providers. The use of mobile devices, smartphones, tablets etc. and social media are the obvious findings to become an integral part of the travel experience. Thus, quality method can attempt to predict Asia Pacific tourism market development in the future.

However, improving the predictive power of travel behavior models and to increase understanding travel behavior which lies in the use of panel data(repeated measures from the same individuals). Whereas, cross-sectional data only reveal inter-individual differences at one moment in time, panel data can reveal intra-individual changes over time. In effect, panel data are generally better suited to understand and predict (changes in) travel behavior. However, a substantial proportion was also observed to transition between very different activity/travel patterns over time, indicating that from one year to the next, many people renegotiated their activity/travel patterns.

How to apply advanced traveler information systems (ATIS) to predict future travelling behaviour.

Nowadays, information can impact on traveler behavior and network performance. For example, when steadily growing levels of vehicle ownership and vehicle miles traveled information has been identified as a potential strategy towards man aging travel demand, optimizing transportation networks and better utilizing available capacity. Toward, this goal to predict further tourist behavioral consumption. Many countries, government tourism development institutes has applied advanced traveler information systems (ATIS) which travel behavior models and high-fidelity network performance models made increasingly feasible through the rapid advances in computer power. Crucial components of this problem domain are the modeling of individual tourist drivers' response to travel information and the development accurate guidance of relevance to real would trip makers. So, this advanced traveler information systems (ATIS) can assist the tourist who like to rent travelling car tools to travel in any countries own free traveler information systems service conveniently. Also, this travel information system can be intended to assist travelers to make better travel choices. e.g. this system can improve the decision making of individual traveler rather than improvements of network performance overall. So, we need to understand how tourists make their travel plans. Also, understanding decision process that lead to booking of the trip is equally important, as it allows of a potential behavior.

How does online tourism sale channel can influence traveling consumption of behaviour.

Nowadays, internet is popular, it seems that booking air ticket behavior of using internet is predicted to influence overall tourism air tickets payment method. Tourism industry has grown in the previous several decades. Despite its global impact, questions related to better understanding of tourists and whose habits. Using online travel air ticket booking benefits include booking electronic air tickets can be made from entering any electronic travel agents websites in the short time and electronic travel ticket payers do not need leave home, who can pay visa card to pre booking any electronic travel ticket from online channel conveniently.

How to analyze activity based travel demand ? Nowadays, human are concerning the traffic congestion and air quality deterioration, the supply oriented focus of transportation planning has expanded to include how to manage travel demand within the available transportation supply. Consequently, there has been an increasing interest in travel demand management strategies, such as congestion pricing that attempts to change aggregate travel demand. The prediction aggregate level, long term travel demand to understanding disaggregate level (i.e. individual levels) behavioral responses to short term demand policies, such as ride sharing incentives, congestion pricing and employer based demand management schemes, alternate work schedules, telecommuting limitation of travel agent traditionally work nature shall influence oriented trip based travel modelling passenger travel demand indirectly.

Finally, online travel purchase will be popular to influence the number of travel behavioural consumption nowadays. Any travel package products can be sold from websites to attract travellers to choose to prebook air ticket for any trips conveniently. In the past ten years, the internet has become the predominant carrier of all types of information and transactions. Regarding travel decisions, internet has also become an important sales channels for the travel industry, because it is associated with comparably lower distribution and sales costs, but also because ir adapts to hign supply and demand dynamics in this industry. Consequently, the travel and tourism industry tries to increase the internet sale specific share of sales volumes. So, internet sale channel has changed travel consumption behavioural pattern and characteristics and travel experience. For example, Switzerland has one of the highest population-to-computer ratio in Europe. It is also one of the most highly internet penetrated countries in terms of use of the WWW on a day-to-day basis, with more than 75 percent of the population older than 14 years using the WWW daily (ICT, 2005).

The reason of booking online tourism may include: convenience, fast transaction, finding traveling package choice easily, more airline seats available. So, online booking tourism will influence the traditional tourism agents visiting of sales and air tickets and travelling package numbers to be decreased. Finally, the online booking tourism market shares will be expanded to more than traditional tourism agents visits sale market in the future one day. So, the travel agents who still use the traditional tourism visiting sale channel which ought raise whose features to compare to differ to online tourism sale channel if these traditional touriam agents want to keep competitive ability in tourism industry for long term.

Actively based patterns of urban population of travel behavioural prediction method.

Actively based patterns of urban population. It is a method of motivational framework means in which societal constraints and inherent individual motivations interact to shape activity participation patterns. It can be used to predict one city or urban the numbers of travel demand in the year. It has two elements: First, capability constraints refer to constraints are imposed by biological needs, such as eating and sleeping and/or resources, such as income, availability of cars etc. to undertake the urban or city's family activities in the year. Second, coupling constraints define where, when and the duration of planning activities that are to be pursued with other individuals. So, this method needs to gather information (data) to get the relationship between activities, travel and spending work time and space time to evaluate whether there are how many families who have real needs to spend time to go to travel in the year.

What is trip based versus activity based approaches?

What is trip based versus activity based approaches? The fundamental difference between the trip-based and activity based approaches is that the former approach directly focuses on trips without explicit recognition of the motivation or reason for the trips and travel. The activity based approach , on the other hand, views travel as a demand derived from the need to pursue travel activities. So, it is better understand the individual or family behavior basis for individual or family travelling decision regarding participation in travelling activities in certain places or cities or countries at given times and hence the resulting travel needs. This behavioral basis includes all the factors that influence the why, how, when and where of performed activities and resulting individuals and household, the cultural/social norms of the community and the travel surrounding environment.

Another difference between the two approaches is in the way travel is represented. The trip based approach represents travel as a collection of trips. Each trip is considered as independent of other trips, without considering the inter-relationship in the choice attributes , such as time, destination and mode of different trips. As tours are chains of trips beginning and ending at a same location , say home or work. The tour based representation helps maintain the consistency across and capture the interdependency and consistency of the modeled choice attributed among the trips of the same tour.

In addition to the tour based representation of travel, the activity based approach focuses on sequences or patterns of activity participation and travel behavior, using the whole day or longer periods of time is the unit of analysis. Such as approach can address travel demand management issues through an examination of how people modify their activity participation, for example, will individuals substitute more out-of-home activities for in home activities in the evening of who arrived early form work due-to a work schedule change?

The major difference between trip based and the activity based approaches is in the way, the time dimension of activities and travel is considered. In the trip based approach, time is reduced to being simply a cost making a trip and a day's viewed as a combination, defined peak and off peak time periods. On the other hand, activity based approach views individuals' activity travel patterns are a result of their time use decisions with a continuous time domain. As individuals have 24 hours in a day or multiples of 24 hours for longer periods of time and decide how to use that travel among or allocate that time to activities and travel and with who, subject to their socio-demographic, transportation system and other and scheduling of trips. So, determining the impact of travel demand management policies on time use behavior is an important step to assessing the impact of such policies on individual travel behavior. The final major difference between this two approaches relates to the level of aggregation. In the trip based approach, most aspect of travel, e.g. number of trips etc. are analyzed at an aggregate level.

Consequently, trip based methods accommodate the effect of socio-demographic attributes of households and individuals in a very limited fashion, which limits the activity of the method to evaluate travel impacts of long term socio-demographic characteristics of the individuals who actually make the activity travel choices and the travel service characteristics of the surrounding environment. So, the activity based models are better equipped to forecast the longer term changes in travel demand in response composition and the travel environment of urban areas. Also, using activity based models, the impact of policies can be assessed by predicting individual level behavioral responses instead of employing trip based statistical averages that are aggregated over defined demographic segments.

Why senior age will be main travelling target.

In the past, Germany government had established tourism survey analysis to analyze survey data in order to arrive at reliable conclusions on future trends in travel behavior. To aim to find how demographic change will influence the tourism market and how the industry can adapt to those changes. The travel analysis provided data on tourism consumer behavior, including attitudes, motives and intentions. Since, 1970 year, it is based on a random sample, representative for the population in private households aged 14 years or older. Then, a continuous high scientific standard combined with a national and international users makes the travel analysis a useful tool and reliable source for tourism industry and policy decisions. It aimed to gather statistical data. e.g. on the age structure and on demographic trends, quantitative and qualitative analysis with time series data from the travel analysis. It shows e.g. not only the future volume , quite different from today's seniors, or how who will travel of family holidays will change, e.g. single parents of low, but grandparents of growing significance for tourism.

Demographic change is said to be one of the important drivers for new trends in consumer traveling change behavior in most European countries (e.g. Lind 2001). Because the growing number of senior citizens in the European Union and other industralised countries, such as the USA and Japan, looks to become one of the major marketing challenges for the tourism industry. United Nations statistics predict that the share of people being 60 age or older will grow dramatically in the coming future, and is expected to rise from 10 percent of the world population in 2000 year to more than 20 percent in 2050 year (United Nations Population Division, 2001). From its statistic, some data showed that travel propensity increased throughout life until the age of about 50 years of age and was then kept stable until very late in life 75 age. The most important results is that the travel propensity when getting older is not going down between 65 and 75 age of course, the overall development of this variable is influenced by a lot of other factors which are rsponsible for quite a variation over time. It is now possible to suggest that the general pattern of travel propensity is one of the key indicators for holiday life cycle travel behaviour, includes three stages. The growth stage tends to increase from early aduithood until 45 age old or when reaching some 80%. The next stage is stabilisation from the ages of around 50 age,until 75 age old, starting with a lower increase. Finally, the decrease stage is a slight decrease occurs once people reach the more advanced age of 75 age to 85 age old (Lohmann & Danielsson 2001).

So, it seems Germany government tourism prediction to future travellers' behaviour indicated these findings, such as on how future senior generations will travel, who had used survey data to examine the patterns of travel behaviour of a generation getting older and applied the findings to draw conclusions on the future. Also, it predicted that on the future of family trips, family semgmentation will be the travel behaviour patterns in the future. These findings together with the statistical data on demographic change allowed for a better understanding of the coming tends in family holidays. It's aim developed in consumer behaviour related to demographic change and predicted what will happen future of tourism one had to consider other influences and drivers as well, for example, trends on the supply side. e.g. low cost airlines or in travelling consumption behaviour in general whether how the past may provide a key to predict travel patterns of senior sitizens to the future.

Given the projected growth of the senior citizens market, designing specific marketing strategies to meet the prospective needs of elderly tourists will become increasingly important. It has been an implict assumption that it will be a close relationship between the travel behaviour of today's senior citizens and the those of future ones. The growing number of senior citizens in the world. e.g. China, Hong Kong, Japan, USA etc. countries. Global senior citizen tourism market will be based solely on demographic predictions about the future of the population's age structure. However, many of these seniors won't only live longer but will be fitter and more active until later in life. Many of the will also have plenty in life. Many of them will also have plenty of time and money to spend on travel. So, will these new seniors behave like today's senior citizens? Will they adopt the same travel behaviour as the previous generation or become a new market of oldies for the leisure and tourism indudtry? However, to determine the actual number of senior citizens who will be travelling and to sought to evaluate and specify certain difficult to predict the actual numbers of senior citizen to any country. However, they can be based on the implicit assumption that there is a close relationship between the travel behaviour of past, present and future seniors. But is this a valid assumption? As the reiseanalyse travel analysis survey, which was conducted in Germany every year, offered some interesting data possibiltieis. It was designed to monitor the holiday travel behaviour, opinions and attitudes of Germans and has been carried out since 1970 year, questions in the questionnaire. Data are based on face to face interviews, with a representative sample of more than 7,500 respondent, the interviews being carried out in January each year. All results refer to the average for the defined generated, which ranges generally over ten years. The group of people then at the age of 60 to 69 age is described. This corresponds to the same generation ten years ago, when they had an age of 50 to 59 age. When this methodological approach is not necessarily very sophisticated, it does have the important advantages of being cost effective.

Psychological method to predict travel behavioural consumption.

On the psychological view point, I think individual traveler's character will have those kind of personal characteristics. First, simplicity searchers value above everything ease not transparency in their travel planning and holiday making, and are willing to avoid having to go through extensive research. Second, cultural purists use their travel as an opportunity to immerse themselves in an unfamiliar looking to break themselves entirely from their home lives and engage. Sincerely with a different way of living. Third, social capital seekers understand that to be well travelled is a personal quality, and their choices are shaped by their desire to take maximum of social reward from their travel. They will exploit the potential of digital media to enrich and inform their experiences, and structure their adventures always keeping in mind they are being watched by online audiences. Finally, reward hunters seek a return on the investment who make in their busy , high-achieving lives. Linked in part to the growing trend of wellness, including both physical and mental self improvement who seek truly extraordinary and often indulgent or luxurious' must have experiences.

Why needs to know the personal character of individual traveler's characteristics. Because if travel agents could feel which kinds of individual traveler's character, then who can predict which kind of travel package to design to them more easily. For example, how to determine future travel behaviour from past travel experience and perceptions of risk and safety? We need to concern that the influences of past international travel experience, types of risk associated with international travel and the overall degree of safety feeling during international travel on individual's travelling experiences likelihood of travelling to various geographic regions on their next international vacation trip or avoidance of those regions, due to perceived risk. Because individual traveler's experience of safety risk degree to the countries, it will influence who chooses to go to the countries/country to travel again.

Why travellers avoid certain destinations are as relevant decision making as why who choose to go to the country(countries) to travel. Perceptions of risk and safety and travel experiences are likely to influence travel decisions; efforts to predict future travel behaviour can benefit to individual tourist's decision making. As Weber & Bottorn (1989) defined risky decision is as "choices among alternatives that can be described by prodability distributions over possible outcomes" (p.114). Some psychologists judge subjective perceptions of physical reality, i.e. image of a particular tourist destination, whereas value judgement refers to the way individual rank destinations according to whose attributes. i.e. attractiveness, safety, risk etc. factors to form on overall image. So, if the individual traveler had unhappy and worried and unsafe experiences to go to where the place(country) to travel during whose vacation time before. Then, this negative travel experience will influence who is afraid to go to the place (country) to travel again. Risk of place, country, destination or region means the danger is relatively high to the place, ie. increasing in airplane accidents, crime or terrorist activity targeting citizens of potential traveler's nationality or the probability of occurrence is great , ie. recent occurrences involving travel regions/destinations under consideration or effective actions to control consequences exist. i.e. selecting safe regions and destinations, taking extra precautions when traveling to risky destinations. These risk factors will influence the individual traveler who chooses to cancel travel plan to go to the country again.

Another interesting research, how to predict behavioural intention of choosing a travel destination, which has focus of toursm research for years, but the complex decision making process leading to the choice of a travel destination has not been well researched. The planned behaviour model using its core constructs, attitude, subjective norm and perceived behavioural control, with the addition of the past behavioural variable on behavioural intention of choosing a travel destination.

Understanding why people travel and what factors influence their behavioural intention of choosing a travel destination is beneficial to tourism planning and marketing. Understanding travel motivation is the push and pull model. The idea of the push and pull model is the decomposition of an individual's choice of a travel destination into two forces. The first force is the push factor that pushes an indvidual away home and attempts to develop a general desire to go somewhere else, without specifying where that may be. The second force is the pull factor, that pulls on individual toward a destination, due to a region specific travel location or perceived attractiveness of a destination. The respective push and pull factors illustrate that people travel because who are pushed by their internal motives and pulled by external forces of a destination. Nevertheless, how push and pull factors guide people's attitude and how these attributes lead to behavioural intentions of choosing a travel destination have rarely been investigated. The decision making process leading to the choice of a travel destination is a very complex process. The planned behaviour model is as a research framework to predict the behavioural intention of choosing a travel destination. The model based on the three constructs of attitude, subjective norm, and perceived behavioural control (Fishbein & Ajzen, 1975).

In conclusion, the factors can influence travelers who decide to choose to travel the country, which include personal safety was perceived to the highest motivation factors among the important factors which include, scenic beauty, cultural interests, friendliness of local people, price of trip, services in hotels and restaurants, quality and variety of food and shopping facilities and services. The factors include both push and pull. Push factors include knowledge, prestige, and enhancement of human relationship etc., whereas, the most significant pull factors include high technologic image, expenditure and accessibility etc. For example, Japanese travelers visiting Hong Kong. Push factors are such as exploration dream fulfillment and pull factors are such as benefits sought, attractions and good climate city. It will be the factor of future travel patterns and motivations of sub-cultural and ethic groups for Japanese choice to go to Hong Kong travelling.

Bibliography

Backman, K., Backman, S., Uysal, M. And Sunshine, K. (1995). Event Tourism : An Examination Of Motivations And Activities. Festival Management And Event Tourism, 3(1), 15-24.

Fishbein, M., & Ajzen, Z. (1975). Belief, Attitude, Intention And Behaviour: An Introduction To Theory And Research, Boston: Addison Wesley.

Hsu, C.H.C., Cai , L.A., Li, M(2010). Expectation, Motivation And Attitude: A Tourist Behavioral Model. Journal Of Travel Research, 49(3), 282-296. http://dx.doi, org/10.1177/004728750 9349266.

ICT Information And Communication Technology Switzerland, 2005. ICT Fakten (ICT facts). Available from http://www.ictswitzerland.ch/de/ict%2fakten/factsfigures.asp(retrieved Dec.12, 2005) in German.

Lind, (2001): Befolkningen, Familjen, Livscykeln- Och Ekonomisk Tillvaxt. Institutet For Tillvaxtpo-litiska studier/ Vinnova/Nutek.

Lohmann, Martin (2001): The 31 st. Reiseanalyse-RA 2001. Tourism: vol. 49, no.1/2001;pp.65-67, Zagreb.

United Nations Population Division (2001). World Population Prospects: The 2000 year Revision, New York.

Weber E.U., & W, P.Bottom (1989). "Axiomatic Measures Of Perceived Risk: Some Tests And extensions." journal of behavioral decision making, 2 (2): 113-31.

CHAPTER NINE

Pollution environment influences travellers self-driving journey choice

Does every tourist individual driving behavior influence whose travel behavioral choice? However, individual mobility decisions are possible difficulties for measures aiming at tourist individual travelling behavioral changes and links them to the transport need aspect when the tourist arrives the destination to travel. For example, whether the travelling destination has bus public transportation tool supplies or ferry transportation tool supplies or taxi transportation tool supplied to train or tram etc. different public transportation tools to influence the tourist individual travelling destination choice.

When every country decides to develop travel industry. It needs to understand how to arrange what kind of public transportation tools to be supplied to satisfy any countries‘ tourists mobility needs in whose journeys in order to achieve tourism planning for public transportation system to attract different countries' tourists to choose to arrive itself different destinations to travel more easily. So, the country's transportation services supplies will have permanently impacted to every tourist individual travel behavior towards more mobility when he/she arrives to the country to travel.

Can transportation system factor influence tourist individual travelling destination decision? it depends on the tourist individual attitude or transport needs of decisions. For example, if the city , e.g. New York has many tourists, who are high income, young gender, high education level tourists. Then, they will choose more expensive and comfortable train more than cheap and not comfortable bus transportation tool. So, I assume that the year has many high income, high education , high social class occupation tourists arrive US , New York city . Then, they will choose train more than bus transportation tool to go to anywhere to travel in New York city. So, it is not represent that the city has many cheaper public transportation tool, such as many buses number to be supplied , the bus public transportation tool can bring more income to attract overseas tourists to come to New York travel. It depends on whether the tourist individual characteristics, e.g. high or low income, more or less comfortable transportation tool supplies needs or high or low educational level, alone tourist or family tourist or friend relationship tourist. Any one of these tourist individual psychological factors will influence the tourist to choose either cheap and less comfortable public tool system or expensive and more comfortable public tool system to be supplied to the city to travel. So, the city's comfortable or not comfortable public transportation tool supplies which will influence the overseas tourists how to choose the city to travel.

However, on the tourist's habitual behavior of catching which kind of transportation tools, this factor will bring to influence how to choose the kind of transportation tool(s) whether the city can provide choice to let the overseas tourist to make where travelling decision when he/she arrives to the country. However, his/her transportation tool catching habit will be possible to influence whose travel times for public transport use, instead of which kind of transport tool(s) he/she will choose to catch when he/she arrives the country to travel.

In conclusion, the tourist's age, income, occupation, education level will influence how the tourist's transportation choice in himself/herself country, then it also bring this question: will influence the tourist individual destination choice if the country can provide or can not provide the kind of public transportation tool(s) to let the tourist to choose to catch in his/her journey in the country's city. Hence, it explains that why every country's pubic transportation tool supplies will influence the tourist to choose where to travel in the country.

23.1 What are usually travel behaviors
and attitudes to disabled tourists

What factors can affect the travel behaviors of people with disabilities by ages and lifestyle variable factors? When one person is disable, he/she will have different behaviors to satisfy whose needs in whose whole travelling journey. In special , the older age and younger age disable tourists who will have different travelling needs. In fact, the disabled tourists won't easy to go anywhere travelling destinations in whose whole travelling journey. So, it seems that the travelling entertainment needs won't be very much to these younger or older disabled tourists. Moreover, people with disabilities travel will be compare with people without disabilities. So, it is one key to explain why the travelling entertainment purposes or needs to disable people which are lesser than the people without disabilities.

In negative or problematic experience of travel to disabled tourists aspect, I believe that it is one travelling experiences problem is considered to need to be solved to any younger or older age disabled tourists, because they are handicapped people, they will feel walk in difficulty, even they need wheel chairs to help them to walk. So, the visible moving disabled problem will influence how they feel unsafe on public transport in any strange travelling countries considerable. In special, the older aged 50 and over disabled people need to catch any public transport when they need to sit on wheel chairs to go to anywhere destinations in any strange travelling countries. They will feel un convenient and unsafe when they need to sit on wheel chairs to go to anywhere destinations. These travelling places are their first time arriving places. Hence, transportation tools will be consideration problem to any disabled tourists. It seems that renting car travelling providers will be one popular or preferable choice to any younger or older age disabled tourists. Because disabled tourists won't need to catch public transport tools, such as buses, trains, trams, taxis in unsafe, un convenient natural travelling environment. They can drive themselves renting cars to go to anywhere travelling destinations easily or conveniently. Thus, I believe that the renting travelling service which is very attractive to any young or old age disabled tourist nowadays.

In general, instead of renting cars to drive behavioral change to disabled tourists usually ,renting cars behaviors which will replace to choose to catch any public transportation tools behavior to disable tourists. What kinds of other behavioral changes will impact to disabled tourists? Other aspect consideration is disabled tourist individual health problem . For example, if the disabled tourist is driving himself/herself renting cars to go to anywhere destinations in long term in the travelling country. The long distance of driving miles travelling and driving long hours spend travelling behaviors will influence the disable tourist individual nervous health to be more poor, because he/she needs to spend more time and nervous to drive whose renting car to go to anywhere in whole travelling journey. So, it is very dangerous and unsafe to the disabled tourist when he/she needs to concentrate on nervous to drive himself/ herself renting car to go to anywhere destinations to travel in whose travelling journey or trip.

In consideration of the older age disabled tourist groups will be more unsafe and dangerous when he/she needs to spend much time to drive whose renting car to arrive any travelling destinations. So, it is based on this long time unsafe driving factor, the older age disabled tourist groups will choose to spend lesser time to drive to go to anywhere destinations to travel alone or with their friends and/or families in general. Similar patterns are evident in the numbers of miles travelled and the time spent to driving renting car behavior to any older age disabled tourist groups will be lesser than the younger age disabled tourist groups . Due to the long time unsafe renting car self-driving feeling to the older age disabled tourists. It will impact to influence the older age disabled tourists to choose to catch any public transport or walking to replace renting car self-driving behaviors in their trips, when older age handicapped tourists loss hearing, sight, memory, recognizing physical danger, personal care difficulties disabled characteristics.

Thus, the long time renting car driving behavior which will influence the old age disabled tourists to choose to catch public transport tools to replace to rent car to drive in whose trip persuasively. So, the renting car providers will have lesser old age disable tourist number to compare to young age disabled tourist number in common. Also, the old age disable tourists will prefer to choose the travel destinations where have many public transport tools to let them to catch for their travelling journeys.

- 21.2 How social internet networking
impacts driving traveler behavior

Can web site online internet networking influence traveller individual behavior changes? If web site can influence every online traveller user individual behavior change, how it influence every online user individual behavior change in order to impact his/her travelling service or arrangement change choice. For example, when the traveller walks in one travel agent's shop to find the most suitable travelling package for whose trip.

At the moment, he/she plans to find the travel agent to help him/her to arrange any travelling package. But when he/she goes back his/her home, he/she turns on his/her computer to link online travel agent website. Then, he/ she discovers this online travel agent can provide more attractive travelling package similar service and he/she will compare the walk in travel agent's travelling package to this online travel agent travelling package. Although, the walk-in travelling agent can provide lesser service fee to compare this online travel agent. But , he/she feels this online travel agent can provide more attractive and enjoyable travelling entertainment and trip arrangement service to satisfy his/her travelling need. So, he/she decides to choose this online travelling agent's travelling package and it seems that the online travel agent web site can influence his/her original travelling agent target choice.

Nowadays, the most famous online development reshaping traditional marketing methods of tourism business will be possible to replace the traditional walk-in travel agent business. Because travelling consumers like to turn on computer to link to different travelling agents' websites to choose which travelling package is the cheapest or it can provid the most attractive or enjoyable entertainment arrangement in the trip. So, online travel agents will influence travelling consumers to reduce to spend time to walk in to visit any travel agent shops. The traveller prefers to spend much time to find which travelling agents' websites to find the most right online travelling agent to help him/her to arrange the trip service to replace to find the most right walk-in travelling agent at home conveniently. So, travelling agent website development can impact every traveller individual planning behavior to be changed influentially because when he/she plans to walk in to visit the identified travel agent shop, but when he/she has one desk top computer to be installed at home. Then, he/she will have another choice to buy the travelling package service. So, he/she will change his/her walk in to visit the travel agent planning behavior to change to clicking on any travel agent's website behavior.

Moreover, travelling website characteristics or attractive point is easy communication. When the traveller feels any worry or trouble, he/her need to enquire the online travelling agent immediately. He/she can send email to enquire the travelling agent to arrange travelling package similar service to walk in travel agent and he/she will compare the walk in travel agent's travelling package to this online travel agent travelling package. Although, the walk-in travelling agent can provide lesser service fee to compare this online travel agent. But, he/she feels that this online travel agent can provide more attractive and enjoyable travelling entertainment and trips service to satisfy his/her travelling need. So, he/she decides to choose this online travelling agent's travelling package and it seems that the online travel agent website can influence his/her original travelling agent target choice.

Nowadays, the most famous online development reshaping traditional marketing methods of tourism business will be possible to replace the traditional walk-in travel agent business. Because travelling walk-in consumer like to turn on computer to link to different travelling agents' websites to choose which travelling package is the cheapest or it can provide the most attractive or enjoyable entertainment arrangement .

Thus, online travelling information search tool can attract travellers to choose to find any travel agents' websites from internet to replace walk-in travel agents' shops influentially. Also, it seems online travelling service will be popular to replace walk-in travelling service in possible.

CHAPTER TEN

Informal economic solves pollution influences tourism industry development challenge

Why does the country's poor economic environment and poverty influence tourism industry development? It is one issue that governments, tourism organizations need to consider: Can tourism work as a tool to overcome poverty? Some economists believe that it has the relationship between poverty and tourism. Can travelling strategy solve poverty to the country? If the county had many poor people, e.g. unemployed people number is increasing, they lose jobs to do in long time in society, even some employed people their incomes are less. In this social poverty situation, whether country's tourism strategy can assist its economic development in success.

In fact, any country's poverty will influence itself citizen's travelling consumption desires, because travelling is not essential need, it is only entertainment (non-essential) need to any one. In the past, it is only rich people's entertainment because in general, air ticket prices are expensive and any tourism packages arrangement services are also expensive. So, the past tourism attraction is vey low. It only attracts to the rich people to seek this kind of relax activity, such as (catching air plane to fly to other countries to travel). But, nowadays, some many poverty people living countries, such as India, China, Korea , Africa. Although their countries encourage tourism industry continue develop, but due to many people are poverty reason, they can not real encourage tourism industry development easily.

So, the improving poverty strategies to provide economic and other benefits is needed to these poverty countries. I shall indicate the strategy focus on these several aspects: Economic benefits, e.g. expansion of employment and wages through job creation and training for the poor. Expand of business opportunities for the poor through entrepreneurial opportunities, e.g. donations, lease fees assistance, non-cash livelihood benefits, include capacity building, training and empowerment, mitigation of environmental impacts of tourism on the poor. Equitable management of resources between tourists and local people. Improved access to services, policy, process and participation includes supportive policy frame works at the national and local level that enable participation by the poor. Increased participation by the poor in decision-making.

Encouraging international tourism development is also one good method to raise travellers number in poverty countries, e.g. designing the increasing importance of developing country destinations as a market for international tourists, e.g. China can promote many different countryside destinations, they have mountains and rivers more than cities. So, international tourists can ride bicycles or walk on mountains when they travel to any countryside destinations in China.

However, developing countries need to know that poverty is not natural. It is man-made and it can be overcome by the actions of human beings. So, I believe that any countries ought have themselves suitable methods to solve poverty, if they hope tourism industry can develop in success. Any countries' poverty trend to mention income only infrequently relative to assets, such as social network, health, labor power, land and other resources that make self-provisioning possible. Hence, poverty , it is one kind personal feeling more than social feeling. For example, US is one developed country, when one US citizen had no job , he can earn social assistance from US government. Hence, he does not feel very poverty, because he can still buy essential food and pays rent when US government supports him social welfare assistance , when he loses job. Hence, in general, US poverty people still accept to spend extra money to travel when they can earn social welfare to travel ,when they can earn social welfare to assist their daily lives.

Hence, US poverty won't influence tourism industry development very much. Otherwise, such as India, China their social welfare is less to people's perceptions of poverty. The poor social welfare will influence their travelling desires to be reduced. Because they feel absence of basic infrastructure, e.g. health clinics, transport lack of assets (physical, human, social, environment), lack of basic resources, e.g. food, housing, land, lack of voice, power and independence. Thus, they will feel poverty more than rich countries' poverty people. Their tourism entertainment activities or travelling needs will be influenced to reduced also. Thus, it explains that why any developing countries' tourism industry development is slow than developed countries as well as their travelling desires or needs are lower than developed countries in general. For poor countries and small island states, tourism is the leading export, often the only growth sector of their economies and a catalyst for many related sector.

What is pro-poor tourism (PPT) strategy? It is about changing the distribution of benefits from tourism in favour of poor people. It is not a specific product. It is not the same as ecotourism or community-based tourism, nor is it limited to these niches. Any kind of tourism can be made pro-poor tourism. PPT can be applied at different levels, at the enterprise, destination or country level (pro-poor tourism partnership 2005:1).

There are a number of non -economic benefits of PPT , such as the development of new skills, better access to education, and healthcare and infrastructural improvements of access to potable water and improved roads or transport. They also explain how intangible benefits of tourism can make a significant difference to the lives of the poor, including greater opportunities for communication with the outside world and improved access to information, better knowledge of market opportunities, strengthening of community institutions, and enhanced pride in one's culture and the skills and knowledge which exist within the community (Ashley and Roe 2002). So, the poverty countries , such as Africa, China, India ought choose to apply pro-poor tourism strategy to encourage poverty people accept to spend extra expenditure for any kinds of cheap travelling entertainment activities, e.g. one to two days domestic short journey. They ought not only consider the rich people's expensive travelling entertainment needs, e.g. expensive overseas travelling destination package (long time , as one month to three months or more US different cities visiting journey).

A review of PPT practices in 2006 revealed seven key strategic that could directly enhance the welling being of the poor: Employment of the poor in tourism enterprises, supply of products and services to tourism enterprise by the poor or by enterprises employing the poor, direct sales of products and services to visitors by the poor (informal economy), establishment and running of tourism enterprises by the poor, e.g. micro, small and medium -sized enterprises or community -based enterprises, tax or levy on tourism income or profits with proceeds benefiting the poor, voluntary giving/ support by tourism enterprises and tourists, investment in infrastructure stimulated by tourism also benefiting the poor in the locality (UNWTO 2006).

Hence, it seems that PPT (Pro-Poor tourism) strategy focus on attracting many poverty travellers more than rich travelers in the poor countries. It is one kind of nowadays poverty countries' economic improvement strategy. It aims to persuade many poverty people to accept to spend less extra money to travel in themselves countries. It focuses on motivating adocates of tourism as a tool for poverty alleviation as well as building good relationship between the poverty countries' economic and political and social issues.

The PPT establishment and development of tourism in most Third World countries is usually externally oriented and controlled , and mainly responds to external tourism market demands. In consequence, the nature of international tourism is as a luxury and pleasure seeking industry usually entails rich tourists from the (mainly from developed countries) visiting and coming to enjoy tourist attractions (mainly the poor and resource scarce countries). These forms of tourism development builds the economic structure of dependency on enternal tourism market demand, and also lead to which local people can not relate and respond, both socially and economically.

Reference

Ashley, C & Roe, D. 2002. Making tourism work for the poor strategies and challenges in southern Africa, development Southern Africa 19(1): pp. 61-82.

Pro-poor tourism partnership, 2005; Pro-poor tourism: Annual register , 2005, pro-poor tourism partnership, London.

United Nations world Tourism Organization , 2006. World tourism barometer: Interim update April, 2010. UNWTO, madrid.

Living Economy influences our living experiences change

What does living economy mean ? How living economy influences consumer shopping behaviours and worker productive behaviours change. I shall explain as below:

Firstly, we need to know what economy and science difference is. The reason for the gaps is that economics is very far from an exact science. The main actors are people or consumers, we need to work and spend. In my nowadays living, our consumption model has the impacts of the internet, and whether it bring more growth and better living standards for every. In past, we must need go to shops to buy any things. But, nowadays, we can apply internet to enter any business website to choose our preferable product to pay visa to buy among different kinds products' photos. So, e-commerce or e-shopping had change many consumers' traditional consumption model. It can bring exciting shopping experience and convenience to general consumers. Instead of internet influences consumer shopping method hand, internet also influence some offices apply internet to help employees to work at homes. So, Some office staffs do not need often go to offices to work, they can apply internet to do their office tasks at homes. It is one good example internet can bring living economic shopping convenience and working convenience to influence working people and consumers' living consumption and working traditional habit changing. But, internet also cause some people lose jobs, because some companies may dismiss some positions to be replaced by internet or artificial intelligent technology tools. In economic beneficial view, they aims to reduce salary expenditure and raises productivities and efficiencies. So, (AI) and internet technological invention can raise unemployment ratio in our societies, but it also raise efficiencies and productivities for businessmen in possible. These high technological invention can also bring economic growth because a desire for more profits would raise greater productivity, and therefore greater growth. This was achieved via the division of labour. For example, when one vehicle factory applies artificial intelligent robotic tools to assist workers to manufacture vehicles. The (AI) concentrates on manufacturing some vehicles engines as well as the workers need to divide the suitable engine parts to install to finish to manufacture any one vehicle in the factory. So, (AI) can assist workers to achieve division of labour aim. IN long term, if some countries' vehicle companies, even global vehicle companies can select to apply (AI) tools to assist workers to manufacture any one vehicle in the same time. It will raise whole vehicle industry vehicle productive efficiency and manufacture any one vehicle in the most short time. Indirectly, it will bring economic growth effect to these countries in possible, because vehicle suppliers can have enough different kinds of vehicles number to sell to different countries consumers in any time in global easily. Then, vehicle GDP income will increase and it can bring economic growth rapidly. But, (AI) robotic invention can also bring disadvantages to workers, because since the essence of capitalism is to make money, those workers will be increasingly exploited as time goes on. Faced with growing competition, employers may make staff work longer or harder as they may cut their wages and hire cheaper workers like women and children. Either way, profits will increase and so will worker dissatisfaction.

High technological development, it can bring a new change or unemployment, because wages and unemployment will be influenced by new technological development when it is applied to any organizational team work aspect. Classical economists believed unemployment arose because real wages were too high. In other words, workers were asking for too much money, relative to the rate of inflation and output in the economy. To reduce the number out or work, therefore, it was just a case of lowering salary demands. But, nowadays, it is very difficult to reduce wages , because if your boss tries to cut your salary by 10 per cent, you would probably either seek union support or try to find another job. Even if you are one talent worker. You had learnt skills how to apply (AI) artificial intelligent robotics to co-operate to work to help some tasks to change simple from complex working processes. Then, you will not afraid your employer dismiss you because you own this kind of new robotic technological skills to choose to do the tasks when the employers accept to apply robotics to assist workers to finish any jobs in team. So, (AI) would be effective in stimulating job growth and would have at best a marginal , temporary impact to reduce unemployment ratio in society when many workers own controlling robotic knowledge and many factories began to accept to apply robotic technology to assist workers to co-operate to work together to achieve raising efficiencies and productive aim. So, all of future robotic work participation is changed and online shopping behavioural model is changed , due to we believe they can bring positive or better benefits to satisfy our needs, such as businessmen and consumers roles in our societal daily living.

- Why does technology cause inflation?

To understand and predict interest rate changes, when it comes to making decisions about mortgages, savings accounts and share investment, etc. you need to know where inflation comes from. I suppose that any one needs to earn a living and therefore made as much money as we could out of a transaction. If anything, that drive for profits has intensified since then. New technology, cheaper transport and the rise of the multinational mean forms across the global compete for every one's business now. If the opportunity to make more money by increasing prices is one main factor to businessmen.

How does that opportunity arise? Economists divide the cause of inflation into three categories: too much demand, rising costs and too much money. These rarely appear in their purest form, but provide a useful starting point to understanding why prices rise. Psychological factors such as expectations also play a part. I shall indicate the three factors cause inflation as below:

Demand –pull inflation is the most appealing theory, As the name suggests, this arises when there is too much demand in an economy and not enough goods. For example, when the flight flying to US from UK, it has only 10 seats to supply to passengers. Hence, this final ten seats number will cause airlines air ticket price rises , e.g. 10% or more or less. It depends on how many UK passengers expect to catch this flight time air plane to fly to US. So, it is one short time air ticket price rising factor.

Costs too high, there are often forces at work, too. Instead of demand pulling prices higher, costs of raw material may rise. Due to manufacturers raise their cost, then they will raise sale price in order to avoid profit loss. High wages and more expensive raw materials are just two ways cost-push inflation may take hold. Prices could also rise simply because companies want to increase their profits. This is obviously a risky strategy but one that could pay off in the right circumstances.

However, how inflation may being three effects, either consumer number reduces or consumer number keeps no change or consumer number increases. IN economic-speak, demand for the product is inelastic, then consumer number may no change or demand for the product is elastic, then consumer number may reduce or consumers feel worry about the product price will continue rise highly, then many consumers will make decision to buy the product immediately to avoid pay higher price when the product's price continue increase in possible. So, in this situation, the product's raising price may influence many consumers choose to buy this kind of product immediate. SO, it explains why sometimes the product's higher price can raise consumers' shopping desires to the kind of product because they are afraid the product's price will rise seriously later as soon future.

Why the World Wide Web will help to keep inflation at bay for a number of reasons as below:

Anyone who underestimates the potential of the Internet. The creation of a global marketplace via the World Wide could have terrific consequences for everything from growth to jobs to inflation. Exactly how large those consequences will be is open to debate. We are facing website invention causes inflation and it brings prices increase negative effect. I shall indicate reasons as below:

The internet is an online shop window that allows companies to display their goods at minimum expense. There are no high street rents or shop assistants' wages to pay, leaving less room for cost –push inflation, e.g. Amazon.com, it sells books from internet, has around 13 million titles stored in warehouse in the UA and Britain, whereas the biggest bookshops in New York can afford to rent enough space to carry only around 180,000 books.

Greater price range choice, comparing prices on the internet is easy, which puts extra pressure on retailers to offer you a good deal. If you want to buy a new television, for example, instead of your way through the Saturday crowds and visiting perhaps three or four different shops. You will find the cheapest deal available in the time, it would have taken you to get a parking space.

Adding pressure on conventional retailers. High street shops are unlikely easily competition from the internet means they will either have to match prices or offer services the web can't, such as personal advice from shop assistants.

Low start-up costs, Setting up a website is relatively easy. If a site is proving popular with shoppers, it won't be long before someone else tries to steal some market share by doing it bigger and better. The invisible hand of the price mechanism means large profits will attract more firms, which will undercut existing companies in this e-commerce marketing.

Hence, e-commerce market seems to perfect competition. In this ideal e-commerce world, a large number of online companies produce the same or similar things and are able to move their product photos freely in and out from their website. Online consumers have perfect knowledge about all the online display products on offer to buy from their websites (one of those unrealistic assumptions that perfect competition and consumption economic models). Hence, online consumers will feel to seek out the cheapest products from their websites easily, subjecting inflation prices to the full force of Smith's invisible hand.

Hence, it explains why e-commerce market may raise prices to sell more easily to compare general traditional shop visiting market because online consumers will feel there are many products choice when they indicate their prices and photos data to let online consumers to choose from their websites. They won't have much time to research whether their prices are higher than general their competitors' shops sale prices when they turn on computer and click to the enter their websites to prepare to select any online products, when they feel the product is very attractive and price is reasonable , they will make purchase decision and pay their visa to buy the product from the online merchant's website immediately. Even, they doubt that the product's price may be higher to compare general shop's displayed price. However, they may research whether the online product price is higher to compare general shop's product price. But, they must need to spend time to leave their homes by any transport or walking. In general, they dislike to turn off their computer and forgive to pay visa to buy the product when they feel the online product is very attractive and they do not want the product can not buy from the website if either all online stocks are sold out or the product won't be displayed from internet to let any online buyers to buy. So, it explains why online can create inflation chance to any e-commerce businessmen, due to consumers won't like to spend time to leave homes to research whether any online products prices are higher than shops products prices in our nowadays societies.

- Why nowadays firms need to adapt the high technological environment change

In a high technological development environment, it must continually adapt and restructure to meet the challenges of a changing economic environment, if it is to prosper. For example, a firm must respond to its environment in the form of its customers' needs, threats from its competitors, government regulations etc. or else. Such a response will entail reordering and differentiation i.e. modification of its subsystems and their goals, and generation of new subsystems as appropriate.

Time must be an explicit variable in our nowadays living economic systems, because by definition it is not possible to approach a goal or have feedback expect in time. Understanding the mechanism of change requires us to follow each movement throughout time. For internet invention example, internet invention can influence some businessmen model to be changed. When some businessmen feel that they apply websites to advertise their product and/ore sell their products. This website channel can help them to increase consumers number and helping them to achieve the easy sale aim. It is possible that it will have another one kind of new technological invention, it can bring more sale advantage to compare website channel. So, nowadays, businessmen need to spend time to attempt to search whether what undiscovered new technological channels can help them to attract many potential consumers' considerations. Otherwise, their competitive efforts will be reduced and their businesses can not grow up , even close down in possible.

- Why does increasing skills of manufacturing need to future businessmen?

The increasing skills of manufacturing and the of use of more intensive energy resources, such as coal and oil, gave man ever more power to modify the scope of the earth' surface and even to a limited event some of the resources hidden just below They enables to develop new , more desirable objects of consumption and to turn energy into new, more convenient form to be consumed, for example, as electric light and automotive power. The scale and scope of production and consumption grew to proportions which were unimaginable even a few decades before.

In the future, this new living economic processes as the development was the development of mechanisms for suppliers to make contact with buyers of the products. Specialised factories greatly increased the number of commonly available products, such as artificial intelligent products needs , e.g. non manual driving automobile, manufacturing robotic etc. Any one of future (AI) products needs will be increased when human or consumers can accept to use them. It will influence (AI) factories creation. Arrangements to dispose of them led to more trade and more sophisticated (AI) products sale markets , as places for (AI) products buyers and sellers to meet, and the increasing use of a medium of exchange, such as gold or money. The growing scope which these arrangements for supply and distribution permitted, at the same time enables the scale of operations to be increased in even greater proportion to future potential any (AI) products market. Thus, we have identified the earth resources base, the energy need to transform it into new technological products and the knowledge base which catalyses as well as it explains why businessmen needs to consider increasing skills of manufacturing need , if when global consumers are popular to accept to use any artificial intelligent invention of products . Then any kinds of (AI) products' needs will increase and (AI) factories and (AI) manufacturing skills of needs are also increased. So, it is right time, any manufacturers need to consider how to develop future (AI) market, when global consumers accept to use any (AI) products, they need to learn how to improve their manufacturing skills to apply (AI) manufacturing method in order to manufacture any kinds of (AI) products more easily and efficiently as well as supply any kinds of (AI) products number to satisfy future (AI) consumers' useful needs.

Because our time is not limited, human's living need will raise. So, technological innovation will increases, it focuses on one factor in an interacting network, such as non-manual driving automobiles replace manual driving automobiles product invention, non-manual driving automobiles innovation does not only replace the existing manual driving automobiles, but by destroying the interaction, it may eventually destroy the other conversion processes to, a sort of deindustrialisation, such as traditional engine manufacturing factories may be needed to change artificial intelligent factories. A particular case is the attack on one link in an traditional engine manufacturing factory, " optimising " one part may endanger the whole future factory manufacturing industry.

Thus , if future (AI) products are popular to use, it will influence consumers and manufacturers behavioural change because manufacturers need to learn how to apply artificial intelligent manufacturing skills to manufacture any new kinds of (AI) products as well as consumers won't hope to drive any automobile, pilots won't hope to drive any automobile , or any transportation tools won't need any drivers to drive, their tasks are only control the robotic tools to how to drive their transportation tools on roads or on oceans easily. Consumers can apply (AI) to search any information to prepare to buy any things in order to gather the most accurate data to buy the most reasonable price of products as well as manufacturers can apply robotics to replace workers to do any hard tasks in warehouses. So, technological innovation will bring unpredictable change to influence future our living , such as consumers or manufacturers, sellers roles in our future societies as well as our products' useful behaviours and consumption behaviours and manufacturing behaviours will also be influenced to change absolutely. On conclusion, product innovation will influence our future living change on consumption and manufacturing and useful aspects absolutely. So, it is right time any businessmen need to consider this issue because it will influence future consumers useful and consumption behavioural changes.

I shall indicate that whether living economy will change our traditional social model to change as below:

? The Division and specialization of labor manufacturing method change

As early as 1776, when Adam Smith published his trial-breaking treatise in economics, The Wealth Of Nations, economists recognized the importance of the division of labor. BY the division of labor, Smith meant (1) the specialization of labor in a particular production process today, that might be the person in a service station who specializes in changing oil and (2) the specialization of firms in a few activities, such as the automobiles service station. Hence Division of labor implies specialization of economic activity.

But, nowadays, in living economic view, division and specialization of labor has been changed to influence manufacturing method in some nowadays some industries. For publishing industry example, in producing a textbook process, we feel that it involves no extensive division of labor, both types of specialization are important. The production of one book used the services of tens of thousands of specialized people and specialized business firms. The many economists who have researched the topics; the editors, publishers, and printers; the loggers and manufacturing employees who produces the paper; the people who invented and produced the computer hardware and software technological tools in any manufacturing books process. The enormous availability of books today would have been unimaginable to any age readers to read by electronic books reading method. So, nowadays publishing industry will need to apply internet and any computers to assist labor to print or manufacture paper books or electronic books. Publishers manufactured books by hand, copying and beautiful illustrating manuscripts. Dramatically increased division of labor has made books inexpensive today compared with what they cost in the past.

So, nowadays, division of labor concept allows workers become more skilled through higher education, vocational training and no-the-job training. Moreover, specialization reduces the time wasted by subsistence farmers, who did several jobs in a short time. Time management experts currently make a similar point, they recommend that workers complete one task, for example, responding to their e-mail, before they switch to another task. By reserving large blocks of time for each task, people avoid losing time because avoiding to feel mental pressure to do repeat different responding e-mail tasks, locating new materials to prepare to answer any new email enquiries. For Amazon publish example, division of labor concept can be used to the responding email enquires staffs, they need to respond to every author to answer his/her any enquires about publishing issue or loyalty income issue. So, specialization can help them to reduce the time wasted by responding to any one author's enquire. For example, one responding e-mail staff can concentrate on helping authors to check their report to calculate their every month unpaid royalty income or /and tax calculation issue, another responding email staff can concentrate on helping authors to answer any royalty legal issue, another responding email staff can concentrate on helping to answer how to apply Amazon electronic photos and publishing tools to manufacture one electronic or paper book method. So, Amazon publishing responding email staffs need to be specialized to different divisions to indicate whether they ought concentrate mental and time to find any data to help their authors to answer their every different publishing task enquiries immediately and efficiently and avoiding to answer wrong answers or errors easily. Hence, division and specialization of labor concept can be apply to general non-manufacturing industry only, such as oil, car, ship manufacturing. It can be applied to any clerical tasks in service industry, e.g. bank, publishing. So, our nowadays different kinds of industries need to seek whether their which divisions task model needs to be changed in order to specialize labors to achieve more efficient and innovative tasks to every department in any organizations. Because any organizations seem to be living organizations, they must need staffs work in team when their organizations grow up rapidly. Then, specialization and division of labor function will help them to achieve more efficiency and productive and time management and avoiding errors occurrence chance as well as it can let staffs feel more mental concentrate on doing any tasks more easily in their organization. So, one specialization and division of labor organization ought feel to implement easy operating and achieving economic benefit both aims more easily than one non-specialization and division of labor organization nowadays.

? Living economy environment encourages new form of barriers entering method that prevent new firms from entering their market.

Why does living economic environment encourage trading war occurs between countries? Such as China and US trading war, it is one good example, because they do not want their imports and exports are caused between them as well as they hope to earn the more benefits, so earning the more economic benefit issue can influence China and US need to spend long time to negotiate to discuss whether they ought rise how much level import tariff tax or limit much number of any food or product quote , which is the most suitable satisfactory level to let them to feel.

In living economic view, many markets have barriers that prevent new firms from entering, no matter how profitable making may be. Sometimes there are physical or natural barriers. Economists may recommend how long a patent should last or what kinds of innovations should be patentable, but most would agree that the entry barrier created by a patent is an important incentive for firms to make the kinds of investments that lead to new products. The political process creates entry barriers for different reasons too. For example, when the U.S. auto industry was facing intense competition form Japanese automakers in the 1980s, the American car companies had two basic options: (1) They could create better, cheaper, more fuel-efficient cars that consumers might want to buy, or (2) they could invest heavily in lobbyists who would persuade Congress to enact tariffs and quotas that would keep Japanese cars out of market.

However, living economic environment influences new form of barriers entering method causes to some industries. For example, the airline industry is far less competitive than it appears to be in the past. But, nowadays, airline industry competition is raised, you and some college friends could start a new airline relatively easily in the past, but the problem is that you would not be also to land your planes anywhere. There are a limited number of gate spaces available at most airports, and they tend to be controlled by the big guys. At Chicago's O' Hare Airport, one of the world's biggest and busiest airports. American and United control some 80 percent of all the gates. Or consider a different kind of entry barrier that has become highly relevant in the Internet age, network effects. The basic idea of a network effect is that the value of some goods rises with the number of other people using them. So, such as this US Chicago's O' Hare Airport owner who apply internet network technology to control this airport gates number in order to achieve barriers to none any airport operators can build another airport to compete to this Chicago, US Airport easily. So, living economic environment influences some service industries, e.g. airport service industry, some industry airport needs to find the best method, e.g. internet network tool in order to attempt to protect their gates number controlling authority to barriers the other airport investors to enter their countries to compete to them more easily. Although, in the past, some countries encourage other countries invest to build airports to their local to share risk. But, nowadays, airport service business competition is serious, many countries' airports do not hope to allow other/another countries(country) invest to build airports in their countries. It is one global travelers' traveling needs or desires raising, it influences any countries begin to implement strategies to protect themselves airports to avoid to be controlled and reduces their long term economic benefit absolutely. So, global airport service business is influenced by global popular travelling needs increasing factor to cause airport competitors barrier entering strategy implementation nowadays.

? Why does monopolistic competition had not accepted more to compare alternative theories of competition

Nowadays, living economic environment influences monopolistic competition had not popular accepted more to compare alternative theories of competition. I shall the reasons as below:

Some economists believe that the prediction of the standard model of monopolistic competition differ only in unimportant respects from the of the theory of competition. This is a question of fact, and it must resolved by tests of implications of the two choices.

The fact that supporters of the theory of monopolistic competition had not made tests comparing the predictions of the alternative theories of competition. IN nowadays, living economic environment, if choosing theories in accordance with economist's criteria is to be treated as a positive theory, economists would need to adopt a procedure somewhat similar to the following. When a new advanced , economists would compare the accuracy of its predictions, preferable about phenomena not yet observed, with that of the existing theory and would choose that theory which gave the best predictions.

I feel that living economic environment can cause monopolistic competition is not popular to compare other kinds of competitions. For e-commerce is one god example, e-commerce does not encourage monopolistic competition, because it allows different kinds of service or product sale businesses apply internet and website high technological intangible tools to help them to sell their products from tangible computers. SO, any service industries ,such as airlines can apply websites to let passengers to pre paid visa to buy electronic air tickets, or hotels can apply websites to let travelers to pre-book hotel rooms and choice the day check in and day check out , when they arrives the country, they can live the hotel room absolutely. Any product sale industries, such as book publishers can let readers to pay visa to buy their electronic books to read from their websites or pay visa card to buy the paper book and it will be delivered to their overseas or local homes by air plane or lorry in the short time rapidly.

Hence, internet invention can encourage many competitors enter to the e-commerce sale market. In e-commerce market , it must not have monopolistic competition existing to any kinds of service providers or product sellers. It is one platform to let they have fair competition. None any countries can threaten other countries competitors when they choose to apply internet and website intangible high technological tools to replace any shops to sell their products or provide services from internet. So, living economic environment create new technological sale platform and it also avoid more monopolistic competition creates in our future unpredictable changing business market. Even, it is possible that businessmen will have another one kind of new technological sale platform to replace website to help any countries' businessmen to sell their products or provide their services more easily. Consequently, monopolistic competition will be encouraged to reduce when another kind of new technological sale method is invented in future one day.

? Living economic environment encourages automatic factories and artificial intelligent factories and 3-D printer factories cause

Why does living economic environment encourages automatic factories and artificial intelligent factories and 3-D printer factories cause? Recent technological developments have taken place not just in the production of commodities, but in the generation of the energy needed to operate the artificial intelligent factories of the future. Hence one possible future combines labor-saving technology with an alternative to the current energy regime, which is ultimately limited by both the physical scarcity and ecological destructiveness of fossil fuels. This is far from guaranteed, but there are hopeful indicators for our ability to stabilize the climate, find sources of clean energy and use resources wisely. Because since artificial intelligent innovations, may our living useful things will be replaced by artificial intelligent. For example, non-manual driving vehicles are researched. In our future, it is possible that drivers do not need to drive cars. Artificial intelligence can help them to drive their cars on road safely, even (AI) ships or (AI) air planes will be possible invented. Then , when any kinds related (AI) useful products, e.g. (AI) washing machines, (AI) cookers , (AI) computers etc. will be invented to satisfy our needs. SO, (AI) factories also need to build, it means that traditional labor manufacturing factories will be replaced by artificial intelligent factories because any one of these products will need (AI) robotics to manufacture, so every factory's workers number will be reduced and they will be replaced by robotics in possible. Even may products can be copied by 3D printers in factories easily. SO, any products' producing material number and cost will be reduced, when 3D printers can copy many different kinds of products in short time. It can help manufacturers to raise productive efficiencies, reduce time and costs. In living economic view, artificial intelligent technology will bring high unemployment ratio to the factory workers and their wages will be reduced when robotics can real do their tasks to achieve higher productive efficiencies and reduce time to manufacture any kinds of products and use less material and less cost. IT will bring more economic benefits to future (AI) factories.

On conclusion, our living will be possible to influenced by above these living economic environment changing factor in our soon future one day. So, we need to prepare how to change our living method to adapt future new living changing.

CHAPTER ELEVEN

How living economic environment influences our daily living

In the future, when our economic environment causes to change suddenly variable significantly, it can also influence our living environment changes, then it will also influences our living behaviors change in order to choose to earn the most large benefits in effect. I shall our daily some living cases to explain why it has relationship between our living environment and our living economy and our living behaviors.

The first living changing case, I shall indicate how living economic environment influences students' learning behaviors and social employable behaviors change both.

When one country's students have much pressure to learn and there are many students need to enter schools to learn, but the country has less schools to supply to them to learn. Then, this living economic environment changing factor, e.g. there are many parents need to go to work, but they have no enough money to support their adult age students, e.g. 20 years university students to let them have enough money to continue to enrol universities to learn. IN this less universites supplying number and many poor families living economic environment both factors, it will cause many students feel pressure to enrol any one univeristy, if every year, there has about 100,000 number secondary school students at least, they prepare to pass examination to enroll any one university to study in the country. But, every university has only

100 to 200 secondary students who have enroll to any one university successfully. However, the country has only two universities are existence. So, it has possible that there are 98,600 to 98,800 secondary students , they can not enroll to any one university to study in the country every year. These secondary only choose to find jobs to do.

But, their educational level is low, they will feel find jobs to do in difficulty. If the country's jobs supplying number is less. For example, in the year, there are only 80,000 secondary level jobs to be supplied to these secondary level students to do. Hence, in the year, this country will have 18,600 to 18,800 secondary students who can not find any jobs to work , even they will lose jobs (unemployment) in the whole year in possible.

So in living economic view, this low jobs supplying environment and the low university number graduation and many secondary schools students unemployment factor will only cause this society's economic environment to be more poor, because when it have many secondary students who can not find any jobs to do easily, then they do easy to do stealing, fighting etc. crime behaviors to influence the society's living safety to it living people every day. It is due to this country lacks enough universities to provide to these secondary students to learn as well as they must feel more pressure to examination , due to the university enrolling demand must be raised, e.g. five A grades at minimum. They need to earn in order to enroll to any one university to learn. Even, although some secondary students, they can enroll to any one university to study, but many their parents are poor families and they can not continue to them to enroll any one private university to study, I suppose this country has none any government universities existence. So, these private universities are only for the rich families whose children can enroll to learn successfully. I will let many poor students who feel unfair because they have the best examination result to enroll to any one of these two university to study, but because their parents have no enough money to support them to enroll to either one of these two universities to study. So, they will also need to attempt to find low education level jobs to do in society. Hence, it will raise secondary students competitive number, it will bring negative influence in society, e.g. unemployment rate will be difficult to go down and it will climb up in possible, if this country's low education level jobs supplying number can not increase significantly in the whole year. Then, in this poor living environment economic factor will impact social crime rate increases and young's committing suicide behaves will also increases. If this country can not find methods to solve universities supplying number and secondary student education level jobs supply number shortages, secondary students feel learning pressure emotion psychological problem, poor families living and low salary level household earner psychological pressure problem for this poor and low education level age stakeholder in society.Hence, solving the young age stakeholder learning and working problem will be this country's major social problem if it still hopes its economic environment can be improved.

It must need to change their living and learning condition to be better, it can not neglect to take care their psychological need. It can not only depend on take care the rich families stakeholder's living needs, e.g. supplying enough cars to be imported to let them buy or building expensive houses to let them buy. It is one wrong direction to change this country's economic development, e.g. GDP increases aim. This country ought not need only considerate how to import more cars and build house to achieve the business income increasing aim. It ensures to be one wrong direction to raise economic growth in society. Becausc it's living standard of many poor families must not be improved absolutely. It ought arrange resources

to help education investors to invest more money to build universities in order to increase universities number between five to seven more in order to solve the education challenge to let many secondary students can enroll to universities to study. These universities can have three government assistance governments in order to many secondary school students can pay cheap tuition fee and government can support education loan to them to continue to finish their degrees as well as government can provide business loans to assist some businessmen to start up their businesses in order to increase job positions to let many secondary level education level students have jobs to do. I suppose that this country has enough high education level jobs to supply to university graduates to do. Finally, it also needs to support unemployment assistance allowance to some unemployed parents in short time. It aims to encourage them to continue to seek job. When they have jobs to do, they can not get this enployment assistance allowance from government.

So, they will need to continue to contribute their effort to serve their
society. For example, government only provide the unemployment assistance allowance to these building workers and helping them to seek the new construction employers in short time when they unemployed, e.g.within one month. They will need continue to go to interview when government had arranged the construction firm to make appointment to meet them. If they are failure to pass the interview, then government will continue to help them to find another construction firm as well as arranging the another interview time. So, if they can achieve any one time interview, the government will not
provide another interview chance and it also will not provide the unemployment assistance allowance to them. It aims to encourage unemployed workers continue seek any jobs, it does not encourage them to earn any government assistance allowance in long time.

ON conclusion, it is one best method to change any countries' living environment to the low education and low salary people when the country's government can arrange to use the resources from rich people to be used for the poor people's living and job and learning needs, such as building more government schools, providing short time unemployment assistance allowance, building many public and low market price of houses for the poor and low education young age stakeholders in themselves societies nowadays.

- How investment invention and scientific discovery influences our future living economic development

ON the second living economic environment influence aspect, I shall indicate our invention and scientific discovery will be one important factor influences our future living model has much changed to be improved better. I shall explain how it brings our living economic environment changes as below:

Orthodox growth theories regard scientific discvoery of invention as the ultimate determinants of the
rate of growth of productivity. Investment is merely required to match the pace of scientific advance or invention. However, Schmookler has provided evidence for the conclusion that the rate of invention is determined by the rate of investment. IN fact, inventions are best regarded as a form of investment, and their volume depends, in like manner, on their expected profitability. Investment opportunities are recreated by un limit attempting investment. There is no evidence that inventive opportunities in a particular field become exhausted for technical reasons, although they may do so for economic reasons.

Invention may not be succession, but there is a high probabilities that prior circumstances will bring them about , as the existence of near-simultaneous discoveries by different people show. Learning from prior experience is important not just in scientific or engineering matters, but in other fields such as business and social organization. So, the improvement of scientific advance can thus be neglected in constructing a theory of economy growth, at least at the beginning. Research and development can be achieved with other forms of investment and not considered separately at this stage.

So, it brings this question: How can the relation between investment, invention and scientific discovery bring economic growth to improve our living standard in possible? We need to discuss this question is by how we plan to implement the exploitation of scientific discoveries. According to this view, scientific advance that ultimately determines the rate of growth of productivity. Investment is required to match the kind of scientific invention. If it is more than sufficient for that purpose, the rate of scientific invention return will fall, and if it is less, the rate of return will rise. The productivity possibility frontier, or the production function, shifts
outward at a rate determined ultimately by the kind of scientific invention. At alternative view, it is the kind of invention that is the determining factor, with the kind of scientific invention more in the background. BUt is either view, we need to know about the relations between investment, invention and scientific discovery.

Furthermore, there is no evidence that any investment chance must be success to achieve any new scientific invention or discoveries. but since human decides to
continue without limited learning opportunities. Consequently, instead of scientific discovery and invention being the creators of investment opportunities, investment itself creates them. To understand economic growth, therefore, we need to examine the rate, quality, and determinants of investment. It is a mistake to treat scientific invention and invention as processes that are independent of investment. Any new scientific invention or discovery which are needed human‘ talent and attributing time and nervous. So, training new scientists and increasing new scientists number will be needed because we need they solve our social problems, e.g. air and ocean water environment pollution, overpopulation causes food shortage and water shortage, land shortage dues to global warming causes global water level is increasing. Any non discovery scientific products invention, instead of artificial intelligent products, it is possible that scientists can invent any new technological products to replace them to provide to human to use for our living innovative needs.

As Schmookler does not deny that in some " science -based" industries (he mentions the electrical, electronic, nuclear, chemical , and drug and pharmaceutical industries) invention and research is heavily dependent on scientific knowledge, and that in these industries there were many instances of important inventions being directly induced by scientific discovercies. However, he argues that, even in these industries , economically evaluated technical problems and opportunities arising in the normal conduct of business are dominant' (p.68).

Hence, scientific discovery is also one important factor to bring any invention in success. Also, it implies that scientific knowledge is needed, but if out society can have many scientists are created by education. Then, any new kinds of scientific discoveries will have much chances to find in success. So, increasing the number of scientists will bring the more chance to achieve any new scientific discoveries, scientific knowledge is the traditional and basic education concept. In our future, scientific discoveries is more important to compare general scientific knowledge if we hope we societies can be improved to live more comfortable as well as our living standard will also been raising by more new scientific discoveries.

The third living economic environment aspect is human development. The current economic crisis has affected all aspects of life resulting in political instability, personal financial troubles and a growing number of business bankruptcies. How to use effective human development policy to prevent the economic crisis threats. I shall indicate that governments ought to consider how to apply human development strategy to prevent the economic recession crisis occurrence to threaten to influence whose social economic growth in these aspects.

On high quality education and health systems aspect. Different country's government ought to concern, due to it can support the productivity of an economy by providing healthy and highly trained individuals. Because of the country has good human development strategy, then it can use talent labors to assist its economic growth and good governance practices by governments easily. It seems that human development, good governance and economic growth has close relationship, so it can reduce the economic recession during times of crisis occurrence. It means that human development can influence economic growth. Economic development implies both the improvement of people's health education and general well being and the presence of positive economic indicates, such as economic growth and low unemployment with economic development, people will have better education and healthcare and be more productive. Better human development nations tend to have lower crime rates and greater political strategy than less human development nations.

Does it bring positive consequence of human development to prevent economic recession? It will be an important resource to influence economic growth. How does this human development public policy solve economic crisis? Whether can government use of fiscal policy, such as human development to assist economic stabilization to promote growth and the increase of the capital income efficiency? A key issue relates to the effect of how to use public expenditure and its financing to spend human development on effects of fiscal policy by using a time series approach.

A general model that includes expenditure on education and health, which influences human capital, expenditure and health administration, public investment and transfers and consumption of public products four kinds of expenditure. The model can be used to explore and impact of human development expenditure used on long run per capita income. Debt and external and financing are also possible to be spent to human development expenditure in the general model. So, the public expenditure on the long run per capita income can be explored for low, lower, middle and upper-middle income countries policy that is needed to be estimated how to spend for each aspect of human development expenditure to assist to every country's economy development.

A time series perspective is explained on economic growth may be more useful to pursue for growth and human development strategies. A time series can allow to pursue time series studies for particular countries or country groups at particular stages of economic growth. It can allow for a more specific micro behavior of economic agents. In general, any country has three income groups, such as low income, lower-middle income and upper middle income groups. Also, any country may have these four types of public expenditure for human development which including: enhancing education and building up of human capital, public investment to finance general market and subsistence production, e.g. transportation system, such as roads, bridges, harbors, water supply, sanitation, health and care and education.

A 2005 year study had been carried by Dimonson, Marsh & Staunton, which performed an analysis is stock returns in 53 countries, going back to 1900 year for 17 countries, did not find evidence of a significant long term positive relationship between GDP growth rates and equity returns. Also the analysis from Schroders Economics team found that over the past sixty years, there has tended to be a positive relationship between GDP growth and equity market returns during the recovery, expansion and slowdown phases of the traditional business cycle. This relationship has traditionally broken down during the recession phase.

The Schroders economics team also indicated a traditional business cycle model, which has four stages. In the beginning, it is slowdown stage. It means output above trend, growth decelerating and inflation rising. Next is recession stage. It means output below trend, growth developing, inflation falling. Then, it is recovery stage. It means output below trend, growth decelerating, inflation falling. Finally, it is expansion stage, it means output above trend growth accelerating, inflation is rising. The economic team also suggested the traditional business cycle model: In the slowdown stage, GDP growth is positive, but falling, inflation is high and rising, so policy strategy is tight recommended in the recession stage, GDP growth is negative and falling, inflation is falling. So, policy strategy is loosening recommended. In the recovery stage, GDP growth is negative and rising, inflation is low and falling, so policy strategy is loose recommended. Finally, the expansion stage, GDP growth is positive and rising, inflation is rising, so policy strategy is tightening recommended.

It seems that governments ought concern the business cycle period to evaluate themselves country GDP growth to achieve the most effective policy to adopt to achieve different human development policies to invest to present economic recession crisis occurrence. Usually, in the recovery and expansion phases of the business cycle, the stock market tends to perform well as rising GDP and earnings growth drives positive excess returns on equity. In the slowdown phase, inflation is still high and monetary policy remains tight, resulting in s difficult environment for corporations. reducing earnings and stock valuations tends to result in negative excess returns for equities: declining GDP growth is therefore usually matched with poor equity performance. It also explained that during the recession phase, there is often GDP growth is falling, but the excess return on equity tends to be positive. Historically, falling inflation and an accompanying loosening of monetary policy is needed to rise re-rating.

Thus, it seems the business cycle and human development policy has close relationship. During in the slowdown stage, GDP growth is positive, but falling, inflation is high and rising, then the country's government ought spend less expenditures to human development because GDP growth is stable growth. Otherwise, during it is recession stage or recovery stage, it means output below trend, growth developing, inflation falling. Then the country's government ought spend more to invest to any human development needs to prepare to raise whose labor productivity and GDP growth. Finally, during the expansion stage, GDP growth is positive and rising, inflation is rising. Then the country's government can spend less expenditures to invest human development. Thus, any country's government ought concern what is whose country's business cycle stage to arrange to spend more or less expenditures to achieve its human development policy in different business cycle stages.

Nowadays, political scientists began to apply quantitative methods to classify and measure political interactions. In general, any countries‘ policies that maximize growth are optimal that cares solely about pure " capitalists". The greater, the inequality of wealth and income, the higher rate of taxation and the lower growth. It shows that inequality in land and income ownership is negatively with subsequent economic growth. Many economists have tried to explain lower growth rates and unemployment with a growing tax burden in many developed countries. Although, the impact of taxes on growth can be observed both from the aspect of efficiency and aspect of changes in equity that taxes introduce to economy.

I shall indicate how to apply quantitative evidence to review policy to review human development strategy. In fact, economic or welfare outcomes to changes in regulatory policy has close relationship to be suggested outcome indicate to reduce risk face economic recession occurrence to any countries. Every country government ought design to gather quantitative data to prepare any policy implementation to support mutual learning and best practice in different societal and market conditions. The goal is to help countries to build better government systems and implement policies at both national and regional level that lead to sustainable economic and social development.

The critical public policy challenge is to ensure that the expected economic benefits from regulatory changes are both achieved and outweigh any economic cost imposed. I shall indicate evidence on the outcomes of regulatory policies to help policymakers how design regulatory measures that work better. This method is called "regulatory management". This regulatory management study suggests some conclusions to any policymakers as below:

- Firstly, poorly designed policy regulation can not raise economic activities and ultimately reduce economic growth.
- Secondly, it is impossible between a regulatory policy change and the impact on economic outcomes, such as economic growth is from statistic method easily.
- Thirdly, the reliance on economic recession analysis to investigate the relationship across countries between regulatory variables and economic outcomes may not be readily applicable to any countries and may not always be expressed in economic values. It is particularly useful in developing countries regulatory policy measures for recommendation to policymakers only.
- Fourthly, most quantitative studies deal with the costs of regulation and give little or no attention to quantifying the benefits of regulation. For the policymaker, it is important to compare the estimated costs of regulation. Any policy regulation is intended to correct market failures and assist to economic efficiency and growth. The public policy aims to reduce socially unacceptable income and wealth distributions or it can satisfy expectation that the public should have access to certain products and services, e.g. health care and education irrespective of ability to pay, such as merit products. Some of regulation, that governments need to concern, e.g. of property rights, company law, law of contract etc. and regulation can provide important economic and social, including environmental benefits.

Of course, those benefits need to be set against the costs. Because regulations are the operations of effective economies and societies to market rules, e.g. law of contract and protecting property rights and the rights of citizens. It seems regulatory management is important to influence any policies can be achieved effectively, due to one good regulation can supervise the leader's behavior and otherwise one bad regulation can not supervise the leader's behavior, even it can not assist the country economic growth for long term. So, any leader needs to concern how to use quantitative evidence to review human development policy if who hopes whose policy's regulations are achieved effectively.

At the same time, economic, environmental and welfare pressures raise the demand for regulation above minimum needed for operating a market economy to prepare to face the economic recession occurrence. So, evidence on the outcomes of regulatory policies should help policymakers design regulatory measures that work better. Similarly, evidence on the success or failure of regulation can be used for public accountability purposes.

Regulatory policy defines as the process by which government, when identifying a policy objectives, decides whether to use regulation as a policy instrument and proceeds to draft and adopt a regulation through evidence based decision making. The strategy shall commit governments to remain a regulatory management system, articulating regulatory policy goals, and the impacts of regulation on competitiveness and economic growth. For example, regulation, such as employment law or competition law, the regulation of employment law is applied to control any employers' behaviors to give the fair treatment to whose employees and to protect employees' benefits.

Besides the regulation of competition law is applied to control the fair competition in market. Why this regulations has direct relationship to economy growth. An identifiable economy theory of specific regulatory policies, e.g. administrative simplification and specific economic and welfare outcomes, e.g. high economic growth. The result is a series about the impact of regulatory management on economic indicators. There can be set out as a causal. Thus regulation can be supportive of market transactions and may result in significant economic, social and environmental benefits.

At the same time, ill-designed regulation can have appreciable economic costs, leading to the concept of regulatory burden. In particular, good regulation can reduce the chance of lower economic growth or GDP occurrence, damage investment and competitiveness. But, it has also weakness, such as regulatory costs may act as a barrier to entry into industry in the form of set up cost, e.g. installing equipment to meet health and safety laws and on going annual cost, e.g. preparing returns and facilities inspections.

However, regulatory can be unduly costly to comply with administrator and enforce, but it simplification can reduce the regulatory burden. For example, regulation may not only affect the behavior of those targeted by a rule (direct effects), but invoke behavioral change in the economy (indirect effects). Whether regulation can support governments to avoid or reduce the threats of economic recession occurrence, it depends on the leader's concern how to use quantitative evidence to review policy before who decides to implement which kinds of regulatory management methods.

In recent year, some countries had considered how to achieve policy field with a view to introducing better regulation. The aim is to ensure that regulation occurs only when it does improve social welfare and that regulatory changes do, so with the minimum net cost or maximum net benefit to society. For a policy making perspective, it is important to appreciate how and why a regulatory achievement can be expected to result in a particular impact.

Causal chain analysis is a technique for explaining the way in which a caused regulatory results in an economic impact. By helping to understand the how and why questions, regulatory impact, so causal chain analysis can provide policymakers, with relevant information on the consequences of their policy decisions. It seems that regulation can lead economic improvements, such as higher GDP growth, higher productivity, move business start ups. etc. Due to the causal chain analysis relates to each component separately. So, any decision maker hopes to achieve better regulation, who needs time to attempt to different regulations to achieve whose policies every year. Then, who can review why whose policy can not improve whose country's economic growth as well as to attempt to find reasons how to apply better regulatory to achieve better policy to improve its country's economic growth. It seems review regulatory policy which ought to concern to any decision maker, if who wanted to achieve better regulatory policy to raise economic and welfare gains every year.

In capitalism view, capitalism tends equal systematically, through not uniformly to reward business behaviour that is honest, fair civil and compassionate. When does irrational honesty behaviour influence social economy development? It concerns behavioral economy to individual decision maker whose individual psychology, social psychology into economics. It helps policy makers to incentive in market transactions and in response to policy interventions. So, policy advisers are already using the finding of behavioural economy to advantage to public policy, there is nothing about behavioural economy, but for a long time, it has tended to be concerned how the social economic development, particularly in macroeconomy. For example, policy makers concern of money in nominal rather than real terms in whose how to solve to unemployment. Also, policy makers neglect to recognize how economic motivations apart from those based on rational calculation usually. Most, probably of policy decision makers' decisions to will be drawn out over many days to come, who feels action rather than inaction to any decision immediately, and not as the outcome of a weighted average of probabiities. It seems that the policy decision maker's irrational honesty behaviour will influence how our social's economic development to be good or bad.

On the fourth aspect is how to implement political stability aspect, whether it has relationship between political instability and national economic performance. By past history indicated that the depletion of resource during wars may be one reason why some countries fail to sustain adequate economic growth. However, because economic growth affects a population's well being, this question concerning how was related to growth is important from a policy perspective. So, civil wars can influence any country's economic growth because war can cause the falling changes in a country's physical and human capital as well as lacking technology supporting can reduce GDP per capita to be country during war occurs. For example, during war does noe occur, then trade liberalization, democracy, government stability and a legal system that strongly protects private property rights enhance growth.

During the political instability is occurring, whether tax policy can assist economic growth and social welfare growth. On of central questions in macroeconomics and public policy is how changes in tax policy affect economic activity and social welfare. Consequently, it is possible that sometimes, taxing leads to inefficiency in economy. Whether can taxes stimulate people to change their behavior. For example, the person could either work so hard as before introduction of taxes and reduce whose spending, or work more and spend less time at leisure, thus not needing to reduce spending substantially. However, the inefficiency is caused by taxes, will be presented with a simple supply and demand diagram. In other words, taxes have impact on the amount of supply and demand for products and services.

The purpose of understanding of the impact of taxes on welfare, the decrease in welfare of consumers and producers should be compared with the tax revenue by the country. Such an analysis will show that the decrease in consumers' and producers' welfare exceeds the tax revenue collected by the country. The loss of welfare that takes place after introduction of taxes (a part of which belongs to no one either to a consumer or producer, nor to the country) represents a weight loss or excess tax burden as a degree of inefficiency that taxes introduce to economy. However, full understanding of weight loss requires a detailed tax burden of analysis is needed to governments.

What determines the size of the heavy weight loss to tax? A higher price elasticity of demand curve, or a higher price elasticity of supply curve can lead to a higher weight loss to tax. The more elastic the curves are, the higher is the inefficiency that taxes introduce to the market. The fact is taxes introduce heavy weight loss to the economy because which stimulate people to change their behavior. Since elasticity of supply and demand is a measure of change in the behavior of consumers and producers in relation to change of prices , it also determines the rate of market distortion. The more elastic supply and demand curves, the higher is the heavy weight loss. Another important determinant of the size of heavy weight loss is the tax rate. When price elasticity of supply and demand is the same, heavy weight loss is low when taxes are low and it grows when which both grow. Indeed, heavy weight loss grows faster than most taxes: we can sat that the size of heavy weight loss provided that production costs are constant is equal to 1/2 (elasticity / product quantity), where it is tax rate. Elasticity is price elasticity of demands, product is price of Q is quantity of products.

What is taxation of savings and investment relationship? Taxes can reduce economic growth by affecting savings and investment. The higher the proportion of income that is being saved and invested, the higher will be the future income level, In other words, through its impact on the amount of the income being saved or invested, taxation policy has a crucial effect on the future level of income per capita. The impact of taxes on saving of individuals and companies, investment in fixed capital and investment risk is briefed represented below: How impact of taxes on savings of individual? The gross savings in private sector and accumulated in households and companies.

However, a large past of the gross savings is used for covering depreciation and is needed for the existing capital. The net savings, consisting of savings to householders and earnings of companies, represent the real potential, available for new investments. If all householders would save the same proportion of income, then the impact of income tax on the total savings would be the same, regardless of the pattern of the distribution of tax burden to individuals. But, wealthy individuals shall save more than poor citizens. So, it is expected that the tax collected from higher tax brackets create more burden on savings than the ones collected from lower tax brackets.

Consequently, on individual tax behavior view, a more progressive income tax seems to be creating a heavier burden on savings than a less progressive tax system. So I suggest a less progressive income tax policy will encourage more savings of individuals. However, it is a only assumption, it has another factors to influence citizen's tax behavior: such as, a varies during a life cycle in youth and in old age, it is much lower saving than in middle are when income in highest and when people save for education of their children for a house or flat and for the old age to prepare retirement. So, tax policy is not considered by firms or policymakers in isolation from other aspects of site selection including benefits from public products which are needed to use by citizens, e.g. gardens, swimming pools, entertainment facilities etc. different public facilities.

Finally, I shall explain why individual tax payable honest behavior has moral consequences to cause economic growth. For citizens of all too many of the different countries, where poverty is still the normal. But the tangible improvements in the basic of life that make economic growth, so important whenever living standards are low, greater life expectancy, few diseases, less infant mortality and malnutritian have mostly been played out long before a country's per capita income reaches the levels enjoyed in today's advanced industralized economy.

In fact, immoral or dishonesty business or economic behaviours are caused by some people who pursue material well being and who aim to do benefit to themselves, but it will cause illegal money transactions to raise any overall country's economic or GDP growth. In fact, this business transactions are not legal. So, which can't cause GDP or economic growth to any country. Also, the illegal businesses can not contribute any benefits to any society, so which can not bring any economic benefits or welfares to any countries to satisfy any citizen'e needs ensurely. Even, in parts of the world where the need to improve nutrition and literacy and human life expectancy is urgent, there is often aspect to the recognition that achieving superior growth is a top priority. So, it seems dishonesty behaviours will not improve and raise low income level people whose life expectancy and life quality because this illegal businesses income is used to spend to the illegal businesses or immoral policy decision makers themselves benefits and who won't spend to social welfare.

It seems that these illegal businesss or immoral policies can not assist any economic growth and raise GDP growth rate as well as dishonesty or immoral economic activities can not bring any benefits to societies in our world, even these bad behaviours will bring harm to our societies. e.g. encouraging illegal drug sale to harm young people health and raising crimes rates; winning illegal gamble to earn illegal profit to increase high interest loan businesses and crimes or causing bad families relationship to raise social challenges.

What is the root of the irrational behavioural problem? I believe that is our conventional thinking about economic growth fails to reflect the breadth of what growth, or its absence, means for any society. There are some people's dishonest behaviours only weigh material positives against moral negatives. I believe this dishonest economic activites are seriously. In some cirsumstances dangerous incomplete, the value of arising standard of living lies individuals live, but in how it shapes the social, political and ultimately the moral character of a people.

Economic growth means a rising standard of living for the clear majority of citizens. So, dishonest economic behaviours can only give benefits to the individual and these irrational behaviours can not give welfare to overall societies. In fact, economic growth bears moral benefits as well. So, it seems dishonest behaviours can not raise moral benefit, then it can not also raise economic growth to any country. Moreover, dishonest behaviours are also caused to any country's political democracy. e.g. Many policy decision makers usually only consider self benefit, so who will neglect to consider social welfare benefits to whose citizen. Themselve benefit behaviours will be unfair to whose citizen. The importance of the connection between economic growth and social and political progress and the consequent concern for what will happen of living standards tail to improve, are not limited to the United States and other countries that already have high income and established democracies. So, economic growth or its absence often plays a significant role not only progress from dictatorship to democracy, but also the democracies by new dictatorships.

Also, for dishonest behaviours are caused by decision makers, such as the link between economic growth and social and political progress in the developing countries has yet other political implicatons as well. For example, the continuing absence of political demoracy and basic personal freedoms in China has deeply troubled many observers in the West. Until China gained admisson to the World trade Organization in 2002 year, these concerns regularly gave rise in the Uniter States to debate on whether to trade with China on a most favored nation basis. These concerns still cause questions about whether to give Chinese firms advantage advanced American oil company. Both sides in this debate share the same objective: to foster China's political liberalization. How to do so , however, remains the focus of intense disagreement. The improvement in nutrition, housing, sanitation and transportation has been dramatic, when the freedom of Chinese citizens to make economic choices, where to work, what to buy, when to start a business is already broader than it was with continued economic advance, the average Chinese standard of living is still only one eighth that in the United states, greater freedom to make political choices too, it will probably follow. So the economy is actually developing, like China won't have to wait until China can achieve Western level incomes before they experience significant political and social liberalization.

To conclude, if any country's policy makers who do not consider citizen welfare and who only consider self benefit, it will cause dishonest behaviours to influence social economic development to cause poor situation for long term. So, policy makers must need concern their behaviors are rational choice to make any economic decisions to let their citizen to give welfares for long term. Also any businessmen ought choose to do rational economic behaviours to benefits for societies and clients and governments in order to achieve economic growth to GDP to their countries if who hope whose businesses can be stable to compete for long term. So, policy decision makers and businesses ought consider rational honesty behaviour before who do any economic decision.

How does every country government teach its citizen to do social moral honest behavior which can brings economic growth? How honesty is influenced to economic positive relationship. The dishonesty behaviour includes: e.g. corruption is as an illegal payment to a public agent to obtain a benefit that may or may not be deserved, or the abuse of public office for private gains to consume, corruption probably amounts are to a large share of the gross national product in any countries. So, corruption worries policy makers and international organizations, who remains the adverse effects of corruption.

However, in the macroeconomic view, the academic literature is less definite about how bribes minimize the waiting costs associated with queuing in a equilibrium. Both of those waiting cost associated with queuing and inefficiency models equate bribes as allocating the true worth of the licenses or permit to the most worthy bidder in public sector.

Forbidding bribes that amounts to prohibiting the use of price mechanism in the public sector. In terms of economic growth, the only thing worse than a society over centralized, dishonest bureaucracy is over-centralized. So, the quality of government institutions, including the degree of corruption, affects investment and growth as much as other political economy variable. e.g. political freedom, civil liberties and political violence. Another example, some firms that pay more bribes also spend more time with bureaucrats in more corrupt countries and have a higher cost of capital, thus countering the view of corruption.

Some countries are likely fairer and regulation is less. How does corruption affect income inequality? In addition, capital market imperfection and government spending have been suggested as two channels for corruption to affect inequality and economic growth. Finally, to what extent can corruption explain the differences in inequality and economic growth? So, it seems corruption is associated with a smaller increase in income inequality and a larger drop in growth rates. Also, corruption raises income inequality to a lesser extent in countries to achieve higher government spending. So, it seems corruption dishonest behaviour has close relationship to influence any countries' GDP economic growth.

Corruption is understood as sale of government property for private gain. However, most economists view corruption as a major obstacle to development. It is seen as one of the causes of low income and is believed to play a critical role in poverty. Perhaps the most quoted example of this is speed money paid by business people to government officials to speed up bureaucraties procedures. At the macro level, there is evidence that corruption affects adversely many of the proxy causes of economic growth. e.g. investment in manufactured and human capital. Moreover, high levels of corruption tend to with a lack of political accountability and disrespect for property rights factors which themselves tend to be obstacles to economic growth.

More fundamentally, however, there is a sense in which the focus on growth in GDP per capita is misguided. Ultimately, development is about how to improvement in human welfare. However, corruption is developing a few with access systematic distort political and economic decisions which might be made systematically with conflict of interest at play. For example, different countries‘ banks which achieve different bank schemes to aim to avoid illegal money saving from drug trafficking to cause false economic growth in any countries. The anti-corruption strategy advocated to economic development, democratic reform a strong civil society with access to information and overseeing the state, and the presence of rule of law. The governance program facilities at the request of client governments, a series and surveys involving broad segments of society and national and local government performance.

The causes of its development and many and vary from one country to the next. It seems corruption dishonest behaviours can cause to seem as one country's false economy growth and even, global false economy growth after any illegal economic activities had been done from any illegal businessmen. So corruption is a global issue which is government all over the world. However, what is the causes and consequences of corruption? It is possible that corruption is the intentional with length relationship aimed at deriving some advantage from this behaviour for oneself or for related individuals. So, in micro-economic view, corruption cause is derived from some advantage from this behaviour for the person. Otherwise, in macro-economic view, corruption cause is also derived from some advantage this behaviour for the organization, even overall country's social benefit, e.g. illegal shares buying and selling trading activities, illegal bank saving transaction source from drug trafficking activities.

On citizen educational honest behavior aspect, many of the assumptions which are attempted to rationalize the process of educational development have been criticized or abandon. However, the education quality role of different educational regulation, the choice of financing methods, the examination and certification procedures or various other regulation and incentive structures will influence educational effect to satisfy public needs. Thus, citizen honest educational policy makers need to satisfy public needs. Moreover, educational policymakers also need to concern any new policy making environment which will seriously constrain their attempts to ensure the early discussion of planning considerations as part of the education policy making process. So, every country's environment factor will influence every educational policymaker's individual decision.

As defined, policy represents decisions that are designed to guide (including to constrain future decisions or to initiate and guide the implementation of previous decisions). It is this time bound nature of policy and of policy making that makes it is such a critical concern for the educational planner. However, the failure of the traditional planning models and the recognition of the lack of nationality that can occur in policy making there combined to create an atmosphere of pessimism among some educationalists.

To capture the details of the decision making process of any educational planning itself, an analytical framework is presented that goes beyond the initial decision point to examine both the preceding actions (contextual assessment, technical analysis and the generation, valuation and selection of policy options) and the subsequent activities (planning and conducting implementation, impact assessment and where appropriate, design). Thus, the framework covers the full policy planning process, but with a focus on the facilitating and constraining effects that policy decisions and how they were derived and have no the choices available to citizen honest educational planners.

There are two ways of value to educational planners. First, the methodology of the framework and conclusions of the any one of educational case studies should help in the analysis of current educational policies and decision making procedures (an analysis of policy). So, it is a present method to gather current data from current case studies to make the update conclusions to achieve any any of eductional policies. Otherwise, Second, the another framework can be applied to have evaluation of proposed policies and used to forecast policy outcomes and the probability of successful implementation, given the country of fiscal and management capacity, political commitment etc. So, this framwork is a futuer predict educational method to gather data how to get the recommedation to achieve the effiective quality of educational policy in the future.

Citizen honest behavioral sducational policy can be lower differ in terms of scope, complexity, decision environment, range of choices and decision criteria. Any educational policy decision deals with large scale policies and broad resource allocation will have these questions to need to answer. For example, on strategic view, how can we provide basic education at a reasonable cost to meet equity and efficiency objectives?

On multi program view, should resources be allocated to university level education? On program view, how would occupational training centre be designed and provided across the country? On issue specific view, should graduated of rural universities be allowed to transfer to any one of city area universities to study easily? On the psychological view, some researches indicated behavioral economics with emotions has close relationship to any policy making, such as educational policy. More recently, economists as well as psychologists who are specifically interested in decision making have begun to take greater concerning emotional influence.

So, it seems any policy decision making whose any one of final policy decisions which is influenced to achieve or not achieve from their emotion indirectly. Usually, then an economy is doing well, there is less incentive to encourage new entrepreneurial firms if the country's citizens and firms have enough jobs supply and have enough labor supply in the job market. It seems that good economic growth country will have this question why it needs to take a risk on something new. So, emotions have close link to our societies to influence any country's citizens real needs and entrepreneurs' business aim to develop any societies' economy to be grown. So, any countries' policies decision makers ought concern whose enterprises and citizens whose real needs, then who can attempt to choose what methods of policies to assist whose countries' economy development more effective.

On natural environment protection policy, whether national environment protection policy can assist economic growth to the country. The natural environment is central to economic activity and growth, providing the resources, we need to produce products and services and absorbing and processing unwanted by-product in the form of pollution add waste. So, environment assets contribute to managing risks to economic and social activity helps to regulate flood risks, regulating the local climate both air quality and temperature and maintaining the supply of clean water and resources both.

Government's environment protection role is to send clear signals and set a long term policy framework in order to provide businesses with the certainty who need to make investments in low carbon and resource efficient technologies. It is also essential that government listens to and works with business, so that environment protection policies are designed in a way that avoids unnecessary burdens and removes potential barriers to success. So, the natural environment plays an important role in supporting economic activity. It contributes: directly, by providing resources and raw materials, such as water, timber and minerals that are required as inputs for the production of products and services and indirectly, through services provided by ecosystems including carbon water purification, managing flood risks and nutrient cycling.

The relationship between economic growth and the natural environment is complex. Several different drivers come into play, including the scale and composition of the economy, particularly the share of services in GDP as opposed to primary industries and manufacturing and changes in technology that have the potential to reduce the environmental impacts of production and consumption decisions when also driving economic growth.

In fact, economic growth involves the combinations of different types of capital to produce products and services these include; produced capital, such as machinery, buildings and roads; human capital, such as skills and knowledge, natural capital, e.g. raw materials are extract from the earth, carbon and services is provided by forests and social capital, such as institutions and ties within communities. So, government needs to concern that national resources can not be extracted too much to lead our natural capital is lacked to produce any products or to provide services in the future.

In particular, market failure in the provision and use of environmental resources mean that natural assets would be over-used in the absence of government intervention. These market failures arise from the public product characteristics of the natural environment, external costs and benefits, where the use of a resource by one party has impacts on others, difficulties in capturing the full benefits of business investment in environmental research and development, and information failure. Market failures may include water quality and to vehicle emissions to influence human's body health.

So I suggest that any countries' government needs to achieve these policies which concerns on environmental protection aspect to achieve its public spending and technology policy, such as below:

- On developing flood infrastructure hand, supporting low carbon technologies electric vehicles. Also on the information provision and other policies to address barriers to influence consumer's behavior change, such as product labelling policies and policies to increase take up of resource efficiency measures to provide environment protection. So, effective environmental policy is likely to require and the use of multiple instruments, each tackling to require part of the problem when avoiding duplication and unnecessary regulatory burdens. Also, pricing environmental inputs can correctly help any businessmen to manage how to use natural resources effectively.

- Environmental policy aims to reduce how the economy and the businesses are to adverse environmental events, by reducing environmental risk both. For example, not just investments that facilities emissions reductions to avoid dangerous climate change, but also those investments that help to economy adapt to climate impacts already locked in by past and current emissions. The natural environment plays a key role in our economy, as a direct input into production and through the many services it provides. Environmental resources, such as minerals and fossil fuels directly facilities the production of products and services. The environment provides other services that enable economic activity, such as carbon, filtering air and soil formation. It is also vital for against flood risk, and soil formation. It is also vital for our wellbeing, providing us with recreational opportunities, improving our health and much more. Human wellbeing in a complex and diverse concept, determined by a wide-range of factors including levels of income absolute and relative, health status, educational attainment, housing conditions and environmental quality.

- National capital contributes to economic output through two main channels: directly as an input to the process of economic activity, indirectly through its effect on the productivity of the other factors of production. However, natural capital is as a direct input to wealth creation, which can provide the raw materials for economic production of products the raw materials for economic production of products and services, it includes non renewable resources like, fossil fuels, minerals metal extracted from the natural environment to produce energy, machinery, consumer products, renewable resources, natural processes or own reproduction. Why do our governments need to concern environmental policy? The reasons include natural areas provide global life support functions, including climate regulation and regulation of the chemical composition of the atmosphere and oceans. When natural areas play a role in the maintenance of life essential services, it is difficult to evaluate and demonstrate the contribution that particular habitat types or areas make. Water regulation can reduce flood and storm protection and prevent damage. Natural processes can also provide water quality benefits, pollution includes the removal of nutrients and pollutants from water, filtering of dust from the air, and providing noise. Waste sink includes all non recycled waste is produced by economic activity. In the absorptive capacity of the atmosphere, the oceans and the soil protection, such as many wetland habitats, provides benefits by preventing soil loss. Nutrient cycling includes storage, processing and acquisition of nutrients essential for plant growth in ecological process and waste decomposition, naturally occurring micro-organisms provide benefits through their ability to break down organization matter and speed up the process of waste decomposition.

As the global financial crisis has reminded as once again of the economic role of trust and confidence, social capital attributes which are difficult to influence any policy decision maker's ration decision making more easily. Referring to recent financial crisis, which is related to any psychological drivers of economy activity, we can not understand the economic developments of recent times without psychological insights which go beyond estabished notions of rationality in its economic sense. As people with weigh the costs and benefits of each possibility.

This above assumption is based on the expectation that individuals and firms will act in a consistent manner, with a reasonably well defined notion of what who like and what whose objectives are, and with a reasonable understanding of how to attain those objectives. In fact, behavioural economy is a complement to deductive processes based on those assumptions. In any discipline with practical applications, such as public policy, conclusion is reached by chains of deductive logic based on those assumptions require the test of falsifiability or refutability, or at least that they be supported by confirmatory evidence. However, a rational means the predictive validity of the rational model holds, but that doesn't mean achieving policy should ignore interventions. For example, most people rationally avoid self-harm, but there will be extreme tails of highly protective and of highly reckless behaviour: the latter may require specific protection. So, it seems it has relationship between global financial crisis and individual or organization's irrational behaviour.

How can government' capturing private investment assist economic growth? How can government's capturing private investment policy attract foreign direct investment or different countries? I believe that Increased levels of trade and foreign direct investment worldwide which has a cause or effect of relationship to the closer interdependence of world economies, they are a reality. What is the relationship among these private, public and civil society sectors? Every country contribution is to add to the public policy stream to understand how the main forces in society operate and cooperate in promoting foreign direct investment. Governments have always been concerned about how to position themselves in an increasingly competitive market for a limited supply of investment resources.

Why should a multi-national firm choose one country attraction ? e.g. tax breaks, profit repatriation, low domestic content requirement etc. How can one country strategically position itself against others? Is there an association between pro-social public policy and levels of global private investment? We are particularly interested in those economies in earlier stages of development, where pro-social policies are a rarer phenomenon, as they provide a testing for our hypotheses. What is the relationship between the ability of an host country to attract private investment and the quality of pubic policies affecting the life of its citizens? Are pro-social host government policies in host countries linked to higher inward flows of foreign direct investment to that country?

There has three country level macroeconomic indicators to represent different facets of size: Host country economy growth rate, host country population and host country's rate of inflation. GDP growth, the annual percent change of output in real terms percent, reflects the strength of local economy and the increase in the size of domestic market, opening the door to large sales and high profits. Thus, higher GDP growth should generally be attracted to larger foreign investment. Population is another indicator of market size. It attracted to foreign investment with both large populations and high GDP per capita. So, encouraging immigration and birth rate can attract more foreign investment. Inflation enters the regression as a proxy for macroeconomic stability and as a reflection of the internal or external shocks suffered by the economy during the period under study, which may attract potential inflation sign of internal economic instability and of the host government's inability to maintain consistent monetary policy. It will influence foreign investment confidence. So stable inflation of the host country can increase confidence to let more foreign investment.

How Capturing private investment policy can affect medium to long term economic growth. It is difficult to measure the factors and to determine causality with certainty, between fiscal policy and economic growth relationship. Fiscal reforms are needed to concern structural reforms, e.g. labor or trade and supportive macroeconomic policies. At the macro level, fiscal policy can help to ensure macroeconomic stability, an essential prerequisite for growth at the micro level, tax and expenditure policies can boost growth by altering work and investment incentives, promoting human capital accumulation and enhancing total factor productivity. For example, combining fiscal reforms, e.g. sealing up infrastructure investment when improving the public investment process can increase their effectiveness. Complementary reforms, such as liberalizing trade of fiscal reforms by promoting savings, stimulating investment and not lacking productivity gains, policy uncertainty and high levels of public debt large fiscal deficits reduce aggregate savings in the economy and may lead to inflation, high interest rates and balance of payments pressures, with negative growth consequences. Policymakers need to concern the durability and equity. For example, Netherland, an expenditure cut of 15% of GDP between 1982 year and 2000 year created room sector job-creation. At the same time, both countries managed to avert adverse consequence on income inequality. In advanced and emerging market economies, age related spending on public persons and health care accounts for a large share of government spending (40% and 30%, respectively, IMF, 2014 f). Otherwise, Poland shifted from a financially defined benefit system to an actuarially solvent defined contribution system, and Germany put its pension system on a more sound financial by linking pension benefits to the old age dependency ratio, tightening access to early retirement and rising the statutory retirement age. In health care, Germany and the Netherlands introduced a combination of macro and micro level reforms to contain cost and enhance efficiency, including price controls on pharmaceuticals, higher co-payment and contributions and budget.

Can national leadership and economic growth has close relationship? Can leader individual behavior affect economic growth? Leaders have strongest effects in autocracies, where who appear to substantially influence both economic growth and the evolution of political institutions. I shall indicate to explain why substantial roles for individual leaders and national institutional change, which can further influence the growth environment. In the past, examinations of the fundamental causes of growth debate between institutions, culture and geography, which typically operate without reference to the actions of particular personalities. However, economists may imagine leaders indirectly as policymakers, leaders, themselves are rarely the subject of focus.

The constraints imposed on leaders from electoral pressures, opposition parties, independent legislatures and judiciaries all vary across countries. To the extent that the authority embedded in formal institutional rules and the authority embedded in individuals act as substitutes, the increasing visibility of institutional variation in explaining paths may indirectly motivate leaders' behaviors. Theories of economic growth that emphasize public products, e.g. education, health, public entertainment facilities, such as parks, swimming pools etc. Also, national policies include international trade, monetary policy and fiscal policy etc. or all suggest possibly important roles for a national leader. However, identifying a causative effect of leaders on economic growth is challenging. Even, if it has relationship between particular leaders and particular economic growth in particular economic environment. However, it may be that growth changes drive leadership changes, without a causative effect of leaders. Assumption that a leader quality is independently, it seems the leader has no influence on economic growth. An important additional assumption is that the leader effects are strongest in autocratic settings, especially in the absence of political parties or legislatures to support the leader's any personal view points to achieve any regulations to influence economic growth effectively. These results point to an important effect between institutions and leader individuals in understanding economic growth paths. However, it seems institutions can influence the impact of national leaders behaviors and that national leaders can also influence the path of institutions. If leaders can influence economic growth, then may further these questions are raised: Do leaders act to obstruct economic growth or do they actively promote it? In this view, leaders can be actively good for economic growth, e.g. by investing in public products, choosing pro-growth trade policies, or overcoming national scale coordination problems. However, related questions of how leaders influence growth are related to the role of national policies in explaining growth. If policies might be well matter, even if leaders do not, if national policies care the expression of broader social forces. So, it seems national policies can also influence economic growth, instead of the leader's personal quality. So, it can get this question and conclusion. When asking how do we make poor countries rich? The unexplained, non-deterministic past of economic growth variation becomes especially relevant and given the results about leadership, more within reach.

However, nation leader's behaviour can influence the country's economy development. Concerning irrational honesty whether this behavior can influence social economic development. I shall indicate those questions to attempt to be considered, such as: Can there be a growing scaraity without a growing shortage or a growing shortage with a growing scarcity? Can a decision be economic if there is no money in involved? Can there be surplus food in a society where people are hungry? For example, building ordinary and building luxury housing both involves using many of the same resources, such as bricks, pipes, and construction labour. How does the allocation of these resources between ordinary housing and luxury housing tend to change after rent control laws are passed?

When a government institution or program produces counter productive results, is that necessarily a sign of irrationality on the part of those who run that particular institution or program? Why do American manufacturers of computers or television sets tend to have them transported by others? When Chinese manufacturers tend to transport themselves? How did the movement of population from rural to urban America affect the economy of retail selling in the early twentieth century? Advertising even when it is successful, is often considered to be a benefit only to those who advertise, but of no benefit to consumers, who have to pay the cost of the advertisement in the higher price of the products who buy. Is it irrational economy behaviour to society? Why would luxury hotels be charging lower rates than economy hotels? Whether governments choose to protect competition or protect competitors which method is better? What have been some of the economic and social consequences of the substitution of machine power for human strength, as a result of industralization and the growing importance of knowledge, skills and experience in a high-technological economy? How can per capita income be increasing by 50 % over a period of years, when average family income and average householder income remain almost stable over those same year? Does inequality of income tend to be greater or less in long run than in the short run?

All above questions concern the social and economic influences won't be better if the policy decision makers or businessmen do any irrational honesty behaviours. It seems rational honesty behaviour is important to any policy decision makers or businessmen because whose rational or irrational behaviour can influence social economic development directly are driven to act by economic as well as social ethical and other reasons. So economists need to study of what motivates individual acts, especically regarding economic decisions, offers an intellectual challenge to the human sciences. So, if economists can predict to judge whether any policy decision makers or businessmen whose act is irrational or rational, then who can assist the country's economic development more easily.

Promoting honesty in negotiation can influence social economy growth in global. In a competitive and moral imperfect world, business people are often facing with serious ethical challenges. Usually, many businessmen feel justified in engaging in less than ideal conduct to protect their own interests. However, our commonplace that work to promote credibility, trust and honesty of behaviours can influencc our social economy growth in long term. For example, deception in negotiation behaviour is immoral, due to success in business typically requires successful negotiations.

Given the high value placed on honesty, the incentives for deception in negotiation create a serious moral tension for business people. Not surprisingly, deception in negotiation is a widely discussed problem in business ethics. How many negotiators their views are essentially, who is regarded as a superior moral philosopher, would find them objectionable? For example, philosophical debates about the loss of civilian life in war would be better served by putting resources and intellectual energy into developing political, economic diplomatic and military strategies that resources and intellectual energy how to be chosen to use in military strategies aspect or political aspect or economic diplomatic aspect. The country's leader will influence the whole country's social economy development in long term.

However, individual and social stability are difficult to maintain in a social setting in which there is serious conflict between ethics and personal welfares. Because irrational honesty behaviour is usually caused between the personal welfare and ethics choice.

Can behavioral economy be applied to develop policy and influence economic growth effectively? Such policies stress that changing the way choices are presented or changing the environment in which decisions are made, can substantially alter behavior. Ideas from behavioral economics have helped to develop the traditional economic choice framework, in which people are assumed to make choices that are rational, self interested and consistent. Some of the most important behavioral insights for tax and benefit policy include: Faced with complicated decisions, people may make choices, which are often approximately optimal, in that who maximize welfare, but might in some cases lead to poor choices. There is evidence that how choices are presented affects outcomes.

The environment in which decisions are made would provide cues to make particular choices or made could provide cues to make particular choices, or some aspects of the choice problem may be more or less influence to consumers. When any policy relates to income and spending, or it is label money for another can affect what people choose to do with it. Individuals appear to care not just about their own outcomes, but also about those of others. This might be because people derive value from fairness and cooperation. These motivations could give intrinsic incentive to make particular choices. It is possible that providing extrinsic incentives, such as taxes, fines or rewards could be crowded our desirable behavior.

Consumers may have to exercise costly self control to make certain choices, such as eating health foods or giving up smoking. Commitment devices to help overcome self control problems are therefore values, for example, raising the cost of tempting choices, increasing cigarette taxes, say: when making choices with uncertain outcomes, people will do a number of behavioral features. Such as, attaching subjective decision weights to each outcome and these may differ from objective measures of probability. Usually, outcomes are measured against a reference point, relative to the reference point are felt more strongly than equivalent gains. When welfare increases and ever bigger gains falls, as the welfare cost is from ever bigger losses, then people will appear to be risk seekers when welfare cost comes to cause social loss. How people value the future changes with the passage of time. Usually people hope to earn immediate rewards in present than distant rewards in the future. This means that people make plans who find it hard to achieve. People may also make choices under the assumption that their preferences won't change in the future. So, for policymakers those biases have important implications for why behavior change interventions may be necessary.

Behavioral insights provide new reasons to intervene, issues of self control, for example, making failure, where outcomes are come from the perspective of either individuals or society or both usually. As a common failure is the case of externalities, when individual choices generate costs or benefits for others. Since, these are not taken into account in private decision making, which are come from a social perspective, there is too much or too little of the activity.

In this case, taxes or subsidies can help private and social incentives. So, behavioral economical concept can be suggested these important insights for externalities, such as private decisions are closer to the social optimum, reducing the need for correcting taxes or subsidies. It seems that taxes or subsidies will affect to change people's behaviors if social preferences are important. Externalities can arise not just because of how someone affects the well being of others, but also through how decisions made today affect the individual in the future. This is known as an internality. Taxes or subsidies policies both can influence people's present behaviors to be changed and future behaviors will be influenced to be changed from whose present behaviors in societies. Thus, policymakers can not neglect this policy of method to attempt to solve any social challenge nowadays.

Finally, I shall explain why national leader's behavior can assist policy development. Behavioral economy is a science, includes psychology, economics, finance and sociology to understand human behavior and decision making. Behavioral economics recognizes that constraints in time and mental resources prevent us from optimally evaluating every decision. To deal with our limitations, so we rely on mental decision to judge our face of uncertainty, but we can be leaded to predictably irrational behaviors from behavioral economical concept.

As government agencies enact laws and regulations that are focused in the society. They often rely on restrictions, incentives or public information campaigns in order to change citizen behavior. When well intentioned, those traditional approaches can be accepted. For example, regulations that can be supported to financial advisers disclose conflicts of interest have led to achieve any final results. Disclosures can increase pressures on advisees to comply with the advice provided and in some cases increase greater perceptions of trust rather than the evaluation of biased advice. Similarly, tax incentives can increase retirement savings rates which have had limited impact. Researchers studying the impact of concluded that such policies are an expensive way of encouraging new savings.

On the one hand, governments ought engage their citizens to do any action, whose action is influenced by behavioral economics to discover how behavioral economics can be provided powerful insights into human motivation and behavior. As different countries' government experiments are more from academic laboratories to the real world. So, it is a kind of method to be applied to assist any countries' governments how to use effective policy to improve people's lives. For example, designing what is the best reasonable taxes, subsidies, incentives or educational campaigns level at the rate, donations and retirement savings rates as well as healthy food product label consumption of selection etc. strategic policies which are related how to apply behavioral economy to analyze or experiment to gain the better choice among of them.

On the another hand, Economic agents ought attempt to spend time to gather data to choose to do the best decision, but not perfectly national ones. Also economic research should be used reasonable assumptions about agents' cognitive actives. So, economic models should take predictions that are consistent with micro-level data on decisions, including experimental evidence. Moreover, economists ought spend much time to learn from psychologists. Behavioral economists now routinely combine experimental data, field data and theory to construct their arguments. As behavioral economic continues to gain acceptance, behavioral economists will increasingly find themselves participating in policy discussions. As policy has the ability to do good or to create great mislead, depending on who, leader is in charge of making the rules. Indeed in some cases the findings of behavioral economists suggest that active policies may be quite harmful. Successful policy analysis should be concerned the motives of private actors, e.g. consumers and firms and the public or governmental actors need to design formulate and enforce policy with cooperation to regulators, bureaucrats, politicians.

So, policy analysis must also be carefully concerned the institutional environment in which these private and public actors interact, e.g. , market, elections and bureaucracies. However, any bad decision making is caused from bounded rationality, slow learning, framing and lack of self control with those effects in mind, one might conclude that government can easily improve consumers' welfare by paternalistically helping consumers make better decisions. Such paternalistic policies can improve consumer welfare by enhancing an individual's maximizing whose own welfare. So, this stands in contrast to most public policies, which address externalities or public products problems that arise because of interactions among economic agents.

To conclude, national leader and whose psychology which can influence whether he can do the reasonable policy and which have close relationship, As if the national leader had health psychology, then who will have more possible to achieve good behavior to perform to decide how to achieve any the best public policies to raise growth to make welfare to whose citizens. So any policymakers ought need to concern how to listen to behavioral scientists to let them to give any recommendation how to improve or review or revise whose psychological challenges to let them have more effort to decide how to choose to do the right decision effectively. Because the relationship between psychology and behavioral science has more generally to influence public policy which is particularly painful and frustrating of the success for any similar policy recommendations. Hence, economics and psychology indeed can provide policymakers with vital tools to develop the best policy to solve any social challenges.

Consequently, it seems the leader's psychology will influence whose behavioral performance to be decided to choose to do the more correct policy to influence economic development more easily. It also means that one leader's psychology is an important factor to influence any social economic development directly for long term. So who can not neglect to concern whether whose psychological mind is right or wrong to already to make any decisions to plan any policies before whose any polices are implemented. Because the leader's psychology will influence whose behavior is more correct to decide to decide how to do any policies effectively.

On conclusion, if we hope our future living to be improved, we need follow as several aspects in order to raise our economic growth more easily. Then we will build best between living standard and economic growth.

Reference

Dimson, Marsh & Staunton, London Business School (2005) In The Global Investment Returns Year Book, ABN Amro.

Fiscal Policy And Long Term Growth, International Monetary Fund, IMF policy papers, Washington, D.C. Available from April, 2015, http://www.imf.org/external/pp/ppindex.aspx

reference

Schmokler, J. (1966). Invention and economic growth, Harvard University Press, Cambridge , Mass.

CHAPTER TWELVE

Environment impacts consumption desires change

Why does environment changing impact our living model change? Does they have close relationship between environment and living? How and why environment influences our living model needs to be changed in order to adapt any sudden economic environment changes. In macro view, economic environment and our living environment which have direct relationship. When our social economic environment changes significantly suddenly, then our society needs to find the best methods in order to let us to feel adapt to the sudden economic environment changes to threaten the least living negative effects. I shall indicate the reasons as below:

Any countries must have themselves methods to adapt any time sudden economic environment changes. Such as China and US, China is one non -freedom country, but US is one freedom country. Hence, the relationship of how to adjustment policies, poverty and the environment was complex and different between them. Due to these are different, so they will influence themselves citizen decide how to do behaviors in order to adapt their living when they are living in themselves countries. It seems that any countries citizen need to find the best methods in order to adopt to live in themselves countries easily. Otherwise, some people feel difficult to adapt to live in themselves countries. Then, they will
choose emmigrate to other countries to live because they feel that they cannot adapt to live themselves countries more easily.

Some countries feel macroeconomic stability is one good method to keep their countries can have long term economic growth. But, it is not absolute right because it is not sufficient
to ensure long-term environmental sustainability. For example, lower inflation rates, increased savings, lower budget deficits, and improved trade balances were central to creating conditions for increased investment, a higher growth rate, employment creation, and poverty reduction. However, macroeconomic stability and increased economic efficiency would not and could not solve other basic development issues, such as income inequality and cost internalization, which directly threatened the sustainability of the countries‘ development strategies. Such as
Mexico and Thailand that bring the shortcomings in addressing specific environmental impacts of the price

corrections and government failure to implement complementary policy reforms to bring Mexico and Thailand people often immigrate to US illegal because they feel living difficulty to live in their countries. So, in long term, poor economic development will bring the number of immigrants increases effect to any country in possible. Also, it seems that the immigrants number is more or less, it has close relationship to the country's people how feel their country is suitable to them to live forever.

Why does environment can impact liberalized trade regimes and influence consumers' consumption desires change ? Many criticisms of the impacts of structural adjustment on the environment focus on the negative environmental consequences of liberalized trade regimes. These concern on these aspects: The fact is that liberalized trade discourages internalization of environment costs. IN the logic of competitive advantage , countries that lower the production costs for private enterprises can enjoy an advantage over competing nations by failing to internalize environment costs associated with production and disposal of commodities and

manufactured goods. Such as the General Agreement on Tariffs and Trade (GATT), which prevails trade practices that encourage the externalization of environment cost. For example, GATT rules do not allow countries to distinguish between production processes that internalize environment costs and those that pass such costs to present and future generations. However, this policy failure of trade regimes thereby grants competitive advantage to those who do not internalize environment costs. In fact, environmental standards can be attacked as nontariff barriers to trade that run contrary

to the principles of enhanced international trade. Hence, it creates the difficult international trade co-operation relationship between environment protective countries and non-environment protective countries. For example in agricultural farm industry aspect, it will bring agricultural export difficulty to in Latin America, the trade-offs between short-term economic growth benefits and the long term environment costs of promoting non traditoinal agricultural exports in Latin America. When Latin America evaluates it will bring less and short term benefits to export any agricultural food to environment protective countries. Then, it will reduce export to them, even forever without any agricultural exports to them again. Then, these environment protection countries

people won't eat any Latin America agricultural food easily. Shortage of Latin America agricultural food will be shortage to supply these environment protection countries, then Latin America agricultural food price may raise, if these environment protection countries agricultural food consumers still need to eat much Latin America agricultural food. Consequently, the shortage of

Latin America agricultural food issue will bring long term inflation to any Latin America agricultural food. It will influence these environment protection countries' Latin America agricultural food consumers their eating needs to be reduced and they will decide to change their taste to eat other countries' agricultural food to replace Latin America agricultural food. Finally, any Latin America's agricultural food to these environment protection countries' people, they won't have any higher market worth or higher price or lose any worth to compare other

countries' agricultural food because they will like to eat other countries' agricultural food more than Latin America agricultural food. Hence, environment protection environment will influence some countries' export reduces as well as the import countries' consumers' choices will also changed and their consumption desires will also change in long term.

I shall explain why environment pollution will influence consumer behaviors to be changed also.The findings of behavior analysts on resource conservation and pollution control are interpreted in terms of the classification of consumer behaviors and contingencies
proposed by the model. These environmentally-impacting consumer behaviors are elucidated through discussion of both their consequences and the nature of intervention to a
meliorate them. An appropriate social marketing mix for each class of consumer behavior is suggested. Why does the country some consumers reduce to use some products or reduce to buy some products, e.g. riding bicycle to replace driving car; reducing to use plastic and paper bags at homes or going supermarket shopping; reducing to catch air planes to fly to travel because avoiding air plane's gas pollutes air on sky; reducing to catch ferry on sea number because avoiding gas pollutes on sea. Their living
behaviors changing reaon aimed at environmental preservation. So, these environmentally-impacting consumer behaviors issue will be one good example to explain how and why environment changing and consumer behaviors changing have close relationship.

Applied behavior analysis has contributed substantially to knowledge of economic consumption as it adversely affects the physical and social environment (Cone and Hayes 1980; Geller, Winett and Everett 1982). Skinner's (1953) behavior theory which stresses
that the causes of behavior are found in its environmental consequences. They indicate how environment protection attitude can change consumer behavior, such consumer behaviors as excessive use of private transportation, over-consumption of domestic energy, littering and waste generation, and consumption of scarce resources such as water.

Social advertising from television, radio, newspapers, magazine which is one good example to encourage environment protection behavior to consumers e.g. not purchase cars to drive on road to avoid air pollution from gas. Further, the effectiveness of campaigns intended to change behavior by modifying attitudes has been questioned. To the extent that environment protection aware consumers rely heavily on the use of persuasive communications to change pre-behavioral attitudes and values, social information campaigns have had little impact on consumers' conservation behavior.

Despite vast general public knowledge about the potentially catastrophic consequences of failing to conserve energy, researchers report an inability to identify the required relationship
between attitudes toward energy use and conservation; even those maximally informed are no more likely to save energy; nor does specifically informing people about
the personal costs of current energy use and the benefits of reducing consumption affect behavior (Costanzo, Archer, Aronson and Pettigrew 1986).

However, applied behavior analysis indicates that simply informing people of the consequences of their actions is unlikely to modify their behavior unless they have been systematically exposed to those consequences in the past.

Social de marketing based on applied behavior analysis can be systematically related to marketing mix management by a model founded on the behavior theory that underpins that analysis, the nature of both environmentally-impacting
consumer behavior and its deleterious ecological effects. The major consumers target whose useful behaviors can be changed when they aware the
environment protection , they include transportation, energy consumption, waste disposal, water use consumers.

At the theoretical level, the purpose of the model and its developmental research program is not to supplant these or other structural approaches but to further understanding of the role of contextual influences and consumers' learning histories on their current actions as buyers and users of economic resources. The central explanatory mechanism of the model is the synomorphic consumer situation,
the meeting place of the consumer's history of reinforcement and punishment (representing the personal variables responsible for current behavior) and the setting in which purchase and consumption occur (representing the contextual influences on behavior). The former incorporates the consumer's prior experience of purchase and consumption and the effects of the consequences of these acts on the probability of their performing similar consumer behaviors in the present and future.So, when one person who is living in one environment protection awarerness is strong country, he will be influenced by its country's environment protection message to avoid to do any environment pollution behavior in every day.

Environment pollution is Social and public costs accrue to the community as a whole and not specifically to the individual consumer who is responsible for their being incurred. Consumer behaviors frequently take the form of behaviors that are damaging to the environment: e.g., seeking ever-greater accomplishments that provide
rewards and show forth one's status may result in the consumption of scarce and irreplaceable resources. Beyond a point, pleasure-seeking may also have a deleterious effect on the environment through energy consumption. Accumulation brings with it the need to dispose of packaging and, in societies marked by ever-shortening product life-cycles, the products themselves. And, finally,the consumption of the basic commodities of life themselves, such as water, now threatens further consumption by depleting stocks.

Whereas the environmentally deleterious results of the behavior are encountered, if at all, indirectly and only after a period of time has elapsed. The immediate reinforcement of behavior with ultimately deleterious effects is so great, and the aversive outcomes so remote, that the longer-term consequences can sometimes only be reduced or prevented through active self-management. The relatively open settings
in which these behaviors typically take place and their maintenance by strongly hedonic reinforcers mean that some closure of the setting has been advocated in of self-management in order to compel a degree of prosocial behavior.

Private Transportation Environment Protection awareness

Of the environmentally-impacting consumer behaviors with which applied behavior analysts have been concerned, the use of private automobiles, often carrying a single individual to or from work, falls into this category. Such behavior is apparently maintained by the fun of driving, control of one's journey - and informational reinforcement - speed, low and flexible journey times. In addition to these immediate sources of reinforcement, personal driving is powerfully maintained by apparently available on a variable ratio schedule: social approval, personal safety, simplification of journey planning routines, all of which are contingent on the performance of a number of responses that varies among situations.

In environment protection high awareness countries, private drivers attempt to modify consumers' private transportation behavior which has been intended to reduce fuel consumption, urban congestion, and pollution by discouraging unilateral use of private cars and promoting public transportation. The most successful interventions have offered in the form of financial incentives: provision of small monetary rewards for riding the bus has, for example, increased the number of users of public travel services by 50-180% . Riding the bus and other strategies which avoid private transportation (such as walking, car pooling and cycling) are at best minimally reinforced by social contact and, eventually, feelings of fitness, and informationally by cost savings. But they are punished by aversive consequences: slowness, discomfort, danger, exposure, crowding, noise, inflexibility, unpredictability, and lack of control.

Discouragement of car travel has reduced mileage travelled by between 10 and 50% (Cone and Hayes 1980). The provision of informational plays a strong role in reducing driving.While feedback alone (on the number of miles travelled, operating costs, depreciation, social costs, etc.) had no effect on mileage travelled, performance feedback influences behavior by allowing the driver to monitor his or her behavior in order to achieve the incentives.

In the marketing of alternatives to private car use, notably transportation by bus which for many drivers is likely to prove highly disruptive of their journey routines, Domestic Energy Consumption as 'Pleasure'. Among environmentally-impacting consumer behaviors, pleasure is exemplified by the over-consumption of domestic energy derived from fossil fuels, notably electricity for heating and lighting. The hedonic reinforcements are high and closely related temporally to the responses that produce them - convenience, comfort. While informational reinforcement is less obvious, social approval may follow generous use of these resources in the company of others (meanness will certainly lead to social disapproval and loss of status). The long term consequences are remote: e.g. depletion of resources, social disapproval. Consumption behaviors are apparently controlled by a variable interval schedule: comfort and satisfaction depend upon employing the source of heat or light for a time that varies from occasion to occasion with the individual's task requirements and state variables (e.g. cold, hunger).

Social demarketing should concentrate on making the behavior (including avoidance) more involving, encouraging the avoidance of high bills and a feeling of self-gratification at saving energy and reducing pollution.By increasing the costs of energy. Support for the classification of domestic energy use as pleasure and for the efficacy of this strategy comes from the attempted modification of consumers' domestic energy consumption which has used prompting, feedback, and incentives, separately and in combination. Alone, information relating to the environmental effects of pollution caused by high consumption of electricity at peak

periods
had little if any effect on peak usage. Greater effect was achieved by consumer self-monitoring of current energy usage: peak consumption reduced by up to 30% of mean baseline levels. Overall energy usage (i.e. peak and non-peak consumption) has also proved sensitive to informational feedback, even at times of steep increases
in the price of energy. Combined feedback and monetary incentives have reduced peaking by about 65% of baseline, confirming the efficacy of combined consequences.

Waste Disposal will reduce for environment protection consumers

Waste generation is a consequence of accumulation but it is actually a problem manifested in the opposite of accumulation: disposal. Indiscriminate waste disposal has relatively few hedonic benefits other than convenience but its informational outcomes are extensive if subtle: it confers status through the assumption that someone else will clear up, and it may also imply conspicuous consumption. Such behaviors are maintained seemingly on fixed ratio schedules. Their long term consequences are also remote: gradual spoliation of the physical environment, accruing social disapproval.

The findings of applied behavior analysis in this area do indeed confirm the analysis and classification. Attempts at reducing littering have relied heavily on the use of prompts. The results have been generally disappointing unless the prompts were accompanied by positive reinforcement, usually hedonic. Exhortations, lectures, and relevant general education have proved largely ineffective in this sphere. Even the attempt to reduce littering among children in a theatre by manipulating the physical environment (providing bags for waste) had little effect. Combined with messages pointing out the disadvantages of litter, the provision of bags had a moderate effect. However, when
a reward was given for each bag of rubbish, the decrease in littering was massive. Another form of hedonic reward in the form of a ticket for a movie had a similarly substantial negative effect on littering. Similar results have been found in experimental studies of the reduction of littering in streets, and around and within buildings.

Success is also apparent in the closure of the behavior setting, e.g. providing more litter bins and devising trash cans that are fun to use, and by ensuring the initial cleanliness and attractiveness of the environment; all of these strategies have had some effect by bringing behavior under stimulus control, but only the presentation of positive reinforcers in the form of payments has any dramatic effect on behavior. Prompts, used alone, have little if any effect, perhaps because of their reliance on punishment
for unapproved behavior: the individual who litters nevertheless and avoids immediate punishment is actually likely to be reinforced for his or her littering.

The relative effectiveness of prompts and incentives indicated by litter studies has been confirmed by experiments aimed at increasing consumers‘ willingness to conserve irreplaceable materials through recycling. Attempts at increasing consumers’ purchases of returnable bottles are a typical example. The use of prompts informing customers of the savings to which such behavior would lead and that they would be contributing to the fight against pollution have had mixed effects . Giving consumers small financial rewards for the reuse of such items as egg cartons, milk containers and grocery bags, accompanied by in-store prompts and a pleasant and enthusiastic reaction by salespersons, has led to increases in custom.

Some attempts at increasing consumers‘ recycling behavior have had significant punishing consequences. The Bottle Laws enacted first in Oregon and subsequently adopted by several other states impose considerable transaction, inventory and time costs on retailers who pass them on to their customers (Guerts 1986).

Both are penalized for their participation in the waste reduction campaign and, even though distributors are legally bound to comply, their consumers are in general unlikely to incur the costs involved in prepaying deposits and returning glass bottles unless they are adequately compensated for the punishing consequences of these prosocial endeavours. Experimental attempts to encourage the recovery of waste materials such as paper which can be recycled also indicate that prompts have minimal effects on behavior while the provision of hedonic and, to a smaller extent, informational reinforcers has a substantial reinforcing effect. Hence students offered prizes in contests and raffles are more likely to reduce wastage than those who are only exposed to educative prompting. The provision of convenient containers for the collection of recyclable waste is also significantly more effective than prompting on the promotion of appropriate prosocial behaviors perhaps because it achieves a degree of closure of the setting and the combination of prompts and suitable receptacles for the collection of waste has produced a combined effect on behavior greater than that expected from their individual contributions.

Domestic Water Consumption is encouraged to households useful behaviors at homes

Maintenance is exemplified as an environmentally-impacting consumer behavior by the domestic over consumption of water. The luxury and status of having water continuously available on tap are easily taken for granted but being able to drink, clean, bathe and water the garden are indicative of comparative wealth and power; they are informational benefits directly related to the consumer's state of deprivation. The consumption behaviors in question are apparently maintained on fixed interval ratios, most of the uses of water taking place at some time or other on most days or most weeks.

These methods can threaten householders abuse water useful behaviors. They include punishment, especially involving price would be especially efficacious in reducing consumption; metering, to provide general association between behavior and its contingent consequences and to provide accurate and quick feedback on the outcomes of consumption would be especially effective ; closing the setting by reducing the time and place during which water can be consumed would be effective.

A study of the conservation of metered water in Perth, Australia (Geller et al. 1982) indicates that water consumption decreased by over 30% in both an experimental group provided with daily feedback on water use and a rebate proportionate to demand reduction, and a control group provided only with feedback, though change in climatic conditions may also have affected the results. The low elasticity of demand for water makes financial rebates less appropriate than for other classes of consumer behavior.

Modification of accomplishment behaviors, exemplified here by private motoring, requires the development of a radically more attractive product with strongly reinforcing informational attributes: this may even necessitate the creation of a different product. Price may be important too, but only when the new or thoroughly revamped product has been successfully launched and established: the price of the original might then be raised to punish its use. Until this point is reached, however, such a price rise would have little overall effect on demand for the original product given the abundant hedonic and informational reinforcers it provides.

Indeed, to the extent that private transportation is a good, maintained by informational reinforcement that derives from conspicuous consumption, an increase in the costs associated with it might be counter-productive, encouraging rather than discouraging consumption. During the introductory phases of the new product, its price might be subsidized to ensure that consumers switched to its use: whether the price reduction has to be maintained indefinitely depends upon the effectiveness of the primary hedonic and informational reinforcers provided by the novel product. As far as promotion is concerned, prompts are unlikely to have a strong effect on demand, though coupled with effective consequential stimuli they provide a necessary informative and persuasive role. However, advertisements containing modelling of the prosocial behaviors advocated would probably both increase awareness of the campaign and encourage imitative responses. Finally, as far as place is concerned, the behavior setting should be opened further by increasing competition and making the new product widely and flexibly available.

Consumer behavior modification in the case of pleasure is more changed through the provision of increased, relatively rapid and regular information on consumption. This information can be seen as part of the product provided by the utilities companies. Since the overall goal of the campaign is a reduction in energy use, this must be accomplished by the encouragement of personal and domestic arrangements which promote thermal savings (e.g. better insulation, the wearing of more heat-efficient clothing and the elimination of useless energy consumption such as the illumination of unoccupied rooms). These factors, which might be considered part of the place element of the marketing mix since they determine the location of consumption, contribute to the closure of the behavior setting. Price might also be used to deter over use of resources but, given the highly hedonic consequences of energy consumption, it is unlikely to have a strong independent effect on usage.

The single most cost-effective means of reducing littering is probably the closure of the behavior setting. Since litter is itself a discriminative stimulus for further littering, the provision of bins, bags and other containers that encourage disposal is likely to have a cumulative effect on behavior. Prompting alone also has some effect on litter disposal if it is directly related to the means of acting prosocially, e.g. by pointing out what to put, where to put it and when. The behavior setting for recycling can be closed by the provision of containers for bottles, plastics, papers, and so on in convenient positions for consumers to use.

Competitions and variable person schedules appear to be the most effective means of changing behavior, especially if coupled with promotional campaigns emphasizing modelled prosocial behavior. The costs involved in some prosocial behaviors presently punish the consumer -
e.g. in the case of returning bottles and other packaging; either these costs must be reduced through the collection of waste materials or the financial recompense for their return must be expanded until behavior is economically controlled.

Finally, in the case of household water consumption and conservation, it is important to control the behavior setting by installing water-conserving methods (e.g. smaller cisterns), by encouraging the use of rainwater for garden watering, and the opportunity to use water less expensive than fully-purified drinking water for some domestic purposes such as flushing toilets. The alternative place strategies (rationing, standpipes, etc.) are politically unacceptable and usually unnecessary except during
emergencies, though metering is probably an essential prerequisite of most systems of behavior modification based on consequential stimuli whether informational or hedonic.
Price might be used to overcome overuse, though again this would be politically acceptable only within close bounds.

- Why environment and human's qualify of life and economic growth has close relationship.

I shall explain how this study confirms the invested correlation between economic growth and environmental degradation of hypothesis that is at the early stage economic growth which increases environmental degradation, then environmental degradation decreases after reaching a certain level of average income per capita. Moreover, I shall explain how other factors, such as trade openness, industrial extension also cause an increase in environmental degradation. This study also has been investigated the between environmental pollution and per capita income when have close relationship to influence economic falling down in long term.

The key indicators are used to capture the changes in environmental conditions have been developed and used in many countries. A high rate of economic growth has been a primary and permanent goal of government and society, particularly in developing countries. The increase in economic growth is related to an increase in the production and consumption of products and services. Consequently, it may lead to an increase in the multiplied products of the people and income per capita consumption. However, economic growth may produce negative impacts on the environment pollution, overexploitation of natural resources, degradation and loss of wildlife habitat and climate change. Hence, many countries have been facing the decline in environmental quality issue when which neglect to reduce environmental pollution challenge in long term.

I believe that the impact of economic growth on environment quality is categorized through three different channels: The first is the scale effect, the second is the composition and the end is the technique effect. The scale effect means to happen as pollution increases with the size of the economy, the explanation being that even of the structure of the economy and the technology doesn't change, it is assumed that an increase in the scale of economic activity leads to an increase in pollution and environmental degradation, when the composition effect refers to the change in production structure of an economy from agriculture-based to industry and service. The last effect is the technique effect, which captures improvement in the technique of production and adaption of cleaner technologies and hence a reduction in pollution

● Explaining why the Environmental Kuznets Curve key indicator method is measured to any country's economic growth and environmental pollution relationship commonly

Generally, evidence shows that some environmental pressures have diminished in developed countries, the hypothesis could generalized to the global relationship between economy and environment at all. The hypothesis is called the Environmental Kuznets Curve (EKC) hypothesis because of its similarity with the relationship between the level of inequality and per capita income is posited by Kuznet. According to the EKC hypothesis, it indicated that "at the first stage of economic development environmental pressures increase as per capita income increases, but after a critical turning point these pressures diminish along with higher income levels(Beckerman,1992)". In its most optimistic view, the hypothesis suggests that economic growth is itself the solution to environmental problems, because environmental improvement will be an almost unavoidable.

In fact, energy consumption, environmental protection and economic growth belong to an organic whole. The development of industry plays an important part in the development of the national economy. Meanwhile the development of industry spends lots of energy and makes serious pollution. Energy is a important material basis of human survival, economic development and social progress. Instance, China is promoting energy production and sustainable economic growth. We know that the environmental pollution should be the cost of economic development. Energy consumption and environmental pollution in-depth has a great practical significance for guiding the healthy development of China's economy.

The sustainable economic growth, urbanization and environmental protection in China. China has developed to become the second largest economy in the world next to USA. With fact economic growth , cities in China have been expanding and it is through urbanization to cause serious environmental problems, such as pollution of air, water and solid waste, which have imposed huge challenges to economic growth. In fact, urbanization has led to damage to the environment. So, the China environmental pollution is caused from the relationship between economic development and urbanization and then urbanization is driving economic growth. Also, the major environmental pollution is driving to China's economic growth and the major environmental problems of China are caused by urbanization in China and urbanization will cause negative consequences. However, China industrialization demands are increasing and China economic growth is also increasing, but the environment pollution is also increasing at the same time.

Another environmental pollution of country, such as Australia, its economy has grown an average of 3.3 % gross domestic product (GDP) annually the past 40 years, corresponding to an average annual GDP per capita growth rate of 1.3% (ABS, 2014). There are concerns that growth has been accompanied by excessive natural resource use and declines in environmental quality. However, economic growth can also stimulate demand for environmental quality and thus environmental policy has been enabling the development and adoption of new technologies. Whether income growth is associated with increasing or decreasing environmental quality issue for long term, which is a question that varies across environmental quality measures and economies growth. The fact is as the scale of Australia economic activity increase, environmental degradation, including increasing resource use and negative externalities tends to increase as well. On the one hand, econometricians indicated that "starting in the early 1990 year highlights the possibility that for some environmental pollutants there tends to be an inverted "U" shaped development path with respect to income, as measured by GDP, such that pollution tends to after some switching point (Grossman and Krueger, 1991)." This relationship could arise from demand side pressures (environmental quality is a normal product) or supply side pressures (technological and structural changes) . It is possible to bring the relationship between environmental quality and economic growth. On the other hand, nowadays, the conflict between economic growth and biodiversity conservation is concerned from many countries' governments. A more compelling response to the conflict is that may be resolved with technological progress. However, I review the conflict between economic growth and biodiversity conservation in the absence of technological progress. The conflict between economic growth and biodiversity conservation is based principle of ecology, such as trophic levels and competitive exclusion, the human economy grows at the competitive exclusion of nonhuman species in the aggregate. However, the conflict via technological progress has not occurred and is infeasible because of the linkage between technological progress and economic growth at current levels of technology. My supportive reason is that surplus production in existing economic sectors is requires for conducting the research and development necessary for bringing new technologies to market. Technologies also reflect macroeconomic goals, and if the goal is economic growth, technologies are less likely to be developed. As the economy grow, the loss of biodiversity may be partly mitigated with end use innovation that increases technical efficiency, but this type of technological progress requires policies that are unlikely if the conflict between economic growth and biodiversity conservation and other aspects of environmental protection is not acknowledged.

In my discussion concerns that environmental damage has not only created obstacles to economic development, but it is also posing great threats to human health and life, to ecological systems and natural world, and to the socio-cultural environments in which human beings lead their daily lives. Hence, I suggest that different countries' governments need to concern mobilization of political risk and socio-economic resources. The concept of "sustainability" was formulated as a result of the linkage between pesticide use and widespread pollution, of the effects of pollution on the health of humans and other animals and plants, and through proposal for managing resources in a way which doesn't destroy supplies of resources needed in the future. A country is considered "developing" when it is experiencing expansion of its productive capacity, the indicator is used, such as gross national product (GNP), and/or GNP per capita. The well being of all people depends largely on economic growth. However, when a country, such as developing countries Hong Kong and India both countries which populations are increasing, indeed it is difficult to imagine development without economic growth. As a result, however, nature has been scarified in the name of economic development. The pursuit of wealth and exploitation of the planet had taken place on an individualistic basic or collectivist basic, environment problems are began to cause increasing concern in growing segments of societies, mainly in the developed countries, such as India and China.

We emphasizes quality of life, but the bio centric view, gives greater recognition to the planet, regarding the pursuit of wealth through industrial expansion and economic growth as incompatible with the earth's resource base. This view also takes the position that economic growth at the expense of natural represents consumption of what belongs rightly to future generations. However, becomes human kind is seen to be living within ecological constraints, economies will have zero growth in quantitative terms. Instead growth should be measured in qualitative terms, such as clean and healthy natural environment level, in other words, on the basis of quality of living rather than standard of living. Quantitative growth may occur only in certain areas, for example, in developing countries, such as China or India and poor areas of developed countries, such as USA, but there must also be negative growth in areas which are already highly developed.

In General, the economy growth is always the attention focal point to every country. The economy growth impacts the protecting environment, on the contrary, the protecting environment also impacts the economy growth whether the environment is a factor considering the economic growth. In fact, environment not only provides the substance foundation and activity space for human, but also is responsible for production. Economic development not only enhances the integration national power and improves the people's life quality, but brings number of environmental problems, soil degradation, desertification etc.

Concerning how to reduce environment pollution and to raise economic growth at the same time. I shall have these questions to be needed to answer in order to give suggestion to solve this challenge. These questions are such as below:

- Whether does economic growth affect the environment?
- On the contrary, whether also does the protecting environment affect the growth economy?
- Whether is protecting economy and protecting environment a pair of contradiction or not what creates the environment problem?
- Is economic development incompatible with environmental quality?
- What is the effect of an increase in employment or wages on the environment in a particular industry?
- How do environmental conditions or regulations influence firm location and expansion decisions and thus economic growth in a community?

However, I feel that poverty is another factor to cause environmental pollution. Instead of factory manufacturing industry, such as India has many poor people neglect to keep natural river, ocean, hill, farming, and any public places environment to be clean and not direct to use these natural places. Solving this problem is that developing countries' economy how to increase economy under the protecting environment. Analyzing poverty and environmental pollution relationship is the focal point. We need to concern problem formulation, such as what the conflict is between developing economic and protecting environment. For example, the problem is concerned the traffic point problem, such as the environment impact of transportation has now become a global issue. Otherwise, environment impacts from transportation in the developed world are now equalized or exceeded by those in developing countries. It is given the relatively high level of car ownership and use in developing countries, such as developed country Hong Kong, which is a small Asia city, but there are many Hong Kong people who like to buy cars to drive to go to office on the roads every day. Hence, it causes much traffic jam transportation problems to Hong Kong roads every day. Otherwise, developing country, Africa. Because people are poor commonly, so there are less many own cars. The air pollution will be reduced also. However, Hong Kong has higher level of pollution to have a negative impact on employment growth due to the following reasons:

Better environmental quality attracts more skilled workers at lower wages and firms have access to whose more easily in regions where environmental quality is higher. Hong Kong has high level of pollution because Hong Kong firms attracts more skilled works to work in high technological manufacturing industry to case air or water pollution.

Production costs may be lower in regions with higher environmental quality if cleaner air and water result in lower rates of sick leaves and higher worker productivity. Hong Kong firms aim to raise worker productivity, so which uses high technological machines to raise whose productivity, but it also brings oil energy pollution to air or water.

I give a hypothesis is that higher earnings and lower employment growth rates contribute to decrease in pollution growth rates, resulting in better environmental conditions in a country. The usual hypothesis is that earnings and environmental quality are positively correlated. Since as earnings rise, the demand for environmental quality increases through an income effect, as do the public and private resources available for environmental improvement. Otherwise, increase in employment might increase pollution activities in the region, due to a scale effect. The scale effect reflects the increase in the level of economic activity in the relevant constant techniques of production and composition of final product. Hence, it seems Hong Kong income growth associated with decreasing environment quality nowadays. Because Hong Kong is lower earnings and high employment growth rates contribute to increase in pollution growth rates, resulting in worse environmental conditions in Hong Kong.

An empirical research on relationship between economic growth and atmospheric pollution was investigated to one sample developing country, such as China, which was based on the panel data analysis, the report was gathered China's economic and environmental data over 1991 year to 2010 year, it showed that there existed the long run relationship between the emission of pollutants and per capita (GDP) Gross Domestic Product to China. According to the panel estimation results from estimator, the relationship between emission and per capita GDP of China was inverse "N"-shaped. However, GDP relation of China could be considered as inverted U-shaped for the reason that per capita GDP of China of left turning point was to small. The relationship between economic growth and atmospheric pollution in China which was based by Environmental Kuznets Curve hypothesis measure method. It was seemed that Environmental Kuzents Curve hypotheses measure method might be an effective economic method to measure the indicator of relationship between environment pollution influence and economic growth to the sample research country, China. The China economic and environmental pollution sample report aimed to research whether China's economic growth would cause greater damage to regional, national and even global environment or environmental quality could be benefits from the increase of income and wealth to China. Finally, it reflected that China has have a positive impact on employment growth and economic growth, but it has also a high level of pollution at the same time nowadays. Because China is lower earnings and high employment growth rates contribute to increase in pollution growth rates, resulting in worse environmental conditions in China.

In fact, many environmental problems happened, due to many factors caused, such as (external diseconomy, regional development, strategy etc.). However, EKC (Environment Kuznets Curve) provides an alternative solution: the increase of capita income will improve environmental quality at last with the increase of income, the pollution level increases at low income level, but pollution finally reduce high income level. However, I recognize that Environmental Kuznets Curve (EKC) has this weaken point which describes an objective phenomenon, but it can't be used a rule to prove the environmental pollution and the increasing or decreasing environment quality measure absolutely.

In fact, China has not a good performance in environmental protection. It has serious air and water pollution. There is excess industrial waste gas in the air, the air will become toxic gas, which will threat health and induce many diseases. For China economic growth is evident across the country at the cost of environmental pollution in the cities (e.g. air pollution). It is the China government's responsibility to solve the conflict between the economic development and environmental protection. In general, judging from the environmental and economic report in Environmental Kuznets Curve (EKC), it can be seen that, in general, the existence of (EKC) and a few negative the (EKC). Further, the relationship between economic growth and environment pollution can be well characterized by inverted "U" sharp in a long term. But in the short term, it may appear all sorts of wave, such a "U", "N" or other shapes. However, I doubt (EKC) measure method whether is suitable for every country, especially for developing countries, such as China. As Kuznets Curve did research on income gaps, it found that income gap increasing first, and then decreasing as economies grow. The relation between the two variables is known as " Kuznets Curve" with the help of Kuznets Curve, it pointed out that there may have the inverted "u" curve relationship between environmental quality and economic development, that is the increase of economic growth and per capita income will lead to a drop in the equality of the environment in the early stages of economic development. However, once the economic development beyond a critical value point, the improvement of per capita income will help to reduce environmental pollution and to improve environment quality. So, it implied that the developing country, China if its economic development could beyond critical value point, then it is possible that it can improve its per capita income and it will achieve to reduce environmental pollution and it will improve environment quality at the same time in the future.

Further, I shall indicate another developed country, such as America whether what its relationship between bio-diversity and ecosystems and economic growth is. The findings further indicate that changes in the global economy combined with climate change, social change and increasing scarcity of ecosystem services is changing the cost-benefit analysis, so that the conservation of ecosystem services is increasing in relative value to USA. In fact, USA government is hard to focus on economic costs and benefits (direct and indirect) and non use values are intangible and more difficult for USA government to use to compare and to select over direct financial gains from degradation of the ecosystem (economic growth).

In USA farming growth sector is very large to keep it's country GDP amount per year. However, keeping clean natural environment is important to USA. Because air and water pollution can influence natural resource and crops and fruits etc. foods agricultural growing economic benefit, due to farmers can not grow many crops, e.g. rice, vegetables, potatoes, tomatoes etc. crop of foods to raise sale numbers in long term. In long term, USA will have bad influence if whose farmers can't grow any crop kind of foods to sell, due to water and air is polluted to influence good farms to let farmers grow much crops to sell to overseas or local both supermarkets or food stores. Although, the manufacturing industry sector income will be raised, but , it will also cause farming sector income and GDP to be decreased at the same time for USA.

The Environmental Kuznet Curve (EKC) hypothesis is an environmental pressure tends to rise faster than income growth in early stages, then slows down and reaches a turning point to which it tends to decline with further growth. The last phase is referred to as delinking of environmental pressure from economic growth. The EKC hypothesis points towards a trade off between environment and development, i.e. it seems to suggest that underdeveloped countries will have to forgo environmental quality of attaining a higher level of development. It further suggests that environment quality will be taken care of as developing countries attain further care of as developing countries attain further level of development. The Environment Kuznet Curve (EKC) hypothesis is summed up " at low level of development both the quantity and intensity of environmental degradation is limited to the impacts of subsistence economic activity on the resource base and to limited quantities of biodegradable wastes. As economic development accelerates with the intensification of agriculture and other resource extraction and the take off of industrialization, the rates of resource depletion begins to exceed the rates of resource regeneration, and waste generation increases in quantity and toxicity. At higher levels of development, structured and services, coupled with increased environmental awareness, enforcement and higher environmental expenditures, result in leveling off and gradual decline of environmental degradation." (Panayotou 1993). (EKC) studies are based on data of developing countries have not come out as yet, the possibility of such studies refuting the trade-off, the way of the Kuznet;s inverted "U" hypothesis was refuted by such studies that came up in 1970 year can't be rules out. Even if the trade off was valid for the past, experiences its policy implication for future of developing countries may not be very useful. An obvious policy suggestion which can be drawn from the trade off is that developing countries should focus primarily on bordering much about environmental protection in their early stages. Because growth itself will take care of environmental quality at a later stage. However, such a strategy can be mistaken (as the economic growth oriented strategy of developing countries, like India in the early planning without much effort for reduction of poverty, believing that poverty was supposed to be mitigated by trickle down effect of high grown.) Moreover, it is important to note that many components of environmental quality, such as bio-diversity are nonreversible of degradation exceeds a level. Anyway, a developing country today need not go through the same course of development on which th rationale for the EKC hypothesis has been formulated. For instance, countries like India have made the transition from a primary sector dominated economy to a service sector dominated economy without going through the phase dominated by the industrial sector. So, it seems that the developed country, USA and developing country, India income growth associated with increasing environmental quality nowadays. Because Hong Kong and India both countries are higher earnings and low employment growth rates contribute to decrease in pollution growth rates, resulting in better environmental conditions in these two countries.

Why countries need to pollute environment to develop economy, such a need for industrialization related environmental degradation in the course of economic development. A country needs and chooses to achieve industry production it can raise technological advancement and adopt technologies, which are substantially less polluting than the technologies used by countries which industry in the past. The environmental development trade off might have existed historically. But it is not bad to developing countries to scarce environment quality for industry development. Nowadays, different countries' governments need to concern how to reduce environmental pollution and to raise economic growth at the same time. In fact, human are facing these challenges, such as energy crisis is from 1970 year is precipitated by oil price jumps, market failure in allocation of environmental resources. At the same time, human are also facing economic development that meets the needs of the present without compromising the ability of the future generations to meet our own needs. Due to natural resource is limited to be supplied in the future, industry needs manufactured, human and natural is left undiminished, so this needs restricting consumption to save natural resources for asset creation and conservation and protection of the natural environment. Efforts and indicators for monitoring sustainability indicates the environmentally adjusted national income or Green Domestic Product (GNP)=NDP less depletion of natural capital-environmental damage and green national accounts indicates degradation of environmental capital is like depreciation of man -made capital. Hence, it implies environmental pollution is a damage cost to any countries. Hence, if the country can reduce or avoid the environmental pollution, then its environmental damage cost will not influence its GDP (Green Domestic Product) income amount indicator to be reduced for the country's national income in the year. Then, it's economic growth will be better in the year. Due to GDP is the country whole year income financial performance indicator. It will concern the country's economic growth level in the year.

Environmental pollution is an important issue in the process of economic growth. Instance, China has obtained remarkable economic growth with an average annual growth rate of 9.6% in gross domestic product (GDP) from 1979 year to 2004 year. Despite the impressive economic performance, the environment qualities have become worse during the past two decades. China government began to concern about to following these questions: will the high economic growth be able to sustain within environmental constraints or without exceeding ecological system? What is the effect of economic growth on environment quality? Are there any tradeoff between attaining high economic growth and protecting environment? And will the environment conditions become improved automatically at higher income level? What should the government do to the environmental degradation? When environmental sustainability, due to the increasing scarcity or overuse of renewable natural resources, arisen non renewable commodities, such as fossil fuels or industrial metals which cause problems, such as water and air pollution, atmosphere or the ozone layer. Thus these bad happening(result) have cause-effect relationship between pollution and public health.

Environmental policy aims at putting environmental resources, such as land, water, air, the atmosphere regime, with clear and enforceable rules. The tools various forms of restriction on activity: access to these resources may be limited, for example, by placing limit values on emissions or their use may be limited (by restricting the kind of activities allowed in natural habitats or drinking water reservoirs) or make subject to specific conditions (such as paying a tax or an environmental levy or the obligation to clean and recycle them after use). Rising incomes and rising pollution have brought with them a rising demand for environmental protection of policies. Market forces themselves have led to a reduction in the pollution in intensity of economic activity of the dynamic growth of the " cleaner" rates of return for local and regional pollution are closer to social rates, then for global commons. However, policy action has nevertheless been strong needed to decouple economic activity and emission levels. In fact, environmental policies cause an adjustment of economic structures. The price of using environmental resources and of exposing the public to health risks should be brought closer with social cost, with consequence that pollution and risks to public health should decline and GDP becomes less pollution intensive. Besides, polluting industries will be held in check when cleaner industries will be boosted and net effects on welfare though not necessarily on economic activity as measured in national accounts statistics. This adjustment comes at th price of fiction between regulated industries, their supplies and customers which could offset potential welfare gains. A cost effective environmental policy should aim to minimize costs incurred in achieving an environmental objective by dynamic character of adjustment needs and cost and benefit can be estimates in the absence of well functioning markets. In this way, it could contribute to significantly relaxing potential trade off between environmental protection and economic growth aim and supporting welfare enhancing structural adjustment.

In conclusion, in the future, environmental behavior change will be limited by unclear solutions and low political profile, but models of human behavior can help in understanding how to support change. I shall recommend three methods to solve environment pollution challenge to influence economic growth for long term at the same time.

The first point, it is practical for example, governments need to promote teaching behavior to let their countries' citizen to know the corrective attitude to putting rubbish to rubbish boxes in streets and to promote recycling schemes to achieve more environmentally friendly products. For example, Hong Kong have 7 million people are living in one small city. If HK citizen put their rubbish to any streets, gardens etc. public places. It will influence natural environment to be worse, then it will influence the flowers, trees plants and bees, butterflies, ants etc. insects which can not be alive, due to their natural environment has been polluted by HK citizen. Hence, human have responsibility to protect their natural environment to let any animals and plants can be alive safely and healthy. If our world could have health and good natural environment which can let human and animals and plants to be alive, then pollution can also be reduced, even our countries' economy can grow fast because product manufacturers can have good and beautiful places to let them to build their plants to manufacture their products every day, due to good natural environment will provide good places to let manufacturers to build their plants, then their workers will also have good health to do their jobs in their plants to raise their productivity and work efficiency. Hence, good natural environment and good places provision to be built plants, then workers will have good health to work, so which has cause and effect relationship closely. Manufacturers need to know their workers should not raise their productivity and work efficiency, even they will reduce their productivity and work inefficiency if their work places are polluted. The second point, economic and legislative need, for example, fines and incentives, making the polluter pays and international action, for example, debt relief international pollution control. Air pollution is the discharge of waste products into air and main sources are cargo or airplanes exhausts, power stations and industrial process as well as water pollution is the discharge of waste products into river or ocean and main sources are ferry, cargo shipping exhausts and industrial process. Thus, governments ought have legislative force to threaten the product manufacturers pollute air or water during their industrial process in their plants.

The third point, involving and empowering people, for example, local decisions and resources of allocation, such as economic decisions about the uses which should be made of land, labor and capital leading to an overall of resources, which generally matches the pattern of consumer demand. Consumer demand creates profitable opportunities for entrepreneurs to organize inputs of factors of production so as to meet that demand. In this way, the allocation of resources responds to the pattern of demand exhibited by consumers. However, the idea and the allocation of resources can be applied much more widely to a range of decision which may be taken by individual or by governments. Such as, people decide how to allocate their own resources when they choose between work and leisure or whether to save more or consume more. Also, governments make resource allocation decisions when they consider making changes to different categories of spending: they may consider whether to allocate more towards defense or education or towards health care or environment protection or unemployment benefit. However, it is not always which the allocation of resources conforms to the pattern of consumer demand. The manufacturing firms and governments can sometimes control certain aspects of the allocation of manufacture raw material resources through monopoly power or through administrative decisions. It aims to reduce natural resource waste and reduce air and water pollution issues occurrence to any oceans, rivers, lands etc. places.

The final point, different countries' governments can achieve agricultural stabilization policies, such as many governments intervene in some way in agricultural markets. In developed countries, the objective is to raise farm incomes, usually by keeping prices above the world market price, and perhaps to keep out cheap imports. This tends to raise food prices to consumers. Within the EU, most policy decisions are embodies in the Common Agricultural Policy. These policies are unpopular with food exporting countries, especially those that are also developing countries. Some developed countries sell subsidized food to very poor countries, which useful if these is a famine. But it is counter-productive when it reduces farm prices and thus poor local farmers' incomes and their incentive to increase output and productivity. So, this developing countries, governments, such as China, India etc. can allocate the limited land natural resources to give to the farmers to use to help their to grow a lot of rice, potatoes, tomatoes, vegetables or to feed many pigs, cows to keep themselves countries' farming sector long term development to earn overseas or local both GDP income and per capita farmer income for long term. Beside, they do not need concentrate on developing manufacturing industry sector income and their environmental pollution will also reduce, due to there are less lands are supplied to manufacturers to build factories to use for long term.

In conclusion, every country needs to concern how to keep economic growth and to avoid to cause environment pollution challenge at the same time. Because, which economy will not be grown, even will be fallen if their environment is polluted seriously for long term, although which economic growth will be raised for short term.

● Reference

Australian Bureau of Statistics (ABS), 2014. Australian National Accounts: National income, expenditure and product (cat. no. 5206.0). Accessed 2 February 2015. Australia from (abs.gov.au).

Beckerman, W., 1992. Economic growth and the environment: Whose growth? Whose environment? World development 20, 481-496.

Grossman, G. M., and A.B. Krueger, 1991. Environment impacts of a North American free trade agreement. NBER working paper 3914. Cambridge, MA: National Bureau Of Economic Research.

CHAPTER THIRTEEN

GDP measurement to quality of human life

Why the quality of human life can not be measured by GDP (gross domestic product) statistic method only. There have been numerous attempts to construct alternative, non monetary indices of social and economic wellbeing by combining in a single statistic a variety of different factors that are thought to influence quality of human life. The main problem in all these measures is selection bias in the factors that are chosen to assess quality of life and, even more seriously in assigning weights to different indicators (measured on a comparable and meaningful scale) to conclude a single synthetic measure. Substantive meaning and prices are the objective weights (although there are also very big problems in estimating the purchasing-power partities that have to used instead of market exchange rates in order to express countries‘ incomes in the same currency). However, some researchers have showed that human rights to identify the factors that need to be included in a quality of life measure. But, even if accepted as a starting point, that still does not point to clear to indicators or how which are to be weighted. So, a technocratic and unsatisfying device that is sometimes used is to recort to " expert opinion".

How to use life satisfaction surveys to measure human quality of life? Some researchers had been carrying on researching a methodologically improved and more comprehensive measure of qualify of life satisfaction surveys. Surveys of life satisfaction is as opposed to surveys of the related concept of happiness, are preferred for a number of reasons, such as GDP statistic method. These surveys ask people the simple question of how satisfied who are with their lives in general. A typical question is on the four point scale used to the surveys studies. For example, on the whole are you very satisfied, fairly satisfied, not vey satisfied, or not at all satisfied with the life you lead? The results of the surveys have been attracting growing interest in recent years. Despite a range of early criticism, such as cultural non-comparability, the effect of language differences across countries, psychological factors distorting responses, tests have disproved as migitated most concerns. One objection is that responses to surveys don't adequately reflect how people really feel about their life. However, responses to questions about life satisfaction tend to be promoted, non-response rates are very low. This simple measure of life satisfaction has been found to correlate highly with more sophisticated test ratings by others who know the individual, and behavioral measures. The survey results have on the whole proved far more reliable and information then might be expected to measure quality of life.

Another criticism is that life-satisfaction responses reflect the dominant view on life, rather than actual quality of life in a country. So, life satisfaction is seen as a judgement that depends on social and culturally aspects, but this relativism is disproved by the fact that people in different countries report similar criteria as being important for life satisfaction, and by the fact that most differences in life satisfaction across countries can be explained by differences in objective circumstances. In addition, it has been found that the responses of immigrants in a country are much closer the level of the local population than to responses in their motherland.

In the view point of economists, who disagree to take the survey results completely at face value and use the average score on life satisfaction as the indicator of quality of life for a country. There are several reasons. First, comparable results for a sufficient number of countries tend to be out -of -date and many nations are not covered at all. Second, the impact of measurement errors on assessing the relationship indicators tends to cancel out across a large number of countries. But these might still be significant errors for any given country. So, there is a bigger chance of error in assessing quality of life between countries if we take a single average life satisfaction score as opposed to a multi-component index. Finally, and most important reason, although most of the inter-country variation in the life satisfaction surveys can be explained by objective factors, there is still a significant unexplained component which, in addition to measurement error, might to related to specific factors, that we want to net out from an objective quality of life index.

Instead we use the survey results as a starting point, and a means for deriving weights for the various determinants of quality of life across countries, in order to calculate an objective index. The average scores from comparable life-satisfaction surveys (on a scale of one to ten) can be assembled for 1999 year or 2000 year in a multi-variate regression to various factors satisfaction in many studies. Together these variables explain more than 80% of the inter-country variation in life-satisfaction scores. The surveys showed the weights of the various factors, included health, material well-being, and political stability and security. These were followed by family relations and community life. Next, in order of importance were climate (environment factor), job security, political freedom and finally gender equality. The surveys showed that the values of the life-satisfaction scores that are predicted by nine indicators represent a country's quality of life index or the corrected life-satisfaction scores, based on objective cross-country determinants. The method also means that the original units or measurement of the various indicators can be rely on the potentially distortive effect of having to transform all indicators to a common measurement also. The survey results indicate the determinents of quality of life factors, and the indicators used to represent these factors are: material wellbeing, health, political stability and security, family life, community life, climate and geography (environment factor), job security (unemployment rate), political freedom, gender equality. However, a number of other variables were also investigates but, upward trend in average life-satisfaction scores in developed nations, whereas average income has grown substantically. However, there is no evidence for an explanation that it has relationship between increasing incomes and stagnant life-satisfaction scores: otherwise, the idea that an increase in someone's income causes enemy or disadvantage and reduces the welfare and satisfaction of others. In the researchers' estimates the level of income inequality had no impact on levels of life satisfaction , life satisfaction is primarily determined by absolute, rather than relative, status (related to states of mind and aspirations).

- GDP measurement to environment economic cost

Can GDP measure the environment economic cost ? The explanation is that there are factors associated with modernisation that, in part offset its positive impact, such as crime, and drug and alcohol addiction, a decline in political participation and of trust in public authority, the erosion of the institutions of family and marriage. In personal terms, this has also been manifested in increased general uncertainty and personal risk. These pheonomena have accompanied rising incomes and expanded individual choice (both of which are highly valued). However stable family life and community are also highly valued and these have undergone a severe erosion. The survey results also showed that four of the indicators are forecast for 2005 yar (GDP , life expectancy, unemployment rate, political stabiliy); one geography is fixed and the remaining four, which represent slow changing factors and quality of life has relationship.

Thus, the researchers implied that GDP method is not accurate to measure human's quality of life. It ought have those other different methods to measure human's quality of life, such as survey method etc. as well as income is not only one factor to influence material wellbeing of human's quality of life; there are other different variable factor to influence human's quality of life, such as health, political stability, security, family of life, community life, climate and geography (environment factor), job security (unemployment rate), political freedom, gender equality etc. factors. McGregor & Goldsmith (1998) explained that " quality is life is relative and difference between individuals, but it can be perceived as the level of satisfaction or confidence with one's conditions, relationships and surroundings relative to the available alternatives. The concept of quality of life is multifaceted. Quality of life consists of among other things: hope for the future, land, adequate food, clothing, shelter, income, employment opportunities, maternal and child health, and family and social welfare." The concept of quality of life is indeed multi-dimersional, complex and very subjective. For example, someone who has changed their consumption habit to better ensure that their choices with make a better quality of life for themselves, the environment and future generations, may be seen by others as having a lower or inferior quality of life since which have removed themselves from the materialistic mainstream characteristics of our consumer society. Someone may feel that an absence of violence and abuse in their life and natural fresh air and clean water good quality supply can lead to even though who have fewer tangible resources, money or shelter; peace of mind and freedom from abuse has increased the quality of their daily life relative to what it was like before.

Otherwise, standard of living is often equated with quality of life, but it is not the same thing. A standard of life is a way of life to which a group of people are accustomed. Some people's standard of living includes only basic food, clothing, shelter and safety. Other people expect to eat at expensive restaurants, wear designer clothes, live in huge homes and travel extensively. Different people expect and want different things, who have different standards, which are very much shaped by values, goals, money, past experience and socialization. However, standard of living are most commonly assessed in terms of annual household income levels and to a lesser extent, wealth, community assistance, family contributions, special family needs, distribution of income within the family or household and geographic location.

Thus, it seems that standard of living or GDP alone is not a good measure of quality of life and environment economic cost. Quality of life is a personal and inward looking concept that has both objective (factual) and subjective (perception) components. However, an individual's quality of life is also affected by external factors (build and natural environment; services and facilities) and this directly links quality of life to regional issues. The subjective aspect of quality of life is particularly important as if reflects how people feel about their situation and this can't be gauged from objective indicators. Subjective quality of life is often broken down into seven life domains: standard of living, health, achievements in life, personal relationships, safety, community connection and future security. For example, the measure of domain, such as standard of living includes as on income and wealth and housing aspect. The subjective measures: satisfaction with standard of living, distribution with wealth in the region, perceptions of personal income, wealth, housing affordability, housing density, green space and facilities near to homes. Objective measures may include distribution of income, welfare dependence, levels of housing stress. On health aspects, the subjective measures , satisfaction with personal health, region's health services, self assessed health status, needs and service usage. Objective measures may include services available per capita, suicide rates . It seems environment pollution factor can be one part to influence human quality of life.

Many studies of quality of life suggest that personal relations are an important aspect, or perhaps the most important aspect of quality of life. For example, Cornelia, B.F. (1999) found that change in interpersonal relations appear to contribute more heavily to satisfaction with quality of life than does either socioeconomic status or social participation. Who found that quality of life is not related of living, having choices is the productive work that you do is the most important dimension of quality of life. However, on environment aspect, rural development is most effective in increasing quality of life when it can increase diversity, both in the environment and in the economy, which can increase social capital, the norms and networks that provide for a collective identity and mutual respect. It can also increase standard of living. Efforts need to promoted standard of quality of life may have.

● GDP measurement to the difference living of quality and environment economic cost

In fact, every American community with the problem of balancing environment growth with the need to maintain environmental and social health. For example, efficient agriculture to businesses get information about new technologies to present pollution. Increasing role of quality of life and standard of living took place in countries all over the world, especially nowadays, when numerous affects of the global crisis are felt all over the world. Emerging crisis caused many problems. thereby, in the current situation, it is interesting to examine the level of the quality of life and standard of living. After short overview of general development of concepts of standard of living and quality of life. The different indicators can measure quality of life or standard of living include GDP per capita, shopping basket, GFK basket, households' expenditures, poverty rate, income inequality, life satisfaction and happiness etc. indicators. The measures show an increase in the standard of living and quality of life. Hence, if the result showed the standard of living and quality of life. The high level of human development and the results of the level of satisfaction imply that human are moderately satisfied with their lives and enjoy a rather high level of happiness.

Standard of living and quality of life have been concerning issues in countries for many years, especially nowadays, when numerous effects of the global crisis are felt all over the world. The financial security and prosperity of the economic systems disappeared. The economic storm caused rising unemployment, falling incomes, increasing rates of poverty and declines in overall well-being. Thereby, in the current situation, it is interesting to examine quality of life and standard of living. However, standard of living is defined and the level of welfare available to individual or to the group of people. It concerns products and services, people are able to consume and the resources who have access too. It depends on the quality and quantity of available products and services and the way who are distributed within the population. Otherwise, standard of living is generally determined by indicators, such as real income per person and poverty rate. Quality of life indicates to the overall welfare within a certain society, focused on enabling each member on opportunity of accomplishing objectives. Unlike the concept of standard of living, quality of life refers to not only indicators of material standard, but also to various subjective factor that influence human lives, such as natural environment pollution challenges. However, in the estimation of standard of living and quality of life their are used two types of measures, objective and subjective indicators. Objective indicators are used to determine and to explain the economic segment, when subjective indicators are used as a descriptive indicator of the noneconomic segment of quality of life and standard of living.

Many researchers were done in the field of economics, psychology, clinicial medicine, health care, phiolsophy and social science to measure whether which kind of factors can cause human quality of life to be poor. The understanding of the concepts passed through a long period of evolution. Human need natural resources have enough supply to able to satisfy their needs. It concerns the physical circumstances, such as natural environment in which people live, the products and service who are able to consume and the resources who have access to. So, the good quality of life which depends on the quantity and quality of available products and services and their distribution within the population. Otherwise, the idea of standard of living requires a macro perspective and it is generally measured by standards, such as real income per person and poverty rate. The most common measure is national output per capita, measured such as GDP or GDP per capita. Other measures, such as income inequality and life satisfaction are also used. So, it can be feeling of human intangible measure, psychological feeling to measure quality of life to human. It seems that the environmental pollution can have close relationship to influence human quality of life. Thus, quality of life can be measured by objective as well as subjective indicators. One researcher, Felce and Perry (1995) who defined quality of life is as total welfare which includes objective and subjective evaluation of physical, material, social and emotional welfare, personal development and activity, all together evaluated throughout personal set of values.

- GDP measurement to economic growth and environment economic cost

What are objective indicators of standard of living and quality of life? Objective circumstances refer to the economic and material conditions which are important aspects of the standard of living and quality of life. In the assessment, eight different indicators were used: CPI, GDP per capita, shopping basket, household's expenditures, GFIC basket, poverty rate, income inequality and HDI. However, these indicators is one number measure. It can't measure anyone's psychological feeling, such as health, safe emotion. The challenge concerns whether environmental pollution factor, such as air pollution, water pollution can cause human's health to be poor, even goes down human's quality of life and economy loss. I shall indicate some evidences to give reasons to support my conclusion why I believe that environment pollution is a factor to cause human quality of life to be poor , even it can also cause economy will encounter loss too.

In general, measure of quality of life need include human's psychological feeling indicator. I shall indicate, Hong Kong, China countries air and water environmental pollution challenges how to influence these two countries' people quality of life to be poor, even, it will cause their economy loss. Nowadays, China and Hong Kong and India and Afria are encountering health problems arising from damage to lungs, heart and blood vessels. Hong Kong and India and Afria and China e.g. Shanghai city pollution is a significant cause of premature death from cardiopulmonary disorders. Present level of pollution cause injury to the immature developing lings of children and adolescents. This damage will lead to life-long health problems in many and a reduction in life-expectancy. Although, there is no evidence from analyses of trends in pollutants that pollution measures in recent years have reduced pollutant concentrations in a way which will benefits public health.

There are clear indicators that for some pollutants. The problem is worsening. In fact, air and water pollution is Hong Kong and China and Africa etc. developing countries' the biggest cause of social and environmental injustice. It harms not only citizens today, but because its transquener national effects on the youngest members of the society, it will cause its will health effects well into the later years of this century, even environmental pollution challenge will cause these countries will encounter economy loss.

Human activities have created forms of air and water pollution, such as gases from fuels, uncontrolled emissions from fossil fuels and other chemical sources have long been recognized as a cause of ill health and premature death. For example, in December, 1930 year, a dense fog affected the Meuse Valley in Belgium. Beginning on December, 3 date, the fog intensified over three days and was associated with laryngeal symptoms, chest pain, coughing, and breathlessness. Some patients showed signs of pulmonary oedema. Overall 60 deaths were attributed to the episode. After a long investigation, the cause was considered to be emissions from high sulphur fuels, including suplhur dioxide and sulphuric acid.

What is the current threat to health? the migigration of air pollution following the introduction of clear air has been followed by a period of unprecedented economic development creating new forms of pollution from the combustion of fossil fuels. For example, to the relatively large tar laden particulates from burning dirty coal which caused episodes like the London city, UK. Smog , traffic pollution now fine with a different size and composition and gases, such as which may cause injury to the respiratory system and the effects of other pollutants. Such as particulates and drive the formation of the secondary pollutant ozone. The effects of pollution will therefore to some extent reflect genetic, environmental lifestyle and behavioral factors to develop these distance in a population together with the existing prevalence of diseases which may be polluted. Hence, living in polluted urban environments is associated with increased levels of biological markers of inflammation compared with residence in a clean air environment. The damage is caused by air pollution manifests itself through a variety of common and recognized health problems, such as upper complaints heart and lung disease. Because of this, we can use statistical methods as well as clinical studies to detect the signal of changes in health problems and increased health care demands in the population. However, doctors had proved air or water pollution can cause these both curdiovscular or respiratory disease indirectly. Curdiovscular disease includes formation of arterial plaques, coronary artery, heart attacks, irregular heart rhythm, loss of heart rate variability, high blood pressure, stroke etc. disease. Respiratory disease includes inflammation of nasal, throat and tracheal airways with acute, lower respiratory tract inflammation and infection causing bronchitis, reduction long growth and function in young people. So, it seems environmental pollution can influence quality of life to human as well as environmental pollution and illness and poor health problem has close relationship.

On the other side, environmental pollution can bring health risk, over it will influence social inequalities. Some researchers had found that the evidence has been compiled for six environmental health challenges, such as air quality, housing and residential location, unintentional injuries in children, work related health risks, waste management and climate change. It seems human need to concern air and drinking water quality, waste management and climate change how to influence our environmental pollution challenge. Although, the evidence base on social inequalities and environmental risk is fragmented and data are often available for few countries only, it indicates that inequalities are a major challenge for environmental health policies. Irrespective of development status, environmental inequalities can be found in any country for which data are available. The valid for the exposure to environmental risk factor is also unequally distributed, and this unequal distribution is often related to social characteristics, such as income, social status, employment and education, even environment risk factor can influence human's quality of life.

- GDP measurement to environment risk

However, human need to concern how environmental risk factor can influence in equal health outcomes to different groups. Such as, the first group is social determinants affect the environmental conditions of an individual and may contribute to the fact that specific individuals or population groups more often experience loss adequate or potentially harmful environmental conditions. The second group is the affected population groups could still be more exposed through e.g. the mechanism of education and health behavior. The third group is given socially disadvantaged groups could show more severe health effects of the social disadvantage is associated. The final group is social determinants affect health (what remains unclear is the relative importance of socially determined exposure to environmental risk factors). Thus, human need to concern our behavior can lead environmental pollution to influence poor health to alive. Even, we can not neglect how to protect our natural environment to be clean issue. Due to environmental non health poor issue can lead our bodies to be nonhealth and to be ill and we have no health to work to influence our job inefficiency and low productivity if we often need to see doctor to raise workload to my staffs often. Then, our employers will be probable to dismiss and many not health employee will lose jobs and unemployment ratio will raise and DP will reduce, it will influence our economic growth . Hence, we can not neglect environmental justice and environmental inequity issue, e.g. indoor air pollution and occupational or exposure to environmental tobacco smoke pollution exposure to high traffic roads or to industrial plants pollution in our society.

Surprisingly, most of above countries , among of them, although Africa is a green and natural environmental country, but Africa has encounted poor natural environmental quality to influence it has poor quality of life to its citizen and poor economy growth to its society both. Why does Africa encounter this natural environmental pollution challenge? Afican have now two potential sources of pollution: consumption and production . This looks reasonable to Africa, since maintenance is completely dedicated to improving the environment, when production generates pollution only as a " by product". Capital implies the possibility of a country being trappical in an economent poverty trap by both a bad environment and low longevity. Some countries (or regions) may even experience other time, both environmental degradation and decay in expectancy. The fact that, in some cases, environmental degradation doesn't imply lower longevity may be due to the fact that economic growth might , at the same time, worsen environmental quality, but generate additional resources that can help increasing (or preserving) longevity. However, these is also evidence of countries where environmental degradation is associated with a reduction in life expectancy. It seems worsen environmental quality will influence any country's economic growth and poor quality of life both. For example, McMichael et al. (2004) identify 40 countries that experienced a loss in longevity between 1990 year and 2001 year (26 between 1980 year and 2001), they also support that the resulting world divergence in terms of life expectancy might be explained by ".... (the growing) health risks consequent on large-scale environmental changes is caused by human pressure, by both bad environment and low longevity, biodiversity and sustainable energy".

● GDP measurement to the relationship between environmental pollution and human survival probability of life expectancy.

I shall assure human adult consumption and environmental quality has relationship to influence the future environment (green preferences) to provide human survival probability, it depends on inherited environmental quality. Thus, human will increase or decrease in the survival probability when we need a higher or lower life expectancy. In general, we depend on these environmental conditions to live, which include quality of water, air and soils etc. and resource availability, biodiversity, forestry, fisheries etc.

It is interesting to analyze different possible strategies to escape from the environmental poverty trap as well as factors that could push some economies back to a low equilibrium characterized. To research whether environment factor has relationship to influence human quality of life. We need to give idea of explaining whether environmental care has relationship to an uncertain lifetime. However, I suppose that an environmental kind of factor can be instead of being defined in terms of GDP per capita, capital accumulation etc. economic factors. Poverty is now related to environmental quality. It should be clear, however, I focus only on one specific mechanism lying behind environmental traps. Just as under development traps may be related to a wide variety of factors, ranging from financial to technological ones, including human capital accumulation and life expectancy. So, I should use this assumption to explain why it has relatively between environmental quality and life expectancy.

This " synthetic" indicator (YCELP, 2006) indicated environmental health is defined by child morality, indoor air pollution, drinking water, adequate sanitation and urban particulates and ecosystem vitality that includes factors like air quality, water and productive natural resources, A key ingredient of our setting is that survival until the last period is probabilistic and depends on the inherited quality of the environments. This survival probability affects the weight of the future environmental quality in human's utility function to achieve interest aim. Final stage, human will have optimal choices depend on life expectancy: in particular, a higher probability to be alive in the third period boosts investment in the environment and reduces consumption. In this case, a given country may be caught in a high morality/poo environment if low income is associated with a deteriorated environment.

John and Pecchenino (1994) were the first to introduce the possibility of multiple identifying, case for a poverty cause characteristic by poor economic performance and environmental degradation, however, life expectancy is assumed to be exogenous and plays no role in their model. Such as soils deterioration are the like, are all susceptible of increasing human morality (thus reducing longevity). So, the existence of both environmental performance and longevity, with countries being concentrated around two levels of environmental quality and life expectancy respectively. The two-way causes are between the environment and longevity. If the causal relationship between environmental quality and life expectancy involves the existence of an environmental poverty, characterized by both bad environmental conditions and short life expectancy.

Human life stage will encounter generations of three periods to get utility from consumption and environmental quality. During adulthood, when all relevant decisions are taken, adult can work and allocate their income between consumption and investment in environmental maintenance: consumption involves deterioration of the future quality of the environment (through pollution and/or resource depletion) when maintenance helps to improve it. The dynamics of environmental quality may also be affected by external factors on more resourced communities. The most importance, unhealthy physical environments across the region adversely affect everyone, ever though who are likely to be most concentrated in more burdened community which also have less social power to change those environments.

Why life expectancy and the environment has close relationship to influence quality of life? Life expectancy and environmental quality dynamics are jointly determined. Human may invest in environmental quality, depending on how much , we expect to live. However, environmental conditions affects life expectancy. In particular, some countries may encounter in a low life expectancy / low environmental quality. This outcome is consistent with stylized facts relating life expectancy and environmental performance measures. Some expects to live longer, who would be willing to invest more in environmental quality, because who feel which have causal link between life expectancy and environmental quality. However, environmental quality is a very important factor affecting health and morbidity: air and water pollution, depletion of natural resources and quality of life.

- GDP measurement to social and physical environmental factors and economic growth relationship

I shall indicate reasons to explain why social and physical environmental factors have close relationship to influence economic growth, even human health of quality of life. The social and economic burdens of poor education, lack of affordable housing and less than self sufficient income affect, not just those individuals and families who have the fewest resources. The social gradient means that not only do whose in the bottom worse health outcomes to bottom of income group and the top income group whose will have poor quality of life influence. The higher rates of disease and disability and lesser productivity among many communities means a higher public and private burden of life years, particularly life expectancy once one reaches age 65. In rccent decades, research and has increasingly shown how powerfully social and economic conditions determine population health and differences in health among subgroups, much more so than medical care. It seems that environmental factor can influence human's quality of life.

Los Angeles Country Department Of public Health (2016) indicated a country health rankings model, this department explained these three health factors can cause this health outcomes. These health factors include health behaviors (30%), it includes tobacco use, diet and exercise, alcohol use, unsafe sex; clinical care (20%), it includes access to care, quality of care; social and economic factors (40%), it includes education, employment, income, family and social support, community safety; physical environmental factor (10%) , includes natural environmental quality, built environmental quality. Then these factors can cause this health outcomes, such as morality (length of life):50% and morbidity (quality of life) :50%. SO, it implies that physical environmental factor can influence human's length of life. So, on our social environmental problems result is from a complex interplay of a number of forces. An individual's health –related behaviors , particularly diet, exercise and smoking, surrounding physical environment and health care (both access and quality) all contribute significantly to how long and how well human love. However , none of these factors is as important to population health as are the social and economic environments in which human live, learn, work and play. We refer to these factors can be as the social determinants of health to influence our quality of life. How do social determinants affect our quality of life? In the late 19th and early 20th centuries, public health concentrated particularly on the physical environment. Improvements in, for example, clean water supplies, healthier housing, sanitation, workplace safety and safe food lead to sharp increases in average life expectancy . Also our quality of life needed to be concentrated on expanded access to medical care, resulting in further expansion. So, the poverty tap is now characterized by those elements, such as low levels of : (i) environmental quality, (ii) life expectancy and (iii) human capital.

In fact, environmental degradation can have a significant impact on human health. De Hollander et. al (1999) & Melse & De Hollander (2001) showed that estimates of the share of environment, related human health loss are as high 5% for high income countries, 8% for middle income countries and 13% for low income countries. Air pollution and exposure to hazardous chemicals are important causes of the related burden of disease in countries. The transport and energy sectors are major contributors to air pollution, when important sources of chemical pollution are agriculture industry and waste disposal. Opportunities for reducing environment-related health risks are considerable. The benefits of many environment policies in terms of reduced health care costs and increased productivity significant exceed the costs of implementing those policies. So, the impact of environmental risk factors on health are extremely varied and complex. For example, the effects of environmental degradation on human health can range from death caused by cancer, due to air pollution to psychological problems resulting from noise. So it implies environmental factor can influence our quality of life in our societies. However, many factors can also influence human's health of a population, including diet, sanitation, socio-economic status, literacy and lifestyle.

De Hollander et. al. (1999) & Melse and De Hollander (2001) showed that total burden of disease, with estimated environment-related share expenditure, mid-1990 year. The average income group has 15 daily/1000 capita, the middle income group has 20 daily/1000 capita, the high income group has 10 daily/1000 capita. As regards both total burden of disease and the health conditions related to environmental; degradation. The result indicates the environment –related share of the burden of disease is greatly dependent on income, with higher-environmental shares generally occurring in lower-income countries.

On the one hand, it seems the large environmental share of health problems is primarily, due to factors related to poverty, such as limited to access to proper food, housing, health care and drinking water. Environmental determinants of human health in developing or developed countries are related. On the other hand, those to the exposure to air pollutants (particularly in urban areas and chemicals in the environment than to poor living conditions. Also sources of human exposure to chemicals are many and varied. Chemicals can reach the environments, for example, through emissions from industries, anti-fouling paints on marine vessels, pesticides in agriculture, waste incineration and leakage from waste disposal sites. When emissions of chemicals from industries and other point sources of pollution have lead to poor quality of life, source of chemical exposure. Intensive agricultural production uses chemicals in pesticides and fertilizer and in feed additives and medication for livestock. Residues remain in fruit, grains, vegetables, meats and daily products, all of which can reach the consumer.

Other sources of chemicals in food include bio-accumulative chemicals in the environment, such as heavy metals and persistent organic pollutants, which can be found in fish, meat and dairy products. So, environment pollution can influence human need to eat bad or unhealthy food to cause we have poor quality of life to live, such as the high income group or middle income group or low income group of families in our societies fairly. Other human health risks that have recently received considerable attention include unsafe livestock feeding practices through which toxins reach the food chain unintentionally. Dioxins that have accidentally contaminated poultry feeds that contain diseased animal remains can cause the so-called " mad cow disease" in livestock which has been linked to a new form of disease. The effects on health from exposure to chemicals and air pollutants vary from allergies to cancer. Although, the link between exposure and disease is often not clear, Even at low exposure levels, urban are pollutants can cause, asthma, allergies, respiratory diseases and cardiovascular disease if the exposure is continuous or long term. Heavy metals have been shown to cause neurological disorders and various cancers. In addition to , physical diseases, environmental contamination can also cause psychological problems. Noise, one of the determinants of the quality of urban life can have an impact on human health, decreasing the quality of life and potentially contributing to depression.

For Ireland, UK country example, this country politicians and policy makers believe the role of environment can be used to measure quality of life, concerning on either in its own right or relative to economic and social aspects of quality of life. Agreement on what measures quality of life and how it can be measured by the role of environment, not just in Ireland, but everywhere. The conventional approach is used for policy has been to use measure of gross domestic product(GDP) or regional valued added. However, it is acknowledged that such conventional economic measures have only a partial relationship with societal wellbeing. To the extent that economic measures are related to public products and consumption, there are also pressing issues in relation to public products and the sustainability of economic growth. However, the role of environmental factor can influence resource use and human's behavioral consumption.

Aspects to quality of life other than income include the environment, freedom, health, working condition, leisure, social and family relationship. Economists don't deny that these factors do play a role in quality of life. However, environment factor can be one role to influence other factors to influence our quality of life to be good or bad effect. For example, locations which might be desirable as paces to life (in terms of income earning opportunities or other factors) were also likely to have higher costs of living, particularly with regard to house prices or health or unhealthy air/water pollution of environment situation of the place to provide human to live. Alternatively, social indicators are based on normative ideals of literacy, low rates of premature mortality or a quality environment. Other measurement of people's personal evaluation of their quality of life, much depends on personal expectations and experience.

- GDP measurement to the relationship between environmental pollution and house price.

I shall indicate that why environmental factor will influence any country's house price. For Ireland example, citizen average incomes and higher in the east of the country, house prices are lower in the west, who are also more able to afford a property of choices. There are more opportunities to purchase houses, where people own their own houses, who are more likely to have benefits from an appreciation is its value and to consequently perceive a higher degree of health. Generally, levels of property appreciation have been higher in the east. Unfortunately, young people and the more economically active segment of the population are more likely to be faced with rising entry level house prices and the prospect of large borrowings. So, the quality of life, such as education, crime and access to healthcare and living environment are not uniformly better in the west or the east regions. Indeed, many measures of social disadvantage are at their worst in the west regions. Some indicators of environmental quality are , indeed better in the west regions, but there are others, such as drinking-water quality or recreational access that are often worse.

Comparisons can often be reduced to an urban-rural dimension rather than a regional one. Factors such as incomes, house prices, crime levels, air pollution and congestion are all likely to be higher in urban areas in Ireland city, UK country. Why environment and housing price has relationship in Ireland to influence quality of life to its citizen? If Ireland's regional development policy is successful , it will bring with it greater competition in the housing market and greater pressures on the environment in Ireland. Because the forest will be decreased to build house, the natural environment will become wood and steel and stone of housing built environment. In fact, it appears that there is a fair of amount of agreement on the relative rating of factors influencing quality of life. Ability to own one's home and security of income were needed, but respondents also placed almost equal important on clean air and drinking water, low crime were differences. The Ireland's rural respondents appeared to place a slightly greater emphasis on key natural environmental attributes, when urban residents valued absolute incomes and social or leisure activity rather more.

In this respect, the analysis identifies three components to Ireland people of quality of life, each of which was evident in all three locations. There components can be broadly described as domestic security, social/leisure and aspects of the planned environment. The first of these includes indicators, such as security of income, absolute income, house ownership and low crime. As this component includes air and drinking-water quality, it suggests that these indicators may be associated with personal health and well-being. When the planned environment component includes those attributes that affect quality of life over which the authorities have a direct influence, for instance, a clean environment, traffic and reducing vehicle numbers on the roads in busy time.

● GDP measurement to relationship between environmental pollution and social welfare

Environmental quality has an undefined impact on quality of life and various indicators are used to show regional variations in aspects, such as water quality . There are many measures of environmental quality , but is only for quality of life. Moreover, the measurement of societal welfare is important. Societal welfare is not simply , the sum of the parts, but varies depending on the individual in which people find themselves at any time in their life. In principle, it should be possible to apply weights to each element of societal welfare, but as preferences for each of these vary within the population. In the absence of a method with which everybody is satisfied, GNP and GDP are typically the most popular used measures for quality of life or standard of life. But, these are problems with the data itself to measure quality of life because quality of life is feeling or satisfaction of level to the country's citizen and it can not be seen by numbers or statistic method. For example, GDP ignores household production, such as the effort that goes into the rearing of children, the benefits that this provides for society and the public expenditure that is avoided. Neither are costs treated equally with the benefits. GDP counts all economical activities irrespective on pollution appears to increase. GDP even through it is a degree of double counting. Otherwise, environmental products are good to be measured to quality of life. For example, many environmental products are unpriced. Consequently, environmental products that people value, or which are critical to the sustainability of development, are abused or depleted because of their public products have good characteristics and the absence of a market price signal.

Environmental economists try to work within the economic model to measure quality of life. Rather than questioning the link between utility and consumption or choice, the preferred approach is to add an element into the utility function that represents the value of environmental products or the stock of natural capital. By one means or another , the preservation value of these environmental products is estimated in terms of willingness to pay to protect the environment or as willingness to forego other products in return. It seems the quality of people's environment can be represented by objective indicators. At another, their interpretation will vary and can be represented by subjective indicators.

Objective indicators come in two forms: (i) economic indicators and (ii) social indicators. The former depends on an ability to select the products and services that are desires, in other words, the satisfaction of preferences . The economic argument is that people select the best quality of life, who can obtain commensurate with their resources and personal desires. By comparison, social indicators are based on normative ideals on what could be considered the food life. For example, would be infant morality, literacy, crime rates and social indicators are objective measures. Both have guided, much of the research on quality of life, particularly concerning with the urban environment. Quality of life can include natural a significant influence on local quality of life, for instance, natural beauty spots used for recreation.

For environmental quality concept, it concerns with health, safety, wellbeing, residential satisfaction and the physical sustainability can be considered to result from an when live ability can be considered to represent the interaction between the physical and the social domains. As with expenditure on the environment, investment in social capital contributes to quality of life. However, the benefits will again vary amongst individuals, depending largely on the security of their individual circumstance. As with the environment, the government can certainly adopt strategies that provide for public security by taking measures to reduce crime, a measure likely to be appreciated by everybody (except criminal) , at least to one degree or another. In other necessary to enhance social interaction, namely community centers or sports facilities. Furthermore, the creation of social capital has an statement which responds to general social trends to raise Ireland citizen's quality of life.

I shall indicate Ireland to explain whether environmental factor is the main factor to influence our quality of life and economic growth. Is environmental quality higher in the Ireland west regions? And if so, does this compensate for lower incomes in these regions? Is it bad that rural areas are characterized by higher costs of living in areas other than housing by environmental factor? In fact, in Ireland , UK country, population increase has a direct impact on the environment by placing demands on local natural resources, particularly open space and water. It also leads to a sense of crowding that reduces the utility associated with access to the environment. How can environment factor influence economy growth in Ireland? In Ireland, agriculture has gone through a period of significant change that has been accelerated reductions in the amount of mixed cropping and traditional land management. Indeed, changes in the expectations of young farmers will ensure that further change is likely to be characterized by increases in farm size and greater specialization with implications for landscape and wildlife. These characteristics of farm holdings are more familiar in the east regions of Ireland , UK country. As with likely to extend to the west regions as the older generation of farmers retires, although this will probably be accompanied by a trend to more farming of production needs to young farmers. So, good natural environment can provide Ireland young farmers to produce more agriculture to earn income, even who can export more rice, fruits, vegetable etc. agriculture foods to overseas. Hence, Ireland GDP will be raise if it can have good natural resource environment to provide Ireland young farmers to grow foods to sell to domestic and /or foreign agricultural market. Given the rate of economic growth, and its concentration in the east of the Ireland, UK country, it would be easy to presume that the quality of the environment is higher the further away from the mid east one goes. Thus, good natural environment is an important factor to influence the farming industry development in Ireland , UK county to satisfy their needs and to raise their quality of life nowadays.

I shall indicate New Zealand and America two developed countries to explain why which are facing environmental pollution challenge to influence their citizen's quality of life and economic growth nowadays. The first country is NZ, although, New Zealand is a developed and natural environmental country, but it had been envountering air pollution annouance and noise annoyance to influence it's citizen's health-related quality of life. I shall indicate why which has this relationship between of them in New Zealand. Nowadays, New zealand population growth is an increasing demand for consumer products and urbanization have lead to concerns over the lived environments in many of the world's cities, such as Auckland, wellington cities in New Zealand. However, environmental quality is an important determinant of health, such as the bad influence of traffic-related air and noise pollution on health outcomes, specially with respect to at risk groups, both in relation to long term exposure as well as acute effect, from brief exposures. For example, cholesterol levels and in relation to myocardial infaction. Nowadays, New Zealand is encountering the high degree of air pollution and noise annoyance to influence it's citizen's quality of life. Air pollutants can be detected either visually, such as witnessing smoke emanating from a vehicles's exhaust, or by smell, such as when odorants stimulate olfactory receptors. The evidence linking air pollution to adverse impacts on human health.

Many air impacts on human health. Many air pollution health studies have focused specifically on urban area, and vehicle generated pollution in particular, as road vehicles are one of the major sources of pollution across much of the world. Elemental carbon, Nox and ultrafine particles an considered to be pollutants most strongly associated with road traffic emissions. In Auckland and Wellington cities, New Zealand , it has been estimated that 71% of summer and 21% of winter concentrations of fine particulate matter is attributable to motor vehicles. Moreover, poor town planning decisions in Auckland (and in New Zealand in general) over many decedes has meant that may people live in very close proximity to busy road and motorways within " road corridors" and so are the adverse effects of road traffic, including noise and air pollution as well as experiencing on potential for degradation in their quality of life. Such as, New Zealand is highly suitable for studies investigating the impact of roads on the health of its residents. For example, NZ, road traffic noise and aviation noist has been linked to cardiovascular disease, hypertension and ischemic heart disease. It influences NZ resident personal psychological and physical both health challenges. In fact, NZ noise increases morbidity and mortality independently of air pollution exposure, though air pollution constituted a greater burden of disease when arise exposure had a greater impact on quality of life, e.g. NZ road traffic noise and air pollution will be caused from drivers in busy time. Specially in Auckland and Wellington cities. It will influence urban and rural environmental pollution. Some retired old people who will feel annoyance when this road traffic occurs in Auckland or Wellington cities to close to their houses in transportation busy time every day.

Next developed country is America, this country's air pollution is also serious nowadays. Because traffic jam often occurs in New York, Washington, Boston etc. big cities in US. So, U.S. cities' parks and its trees have significant influence to produce fresh air to provide U.S. residents who are living in cities to breach for their body health. David

J. & Gordon , M. (2016) indicated " In U.S. these urban parks are estimated to contain about 370 million trees with a structural value of approximately $300 billion." The number of park trees varies by region of the country, but which can produce significant air quality effects in and near parks, related to air temperatures, air pollution, ultraviolet indication and carbon dioxide (a dominant greenhouse gas related to global climate change). Additional open space and other vacant lands in cities, which may contain trees and other vegetation. Contribute significant additional benefits, effects of parks and open space at the city scale can vary significantly depending on the amount of parkland and amount of tree cover within the parkland.

The reasons why parks can reduce air pollution. Parks generally have lower air temperature than surrounding areas. Temperatures are usually cooler toward the center of a park than around its edges. At night, the center of a large park may be 13 degree cooler than surrounding city areas. The cooler air from parks often moves out into adjacent developed neighborhoods. This cooling of surrounding areas tends to increase with park size and percentage of the park covered by trees. So, cooler air temperature is provided by urban parks can have significant impacts on human health. During heat wave events, which can kill hundreds of people, park areas may provide city dwellers with some respite from high air temperture, particularly in the evening, during hot, sunny days tree shade can greatly increase human comfort. Because park influences on air temperature extend to developed areas outside of parks, local energy use for heating and cooling buildings is also effected. Although, the net around effect of parks on energy costs has been by reducing temperature is difficult to estimate at least in the southern United States the effect will usually be a net annual benefit. Furthermore, large park trees will reduce winds and may provide a benefit of winter heating of buildings near the park. Although, the overall economic effect of urban trees and parks on air temperature reduction is not fully billions of dollars annually at the national scale in terms of improved environmental quality and human health.

In fact, trees and vegetation in parks can help reduce air pollution both by directly removing pollutants and by reducing air temperatures and building energy use in and near parks. There tree effects can reduce pollutant emissions and formation. However, park vegetation can increase some pollutants by either directly emitting volatile orgnic compounds that can contribute to ocone and carbon monoxide formation or indirectly by the emission of air pollutants through vegetation maintenance practices, such as operation of chain and use of transportation fuels. David J. & Gordon , M. (2016) showed "Annual pollution removal and economic benefits by U.S. urbank park trees is estimated at about 75,000 tones ($500 million) or 80 pounds per acre of tree cover ($300 per acre of tree cover). Carton storage and annual removal by urban park trees and soils in the United States is estimated at about: carton storage trees: 75 million tons ($1.6 billion), carton storage (soils) : $102 million tons of carbon removal (trees): 2.4 million tons ($50 million)". Park management is recommended by U.S. environment protection department: considering that most of the effects of trees on microclimate and air quality are beneficial for park users and nearby residents; park designs that include a variety of land cover, areas of dense trees, scattered trees and lawn are likely to provide the greatest opportunities for optimum physical comfort of visitors; increase the number of healthy trees (increase pollution removal and carbon storage); sustain existing tree cover (maintains pollution removal levels) and (carbon storage); maximize use of low volatile organic compound emitting trees reduces ozove and carbon monoxide formation; sustain large, healthy trees (large trees have greatest per tree effects on pollution and carbon removal); using long-lived trees (reduces long term pollutant emissions from removal; reducing fossil fuel in maintaining vegetation reduces pollutant ans carbon emissions)." So, if US had many green parks, then which can reduce air pollution, also it can assist many travellers who prefer to travel to US to raise GDP travelling income growth generally.

ON conclusion, the environment pollution issue will bring negative impacts to influence some environment protection countries consumers behaviors change significantly as well as it also bring poor economic growth to these environment pollution countries, e.g. GDP income reduces because these environment protection countries' consumers will reduce consumption desires when they discovered that they will cause our earth environment is polluted seriously because they only consider enjoyment and entertainment, and

neglect how to protect our environment. So, it will bring impact to the environment protection countries' consumers behaviors and reduced their living of standard absolutely.

● Reference

Cornelia, B.F. (1999) Rural development news, the North Central Regional Center For Rural Development vol. no 24 , IOWA.

David J. Nowak & Gordon M. Melsler (2016) " Air quality effects of urban trees and parks." National recreation and park association, USA.

De Hollander, A. E. M., J.M. Melse, Elebret & P. G.N. Kramers (1999), " An Aggregate public health indicator to represent the impact of multiple environmental exposures" Epidemiology: 606-617.

Felce, D. and Perry, J. (1995). Quality of life: A contribution to its definition and measurement, vol. 16, no.1 pp: 51-74.

Los Angeles Country Department Of public Health (2016), Country Health Ranking Model, Retrieved From www.countryhealthrankgings.org/our-approach. USA.

Melse, J.M. & A.E. M. De Hollander (2001). " Human Health And The Environment", background document for the OECD Environmental Outlook, OECD, Paris.

McGregor, S.L. T., & Goldsmith, E.B. (1998). Expanding our understanding of quality of life, standard of living and well-being. Journal of family and consumer science, 90(2), 2-6, 22.

McMichael, A.J. M. Mckee, J. Shkolnikov and T. Valkanen (2004), " Morality trends and setbacks, global convergence or divergence?", Lancet 363, 1155-1159.

Yale Center For Environmental Law And Policy (2006). Environmental Performance Index. Data available on-line at http://epi.yale.edu

Reference

Cone, J. D. and Hayes, S. C., (1980) Environmental Problems/Behavioral Solutions. Monterey, CA: Brooks/Cole.

Erekson, O.H., Loucks, O.L. Strafford, N.C. 1999.
The context of sustainability . In: Sustainability
perspectives for resources and business
USA, p. 3-21.

Daly, H.E. 1990, Towards some operational
principles of sustainable development,
ecological economics, 2(1), 1-6.

Guerts, M. D. (1986) "The ‘bottle bill’ effect on grocery stores‘ costs," International J ournal of Retailing, 1, 12-17.

Kirkby, J; O’ Keefe P., Timberlake, L. (eds.) 1995.
The earthscan reader in sustainable development.
Earthscan Publications Ltd., London, 1-14p.

Skinner, B. F. (1953) Science and Human Behavior, NY: Macmillan.

Winkler, R. C. and Winett, R. A. (1982) "Behavioral interventions in resource conservation: a systems approach based on behavioral economics,"
American Psychologist 37: 421-435.

CHAPTER FOURTEEN

Behavioral and environmental economic prediction to traveler and energy user behavior

How and why can we apply environmental and behavioral economic methods to predict consumer behaviors? Environment and economics has close relationship to influence consumer behaviors. For example, one of the prime reasons for climate change, global warmth factor influences energy consumer's , e.g. householder, drivers, business office energy users etc. different stakeholders useful behaviors at home, offices, driving etc. different modes of energy uses. Because human begins to feel environment protection needs to avoid to use waste of energy in any time. It has a link between the burning of fossil fuels and global warming relationship to impact human how uses natural resource energy every day. It means that reducing energy to use to avoid global warmth crisis to bring threat for the environment protection energy users. So, their energy consumption desire will be also influenced to reduce, e.g. driving less vehicle, turning off home light when the householder feels that he does not need to turn on light, turn on fans, turn on air conditions etc. electricity waste behaviors at homes. For example, US energy users begin to feel energy waste will bring global warmth negative effect in possible to influence their daily lives to be worse. They have predicted that, should global temperatures continue to increase, within decades the polar ice-caps could melt, potentially raising sea levels, around the world and flooding major including New York, London. Further feared outcomes include the shutdown of the Gulf Stream across the Atlantic, which some claim could seriously disrupt the climate in Northern Europe. So, many US people and UK people begin to avoid to waste to use any energy at homes, at offices, less time to drive cars on roads etc. different kinds of energy useful behaviors in energy consumption view.

According to Sir Nicholas Stern, a UK economist who authored one of the first reports on the eventual costs associated with climate change could mount to around 20% of global gross domestic product, around $6 trillion compared with costs of just 1 % of GDP to tackle the threat now. So, environment production energy consumers will reduce to waste much energy daily and it will influence the energy consumption GDP income to reduce to any countries in the future. It is only technological innovation can be applied to help human to avoid global warming in possible if one day , new technological innovation can be invented to avoid global warming, then the energy consumption GDP income will have increasing chance because the environment protection consumers won't feel waste energy consumption to bring global warming crisis and they will accept to increase energy use again in daily living in possible. For example, during Victorian times in London, one of the main fears of the population was the concern that as the city grew, and with it the number of horses on the streets, the English capital would eventually become buried in a pile of horse manure, such as outcome never transpired because of the birth of the motor car (new technological driving tool invention). Similarly, there is much evidence to suggest that new technologies, whether hydrogen-powered motor cars, nuclear –fusion generators or carbon –capture facilities to allow clean burning of coal, will help solve the crisis without subtracting significant economic growth from today's generation. So, if scientists can invent one kind of environment protection energy to let human to use, then human will accept to use much this kind of energy to instead other kinds of pollution energies and the GDP on energy income will also raise in possible.

Hence, climate change is an example of market failure. It is the worst market failure to influence any energy users' daily energy useful behaviors to be changed to less energy consumption behaviors. In a properly functioning market, the price of something goes up when its supply falls or demand for it rises, this is a key element of the invisible hand theory. So, when human feels that more waste to use energy , this waste energy useful behavior can bring environment pollution more seriously , then it will bring the energy demand is reduced and it will influence energy price goes down because demand is less and supply will also need to reduce as the same time in economic view point. However, because until very recently there was no price put on either fresh air or pollution how have relationship to influence energy price variable to less in energy consumption market. But, the actual implied cost of pollution is very high, if pollution caused more desertification and higher sea levels, any lays waste to towns and cities, it will come at a great price variable influence to energy consumption market. But, it is only since scientists realized the potential of climate change for environment pollution influence to prove that they have possible relationship to waste energy useful effect. In theory, the price of combating climate change ought to be what people are willing to pay in order to ensure that they and their children have clean air and water in the future. So, environment protection people will reduce to waste to use energy to avoid this issue occurrence.

How and why behavioral economics can predict consumers' daily behaviors change. Experience shows that people are by no means consistently rational. Such as one smoker will reduce to smoke suddenly, the reasons may include health factor, air pollution factor, cigarettes price increasing factor, income reducing factor, living habit changing factor, family and friend bad relationship factor to influence whose smoking behavior. So, their emotion will be influenced to be poor and it can bring the smokers' smoking behavior changes to be influenced to less smoking. It is good example to make them act irrationally.

Behavioral economic investigates why and how people act irrationally. It is among the newest and most fascinating are as of academic study, combining economics and psychology and it is an understanding develops as to how the mind and the brain work, so behavioral economists are providing greater insight into what really drives people to act.I shall explain economists can apply behavioral and environmental economic to predict energy consumers' behavioral changing as below:

If the economic process consists of temporarily re-arranging some of the earth's resources, energy is what brings about the characteristics that change of scope. Nowadays, human begins to feel where the use of the world energy has become careless, such as drought and the energy crisis. Although this issue is not tangible commodity, but this issue can let human to feel the worse pollution brings to air and water pollution, drought natural environment damage if we still waste to use energy daily.

To understand the role of energy how acts in economic process. I indicate this example, for one farmer , he has arranged the scope of his economic process in such as a way that he requires energy in high density forms. The reason is fundamentally that he requires much of it for eventual transformation into motion, whether for transport or in fixed installations. The farmer concern how he use energy for his farming activity which it is easily carried either with him in his hand farming tool using or farming agriculture machine tool using method. It needs to be in a concentrated and tangible form to choose either of one method. Whether the farmer consider the environment pollution issue if he use any farming machines to replace hand tools to work in agricultural daily tasks aspect. If the farmer feels that farming machine can bring air pollution more easily, then he will choose to do farming tasks by hand, although he feels hard and spend long time to do farming tasks, but he can protect our earth to be polluted by the dirty air. So, energy need must be reduced when the farmer decides not to use farming machines to work on much time., even he does not choose to use farming machine to work on farm. Consequently, oil or electricity need will reduce to the farmer. It is one good example how air pollution influences energy consumers' behavior.

Then, environment pollution will also influence energy suppliers' market behavior changes, e.g. when they discovered that oil or electricity demand is less, then they will reduce supply number to keep price does not need to reduce or goes down prices if they still keep the same oil or electricity suppling level in economic supply and demand theory. They need to make the better decisions on how to reduce the oil or electricity supplying level to avoid the price reducing result. So, the environment pollution issue will influence the oil, electricity suppliers' price changes and supplying number changes in possible. Hence, behavioral economic view, it also explain that environment pollution can influence economic organizations need react in predictably irrational ways when they feel that environment pollution issue is the important factor to influence oil and electricity need to be reduced at the moment.

Moreover, energy shortage will influence products need, such as car industry. Because oil or gas will have shortage problem. When scientists do not real invent another new energy to instead them to use on cars. But, since the electric cars invention, it can replace the traditional cars, it can use electricity to replace oil and gas resource and it is one kind of environmental protection new energy to reduce air pollution. SO, when global drivers can accept to drive electric cars on roads , then the electrical cars need will also increase and its supply will also increase in global vehicle industry. So, the electricity need will also increase when one day global cars are used by electrical energy. So, environment pollution issue can also influence car manufacturers choose to manufacture many electric cars to prepare to sell if they believe that artificial intelligent or non manual driving and electric cars are accepted to drive on roads in popular. Although, electric cars prices are not cheap nowadays, but when human feel global warming, air pollution crisis will damage our natural environment and cause food shortage crisis. Then, electric cars number will not be influenced to demand less ,even its price is higher than traditional oil energy form cars. So, the inelastic price change will be future electric cars market characteristics. I suppose that electric car buyers will not be an irrational decision buyers in common.

Moreover, environment pollution will influence travelers travelling needs because when one traveler feel that his travelling times and long journey number can influence air pollution when the air plane needs much oils or gas energy to fly long time on sky. Then, the environment pollution awareness can influence his catching long time flying number to be reduced. Consequently, the airlines' freight travelling journey time and flying number will also reduce when many travelers begin to reduce to choose long journey and reduce travelling number. Then, the oil or gas needs on airline will reduce , even the oil and gas price will also reduce because oil and gas demand on airlines industry , it is reduced. If the oil or gas supplier does not hope to reduce price , due to the oil or gas demand on airlines is reduced, it can choose to reduce the supply to airlines . Hence, on environmental and behavioral economic view, environmental pollution may influence oil/gas suppliers' income and it can change any consumers who need to apply oil or gas energy to enjoy their entertainment activities to change to less really.

● Household energy use: Applying behavioural economics to understand consumer decision-making and behaviour

Household energy conservation has emerged as a major challenge and opportunity for researchers, practitioners and policymakers. Consumers also seem to be gaining greater awareness of the value and need for sustainable energy practices, particularly amid growing public concerns over greenhouse gas emissions and climate change. Adequate knowledge of how to save energy and a professed desire to do so, many consumers still fail to take noticeable steps towards energy efficiency and conservation. There is often a sizeable discrepancy between peoples' self-reported knowledge, values, attitudes and intentions, and their observable behaviour—examples include the well-known 'knowledge-action gap' and 'value-action gap'. But neither is household energy consumption driven primarily by financial incentives and the rational pursuit of material interests. In fact, people sometimes respond in unexpected and undesirable ways to rewards and sanctions intended to shift consumers' cost–benefit calculus in favour of sustainable behaviours. Why is household energy consumption and conservation difficult to predict from either core values or material interests? By drawing on critical insights from behavioural economics and psychology, we illuminate the key cognitive biases and motivational factors that may explain why energy-related behaviour with either the personal values or material interests of consumers. Understanding these psychological phenomena can make household and community responses to public policy interventions and it can help us design more cost-effective and mass-scalable behavioural solutions to encourage renewable and sustainable energy use among consumers.

Consumer behaviour is complex and rarely follows traditional economic theories of decision-making. When

choosing what products to buy or what services to use, people often think they are making smart decisions and behaving in ways that are highly rational and congruent with their values and intentions. However, in daily life, people routinely deviate from the 'rational choice' model of human behaviour, in which one objectively weighs up the costs and benefits of all alternatives before choosing the optimal course of action. But neither is human decision-making reliably predicted by what people know is the 'best' or feel is the 'right' thing to do. For example, so-called 'green' knowledge and values – such as knowing about or feeling positive towards the use of renewable resources, sustainable products, low-emission technology, public transportation, and so forth – do not reliably translate into pro-environmental choices when buying goods or using services that impact the environment. Many people still rely heavily on non-renewable resources, under-use public transport, fail to recycle, and engage in other everyday actions that harm or neglect the environment—actions they may themselves acknowledge as 'wasteful' Even consumers who face strong material incentives, and/or possess knowledge and motivation patently sufficient to act in more sustainable ways, may struggle to shift their behaviour in the desired direction, particularly over the longer term.
To understand why and how pollution influences energy consumer useful behavior. First, it is clear we need to know what people say and what they do are sometimes very different things. In many domains of human behaviour, we see a knowledge-action gap. For example, people may know about, intrinsically value, hold positive attitudes towards, and/or genuinely intend to act in some socially desirable way. Yet often these things do not translate into actual behaviour. One domain of consumer behaviour where this disjuncture is evident is residential energy use. Many people report that they are concerned about climate change and understand the importance of saving energy, yet this concern does not reliably translate into taking ongoing, practical steps to reduce household energy consumption. It is perhaps unsurprising, then, that traditional education programmes and mass media campaigns – which strive to promote pro-environmental knowledge and attitudes by simply disseminating information.
At the same time, it is also clear that people's behaviour does not generally fall short of their environmental concerns and commitments simply because they are pursuing material interests and extrinsic rewards. Even where energy-saving measures are demonstrably cost-effective (e.g., insulation, low-carbon technology) – making uptake of the technology or behaviour economically rational for the consumer – many people remain reluctant to introduce these things into their lives and homes. In fact, offering extrinsic rewards and financial incentives to encourage pro-social behaviour (e.g., volunteering, reciprocity, civic duty, charitable donations, or other 'public good' contributions), presumably by prompting more favourable cost–benefit appraisals, can sometimes backfire and decrease the desired behaviour by 'crowding out' intrinsic motivation to act altruistically.Though not reliably predicted by either environmental concerns or material interests, individual choices around pro-environmental behaviour and resource consumption are, in fact, predictable—. As with much of human behaviour, energy-related practices are often influenced by certain cognitive biases and 'irrational' tendencies that, while producing decisions and actions that may be surprising from the standpoint of traditional economic models, are actually rather predictable (and even adaptive/functional) from the perspective of psychology and behavioural economics.

- Applying psychology and behavioural economics to explain, predict and change consumer behaviour

Traditional economic theory postulates that human decision-making and behaviour are based on purely rational choice . More recent neoclassical economic approaches also rest on several fundamental assumptions aligned with rational choice theoy, that people have rational preferences among outcomes, always strive to maximise utility, and act independently based on full and relevant information. Based on these assumptions, traditional economic models predict that people will make decisions that yield the optimal result given budget constraints, and that behavioural choices can be improved by providing people with more information (i.e., by increasing knowledge/awareness) and/or more options (i.e., by increasing choices).

In contrast to such assumptions, a growing body of scientific research demonstrates that people are rarely the rational decision-makers envisaged by traditional economic models of human behaviour. Empirical evidence from psychology and behavioural economics shows that consumer choices and actions often deviate systematically from neoclassical economic assumptions of rationality, and there are certain fundamental and persistent biases in human decision-making that regularly produce behaviour that these assumptions cannot account for. Hence, to understanding energy consumption, especially in terms of predicting and changing the behaviour of individuals and households. Among the most powerful and pervasive biases to influence consumers' patterns of energy usage include the status quo bias, loss and risk aversion, sunk-cost effects, temporal and spatial discounting, and the availability bias. In parallel, psychological phenomena such as normative social influence, intrinsic and extrinsic rewards, and trust may also play a key role. A large body of research shows that even where cost–benefit calculations would suggest more materially advantageous choices, people persist in displaying seemingly irrational. For example, people tend to resist change and 'go with the flow' of pre-set options, even where alternatives may yield better (e.g., more financially rewarding or materially advantageous) personal or collective outcomes. Providing a default not only saves people time (by relieving them of having to make an active choice), but it might also be viewed as the best option (since it is apparently being 'recommended' by the provider. Evidence of this status quo bias has been observed across a range of experimental and applied contexts, including residential energy consumption. For another example, people typically process only enough information to reach a satisfactory decision rather than processing all available information to reach an optimal decision, as the latter demands much more time, effort and resources than would ordinarily seem justified by the prospective increase in utility or satisfaction. Yet this tendency to settle for 'good enough' may come at a price, with people often making worse decisions and poorer choices (or avoiding action altogether) when faced with more information and/or options.

Energy useful consumers can feel to avoid loss averse by weighing losses more heavily than equal-sized gains, particularly as the stakes rise. For example, people typically focus on the risks, costs or losses associated with adopting a new behaviour, such as financial costs (what will it cost me?), physical risks (is it safe/healthy?), social costs (what do others think?), ecological risks (is it environmentally friendly?), time costs (will it take longer?), functional risks (does it fit my routine?), and even psychological costs (how will I feel?), and tend to discount equivalent gains and benefits. When faced with making a decision, people perceive the disutility of losing something as far greater than the utility of gaining something (i.e., they feel the pain of losses far more than the pleasure of gains). This tendency is reflected by contingent valuation studies that show that willingness to accept tends to be higher than willingness to pay.

Energy useful consumers tend to become irrationally fixated on 'recovering' losses already suffered, discounting future costs and benefits. Once time, effort or money has been invested in a particular endeavour, they may persist with that course of action and 'throw good money after bad' even as it becomes riskier or increasingly unlikely to yield the desired result. Some researchers have attributed this tendency to an overgeneralisation of the 'Don't waste' rule that many people have learned during childhood, i.e., the notion that avoiding waste is generally advisable, so abandoning a prior investment may seem to 'waste' the resources already expended . In the residential energy domain, for instance, a consumer who outlays time, effort and money to purchase an electrical appliance (e.g., air conditioner, extra refrigerator) may tend to use it more, even when it is not necessarily required. The perceive things as less valuable or significant if further away in time (temporal discounting) or space (spatial discounting), even if such things afford long-term benefits. For example, people often 'discount the future' by preferring smaller immediate rewards (e.g., $5 now) over larger future rewards (e.g., $10 next year), and they may avoid actions that are costly in the short-term (e.g., outlaying time and money to purchase new energy-efficient appliances or making an effort to switch energy retailers), despite offering longer-term benefits (e.g., reduced electricity bills). This tendency to be short-sighted and make time-inconsistent judgements often leads to procrastination, inertia and decreased cooperation in group settings.

Energy consumers can be motivated by rewards and incentives, both intrinsic (e.g., achieving social equity/fairness, the 'warm glow' of acting altruistically)7 and extrinsic (e.g., money) [80], [81]. In general, larger incentives or disincentives lead to greater behavioural responses . However, the effects of financial incentives are often surprisingly short-lived and/or inconsistent, with behaviour reverting back to baseline levels upon removal of the reward. People may even respond negatively to extrinsic rewards (e.g., showing loss of motivation, overjustification, moral licensing effects), particularly if intrinsic motivation for the target behaviour is already high8. For example, if a person is intrinsically motivated to be altruistic, giving a piece-rate monetary reward to incentivise the desired behaviour may have a counteractive effect by 'crowding out' the intrinsic motivation .For example, the efficacy of public awareness campaigns and informational appeals can often depend on the perceived credibility of the communication source [105]. If the source of a message seems untrustworthy, unfair or incompetent, people can be wary or sceptical and either disengage, or react defensively to the information. For example, Gonzales et al. have suggested that when communicating messages to improve householders' energy efficiency (e.g., advocating retrofitting), framing recommendations in terms of loss (i.e., energy and money lost via inaction) rather than gain (i.e., energy or money gained via action) may be more effective. Thus, a statement such as, 'You are currently losing $20 per billing quarter by not switching off your lights' is likely to be more motivating than stating, 'You could save $20 per quarter by turning off your lights'. Likewise, stating, 'What you are currently doing is three times less efficient than doing x' is likely to be more motivating than, 'Doing x is three times more efficient than what you are currently doing'. However, various factors may moderate the motivational impact of a particular message frame (e.g., level of risk associated with target behaviour, who/what the reference point is, characteristics of target audience), and these should be taken into account to maximise the effectiveness of consumer-focused communication, particularly when tailoring messages to different customer segments.

Risk aversion: Focus on the low-risk of energy-saving practices and investments that are safe, stable and secure, particularly where energy-efficiency technology is new, expensive, or not yet mainstream. Uncertainty around electricity supply, market prices, government policies and long-term financial payoffs make investing in energy-saving products and services seem like a risky decision for many consumers , so marketing and communication to alleviate these perceived risks may increase energy-efficient action. Extensive research has examined the impact of different risk-reduction strategies ('risk relievers') on consumer behaviour, particularly in retail environments where perceived risk and uncertainty may prevent people from purchasing new products or services relevant to household energy efficiency and conservation are 'relievers' for financial risks (e.g., offering discounts, rebates, lowest-price and money-back guarantees, no-cost returns/refunds, payment security), time risks (e.g., making the purchase decision and product installation quick), and effort risks (e.g., simplified product design, 'user-friendly' operating instructions, helpful customer service). For example, offering consumers money-back guarantees on new energy-efficient technology (e.g., direct load control devices, smart meters) or obligation-free trials of new services (e.g., renewable or 'green' electricity) may increase consumer uptake by providing a 'safety net' – a sense of certainty and security – around any 'unknowns'. Other useful 'relievers' may include strategies to reduce perceived risks around product/service performance and functionality (e.g., offering free trials/samples, demonstrations, guarantees, extended warranties, free product installation and/or training), physical and safety risks (e.g., providing instructions, expert advice, safety certification, independent testing), the risk of product obsolescence (e.g., promising free or low-cost upgrades, product compatibility with earlier versions), social risks (e.g., securing positive word-of-mouth, customer testimonials, celebrity or expert endorsements, or promoting products or services as popular or socially desirable), and even psychological risks (e.g., building brand credibility, customer loyalty).

On conclusion, to ensure cost-effectiveness and maximise return on investment, it is important to take these phenomena into account when developing strategies for encouraging renewable and sustainable energy use, and for motivating pro-environmental behaviour more broadly. By understanding these predictable deviations from economically rational behaviour, policymakers will be better placed to craft interventions that successfully bridge the gap between pro-environmental knowledge, values, attitudes and intentions, and the everyday energy-related behaviour of consumers. This paper has highlighted the value of applying insights from psychology and behavioural economics to inform the effective design and delivery of consumer-focused communication, messages, and other behavioural interventions aimed at encouraging household energy conservation. So, the impact of haze pollution on residents' green consumption behavior is explored to influence energy consumers behaviors.

I shall indicate Chinese energy users example to expain how pollution influence their energy consumption behavior. At present, Chinese residents have been suffering from the influence of air pollution, especially haze pollution. However, residents' consumption is also one of the main sources of haze pollution. Therefore, residents' green consumption can reduce haze pollution. This paper is to explore the impact of haze pollution on residents‘ green consumption behavior. Shandong Province is taken as the illustrative case to carry on the empirical analysis. Firstly, the grounded theory is used to develop the residents’ green consumption behavior model affected by haze pollution. Secondly, based on the data obtained by investigation, the structural equation model is used to test the theoretical model. Finally, the hierarchical regression model is utilized to study the moderating effect of situational variables on residents' green consumption behavior. The green consumption willingness (GCW) has a significant positive driving effect on green consumption behavior. Furthermore, the haze pollution perception (HPP) plays the most positive role in promoting green consumption willingness, followed by behavioral constrain (BC) and haze mitigation responsibility (HMR). Among all situational variables, the government incentive (IM) has a positive moderating effect on the relationship between green consumption willingness and invested green consumption behavior (IGCB). However, publicity and education activities (PEA) have a reverse moderating effect on the relationship between green consumption willingness and invested green consumption behavior. The difference of the impact of age, income, occupation and household structure on habitual green consumption behavior (HGCB) is significant. However, there are significant differences in the effects of age, income, and educational background on invested green consumption behavior. According to the results received in this paper, more policy recommendations are presented.

As we are entering a new age where industrialization, trades, technology development, and resource exploitation are at their peak, the economy and average income, together with social development have had impressive progresses, while our environment is facing serious problems such as different kinds of pollution and large amount of energy consumption that is almost draining the currently scarce resource, threatening the further development of human beings from communities to countries and even to the globe as a whole

As the environment is getting more and more vulnerable and polluted, the health of people is seriously harmed and many important industries, for example, agriculture, fishing, astronomy, the development of micro machines, transportation, and even building constructions and designations, are also heavily affected due to the significant drop of available resources and the heavy pollution of the air, water, and plantations, sometimes even the changes in climates . The existing problems are getting more and more severe, harming the health of people, blocking the economic development, causing instability among societies, threatening humanity.

However, while much of the pollution emitted and energy used are necessary for human development, for example, fossil fuels and industrial wastes that are necessary to keep the economy going, a lot of energy consumption and pollution are actually unnecessary and are caused by the psychological biases of people, which, if reduced, can strongly mitigate the environmental problems we are facing . So, apart from pure technological development that directly solves the environmental problems by ways like creating more resources or purifying the polluted Earth, etc., methods involving insights from Behavioral Economics that drive people to be greener can also be a focus of our efforts in solving the environmental problems, which can both save large amount of money for individuals, corporations, and even governments, and provide us with a suitable environment for living, working, and developing

Hence, China government needs to impletment many actions have already been taken by different organizations and governments, most having a considerable influence and certain benefits. Many ideas have also been proposed . All of the existing solutions and their results can serve as desirable references for those who are intending to solve the problems. However, since the situations vary from place to place and the solutions working at one place might not be as effective as expected in another, it is relatively hard to come to a specific universal solution for the high level of pollution and energy consumption.

Regarding the problems caused by the status quo biases, which cause people to be unwilling to purchase eco-friendly products that cost at first but save money gradually simply because they feel an irrational appeal to the current product, the government can set up some sort of incentives to offset the unwillingness to change. For example, a factory will be more than happy to change the original equipment into new, eco-friendly one if they receive money or fewer bills for doing so. The same also works with the problems caused by "discounting the future". While people tend to focus more on the immediate benefit, an upfront inventive can never be resisted. Just as the "Green Deal" has done, the government can give incentives in a way of cutting (or even eliminating) the upfront costs of installing green products and get the installing cost back in the following period of time as a little amount of extra charge that is still less than the predicted cost of the original product, which can attract tons of people. Because, facing a large amount of energy consumption saved by installing those products with no upfront cost, everyone gets it that it saves both money and the environment without any cost.

Incentives can also work for the problems of "doubt". For example, one might be more willing to purchase an electric car if it is cheaper, or if it saves the user much more money, of which the value exceeds the "risk" of using a "dangerous product" in the consumer's mind. Incentives can be given in many different ways. I can be given straight to the individuals that contribute to the green work. It can also be given to a certain community to take advantage of group spirits, encouraging communities to produce less pollution, for example, carrying out garbage classification, using less air conditioning, driving more eco-friendly cars, using less water and electricity, or producing less waste, or using less plastic bags, with promised incentives, which can cause people behave in the way we expect because of their eagerness to bring the benefits to both themselves and the people within their own communities And while everyone in a community is doing the eco-friendly things, one will be more likely to carry out the same things due to the "social influences", which adds to the effectiveness of the incentives and provides oversights for the people, since everyone wants the incentives and will be watching those around him or her and make sure they are also doing the things needed to get the incentives for the whole community. Incentives can be given as money. Incentives can also be given as a gift, for example, a meal for free, a phone for free, or even several paid days off. And they can even be given as some sort of discounts at certain stores. Since different forms of incentives have their attraction for different groups of people, the diversity of the forms of incentives should be appreciated. While proper incentives encourage people to be green, several improper incentives might not have such great outcomes. Giving too many incentives might lead to losses for the government or the related companies that outweighs the benefits generated by being greener. And giving incentives that are too small might not have a desirable effect since a lot of people just do not care about the "small stuff". And proper forms of incentives are essential for attracting certain groups of people. So, when deciding to use incentives to deal with the problems, policy-makers have to weigh the benefits and risks and think carefully. Researches are also required to make a wise decision. Hence, incentive is one good method to solve pollution when people consumes energy to use in any time.

www.ingramcontent.com/pod-product-compliance
Ingram Content Group UK Ltd.
Pitfield, Milton Keynes, MK11 3LW, UK
UKHW060008051026
15591UKWH00002B/93
* 9 7 9 8 8 8 5 9 1 4 8 7 1 *